A DICTIONARY OF
CROMER AND OVERSTRAND
HISTORY

Further details of Poppyland Publishing titles can be found at
www.poppyland.co.uk
where clicking on the 'Support and Resources' button
will lead to pages specially compiled to support this book

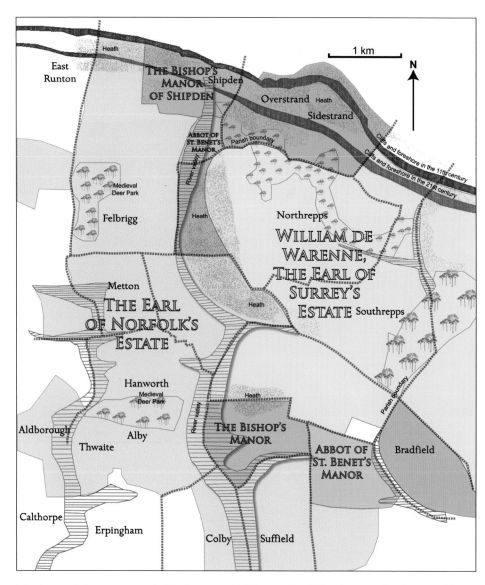

The Manorial areas around Shipden in 1086. The parish of Shipden was flanked on either side by the extensive estates of two Norman barons. To the east of Shipden was the 'Soke of Gimingham', an extensive area controlled by William de Warenne, the Earl of Surrey and the king's son-in-law. To the west the land was controlled by Robert Bigot, father of the Earl of Norfolk. Shipden parish itself was sub-divided into three manors. (the general extent of the manorial land-holdings south of the coast are shown diagrammatically.)

A DICTIONARY OF
CROMER
AND OVERSTRAND
HISTORY

BY
CHRISTOPHER PIPE

POPPYLAND
PUBLISHING

First published 2010 by Poppyland Publishing, Cromer, NR27 9AN
www.poppyland.co.uk

ISBN 978 0 946148 89 9 (hardback)
    978 0 946138 90 5 (paperback)

Designed and typeset in 10½ on 13½ pt Legacy Serif by Watermark, NR27 9HL

Printed in the EU by Latitude Press Ltd

Acknowledgements

The compiler wishes to thank those who have helped find and interpret the varied evidence of Cromer history – especially the staff of Norfolk County Libraries, Cromer Museum and the Norfolk Record Office; David Beasley, Goldsmiths' Librarian; Ron Fiske; Richard Harbord; Peter and Brenda Stibbons; Neil Storey.

Picture credits

Peter Allen: page 141
George Baker: page 168
George Baker collection: pages 18, 91, 143, 212 (top & bottom)
R. W. Brent Magic Lantern slides: pages 152, 255
British Library: page 29
British Museum: pages 6, 23 (© Trustees of the British Museum)

Christopher Pipe/Watermark: pages 15, 19
Benjamin Cabbell-Manners' collection: pages 16, 20, 206, 207, 208
Cromer Museum, Norfolk Museums Service: pages 21, 30, 37, 40, 48, 58, 63, 78, 89, 90, 96, 131, 135, 165, 185, 198 (left), 200
Richard Davies: page 14
Jack Earle's collection: page 32
Goldsmiths' Company (photography by Richard Valencia): pages 144, 171
C. Hall, Provincial Grand Lodge of Norfolk: page 69
Charles Harbord-Hamond's collection: page 65
Crawford Holden collection, Cromer Museum, Norfolk Museums Service: pages 17, 21, 24, 42, 45 (top), 47, 62, 66, 71, 99, 131, 135, 145, 151, 186, 187
Norfolk Record Office: pages 67, 85, 95, 176
University of Nottingham Manuscripts and Special Collections: page 74
Poppyland collection: pages 11 (pier), 12, 54, 57, 114, 142, 167, 184
Poppyland Photos: pages 10–11, 34, 129
Poppyland Publishing: pages 31, 52, 112 (right), 140, 212 (middle)
Randall Salter Magic Lantern slide collection: pages 10, 11, 27, 39, 132 (bottom), 137, 198 (right), 211
RIBA Library drawings collection: page 68
Neil Storey's collection: page 60
Diana Taylor's collection: page 188

Other pictures are from the author's collection.

The maps on pages 2 and 77 are based on original work by Richard Harbord.

CONTENTS

OVERLEAF: *Cromer, looking east, detail from a painting by John Thirtle (1777–1839). Notice the lighthouse (before the building of the replacement tower in 1833); the windmill (near the top of West Street); the sheep grazing in the foreground.*

INTRODUCTION

VISITORS TO CROMER sometimes ask questions which seem simple, yet for which it is not easy to find an answer. How old are the houses? Why is the church so large? Where did holidaymakers stay a hundred years ago?

People who have lived here for years find their memory fading, and can no longer be sure what was on a particular site before the present building replaced it, or exactly when it was that a particular hotel burned down or the traffic was subjected to a one-way system. And though many fascinating details of local history are well known, and found in all the books, others have become lost to living memory and can only be found in newspaper files, old maps and archives – if at all.

Exiles from Cromer may be interested to know what has happened to the town since they left. Entries in this book should help them to form some idea of how it has changed since they knew it.

Family historians, too, often ask about the nature of the community in Cromer in times gone by. They may never have visited the town themselves, but wish to know how life was lived in the days when their ancestors lived here; or they may have old photographs they are trying to date, and need information on the dates of recognisable buildings.

I have tried to provide quick answers to the straightforward questions, whilst also uncovering enough surprising and little-known facts to make the book absorbing to browse in. There are many long-established residents of Cromer who know much more about its history than I do; I would ask them to forgive my boldness in offering this collection of interesting things I have come across in my reading. As Oliver Rackham put it in his *History of the Countryside*, 'facts have turned up and have been filed away until enough has been hoarded to suggest questions and answers'. This is not a complete history of Cromer; for the most part it is a ragbag of titbits which I hope will provide the starting point for further historical inquiry.

Still less does the book contain a complete history of Overstrand. Very little has been written about Overstrand other than the story of the development of 'Poppyland' at the end of the 19th century, but its history overlaps so much with that of Cromer (and indeed a large part of what is now Cromer was once in the parish of Overstrand) that it seemed churlish not to include in the book such information as I have happened across. Entries relating to what is now Overstrand are preceded by the ¶ symbol, and sometimes an entry about a topic in Cromer history has an extra paragraph at the end relating to Overstrand, again preceded by the ¶ symbol so that it makes it easier for those interested in Overstrand to scan for what is of relevance to them.

Source references will be found at the end of the book. For those who wish to find out more, either for topical research or to flesh out the lives of the Cromer ancestors in their family tree, an introduction to the main sources in libraries, archives and the Internet will be found on page 245.

Headwords in the body of the book are of streets, buildings and topics; names of people can be accessed through the index at the end of the book.

Christopher Pipe
CROMER, 2010

Words set in SMALL CAPITALS
invite the reader to look up those headings
for further relevant information.

KEY DATES

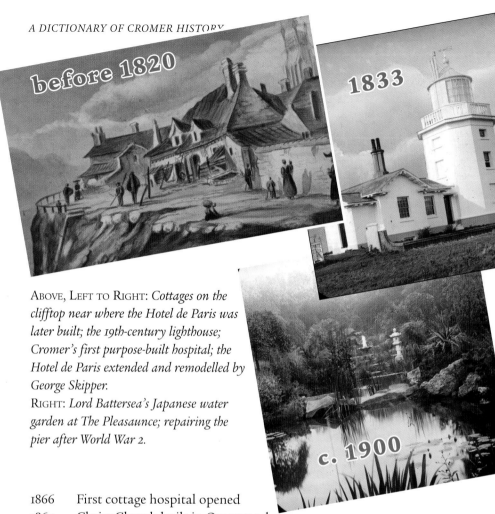

ABOVE, LEFT TO RIGHT: *Cottages on the clifftop near where the Hotel de Paris was later built; the 19th-century lighthouse; Cromer's first purpose-built hospital; the Hotel de Paris extended and remodelled by George Skipper.*
RIGHT: *Lord Battersea's Japanese water garden at The Pleasaunce; repairing the pier after World War 2.*

1866	First cottage hospital opened
1867	Christ Church built in Overstrand
1877	Railway reaches Cromer from London; last of the ship-borne deliveries of coal landed on the beach
1879	Cromer's first police station built
1883	First of Clement Scott's 'Poppyland' articles
1884	Local Board brings conciliar local government to Cromer
1887	Cromer Beach station brings railway from the Midlands; Suffield Park development plan drawn up
1888	Golf course opened; Lord Battersea buys property in Overstrand
1889	Parish church's rebuilt chancel opened
1890–1	Development of Cromer Hall estate on the west of the town
1894	Cromer Urban District Council formed

1901   New sea wall and pier
1904   New cemetery opened at top of Holt Road
1914   Cromer Theatre of Varieties opened (later the cinema);
           rebuilt St Martin's church opened in Overstrand
1923   Lifeboat house opened at end of pier for new motor lifeboat
1932   Hospital moves to Mill Road
1942   Bombs hit Cromer town centre
1974   Local government divided between Cromer Town Council and the new
           North Norfolk District Council
1998–9 New lifeboat house at end of pier
2001–6 Regeneration programme
2010–   Hospital rebuilt

The eastern promenade between 1875 and 1887. Notice the Crescent (on the cliff top) with only two storeys, the Bath House (still weatherboarded), Lower Tucker's (built 1875) and the wooden jetty. The sea wall is clearly built of flint rather than concrete.

CROMER HISTORY A–Z

A

Abbeville (Cabbell Road). Hotel opened in 1898 by Augusta E. Kersey. In the 1990s it was bought by the owners of the Kingswood Centres to accommodate staff of their activity centre at West Runton, but a few years later it was converted into flats.

Actors. Cromer in its heyday attracted numerous actors and entertainers, some coming here to work, some to rest. As early as 1796 the national press, catering as ever for popular interest in the lives of celebrities, carried the news

that 'Miss Leake, the singer, is reported to be much indisposed at Cromer'. *Elizabeth Leak*, born the daughter of a farmer in East Beckham just a few miles outside Cromer, was then in her early twenties and had attracted a good following in London theatres; she retired from Drury Lane in 1801 and is thought to have gone on to teach music.[1]

Lillie Langtry appeared at the Town Hall in 1906.

Gerald du Maurier (1873-1934), the actor-manager and father of novelist Daphne du Maurier, stayed in Overstrand in 1908, together with his family and his ailing mother.[2]

Among guests who stayed at the

CROMER CHARACTERS
PEGGY SALMON

Peggy Salmon is the subject of many stories, not all of them entirely accurate even when she had told them herself. Was she actually born in Australia? She was well spoken and is known to have received a monthly maintenance cheque from a mysterious source in high society, so the exact circumstances of her birth may never be known. She appeared on the London stage, possibly in Peg o' my Heart *though not playing the lead role as is often asserted. In the 1930s she is said to have come to Cromer following the royal and aristocratic personages who used to stay here at that time, and in hope of finding suitable work in the Pavilion Theatre; but, when high society left Cromer at the end of the season, she was stranded here without even the money to return to London.*

Peggy stayed in Cromer and became one of its most famous characters, entertaining the US troops (in more senses than one) and later doing a little work at Cliff House hotel as a cleaner and being paid in lamb chops. (And then there was her cat: 'Have you got anything for my cat? He won't eat fish. Have you got any beef?') She was

also happy to accept anyone's offer of a free Guinness in the pub; as the saying went, when the doctor gave her a blood test, the result showed neat Guinness! Shameless even in old age, she once appeared in the Albion without a stitch of clothing on, and in her seventies appeared topless in Cromer carnival with one breast inscribed 'Mild' and the other 'Bitter'.

Albion were the actor **Cyril Maude** and his actress wife **Winifred Emery** (in the 1890s), and the elderly music-hall comedian **Arthur Roberts**.[3]

Sir **Squire Bancroft** stayed at the ROYAL LINKS HOTEL.

❦ Sir **John Hare** had a house in Overstrand, The GRANGE.

Advowson. The right to appoint ministers to the church was a property right which belonged to Weyland's manor, owned in the late 13th and early 14th centuries by the family de Odyngsels; from 1318 to 1356 it was owned by the Broun family of Tuttington; then it belonged to Hickling Priory until the king granted it to the Carthusians in 1382. They became technically the rectors, and had to appoint a vicar to the church and build him a suitable house 'for hospitality'. On the dissolution of the monasteries, the monarch took over; Queen Elizabeth granted it to the see of Ely, and it was later vested in the Bishop of Norwich. Details are in Rye, *Cromer Past and Present*, pp. 121-7. In 1893 there was an exchange of livings by which the Bishop of Norwich granted the advowson of Cromer to Thomas Fowell Buxton for his lifetime; after Buxton's death (in 1904) it passed to the Church Pastoral-Aid Society, thus enabling Buxton to ensure that future ministers would always be in sympathy with the evangelical wing of the church.

Reymes was a common name among Overstrand landowners centuries ago. This beauitfully incised tablet, still preserved in the rebuilt church, reads: 'Heare lyeth the bodye of Mary Raymes the daughter of William Raymes the yonger who decesid . . . daye of November Anno Domini 1593.'

❧ Patrons of the living of Overstrand, as recorded at the date of appointment of new rectors, were as follows:[1]

1345	Galf' son of Alan
1355	John son of John Reymes
1383	Symon Blicling *citizen of Norwich*
1432	*Sir* Thomas Erpingham &c
1443/47	Roger Reymes
1482/83	William Reymes, *Arm.*
1492	Robert Reymes, *Arm.*
1508	Anna Reymes *widow of Robert Reymes*
1526	Bishop, by lapse
1531	Francis Reymes
1568	Clement Comfort, *gent.*
1577/80	Elizabeth Comfort *wife of Clement Comfort*

1596/1606	William Reymes, *gent.*[2]
1639/41/62	John Reymes, *Arm.*
1670	William Reymes, *gent.*
1714	Nathaniel Life, *Esq.*
1748	Caesar Life
1779	Mary Rant
1794	Edward Hasell *of Ipswich, gent.*[3]
1822	Edward, 3rd Lord Suffield
1841	Edward, 4th Lord Suffield

(At the end of 1848, the right of presentation to various livings, including Overstrand, was advertised for sale by auction.[4])

1871	J. H. Gurney, *Esq.*
1947	The Keswick Trust

Excitement at Cromer in 1914: the town's first chance to get a close look at an aeroplane.

1958/61/74/85   Norwich Diocesan Board of Patronage

1995   The Queen (in right of the Duchy of Lancaster)

1999   Norwich Diocesan Board of Patronage

Aircraft. Cromer's first close encounter with an aeroplane was in February 1914, when a biplane arrived from Yarmouth carrying the pilot and a naval lieutenant who had come to see the wireless station on the cliffs. Landing in the park behind Cromer Hall, they were entertained to lunch by Mrs Bond Cabbell.

Much later in the 20th century, helicopters became a common sight, first in connection with the LIGHTHOUSES and then in air-sea rescue operations, police surveillance and the air ambulance. On one occasion, long before

the air ambulance service began, a helicopter had to be summoned when someone was taken ill at the top of the church tower and had to be lifted to ground level.

Air raids. *See* BOMB DAMAGE.

Albany Court (Runton Road). Flats built on the site of the Albany Hotel, formerly the GRAND HOTEL.

Albion (corner of Brook Street and Church Street). A two-storey building is shown on this site in Bellard's 1747 map. By 1839 the building (probably newly rebuilt) was owned by Francis Pank, a builder, and seems to have been run by a cooper called Sherman Bayfield as a beerhouse, brewing its own beer;[1] water for this enterprise would have been drawn from the well which is still to be found in the pub's cellar. There was also a beerhouse on the other side of Brook Street, in among the old fishermen's cottages, run by Mary Brooks from at least 1843.[2] In 1855, as a widow in her late fifties, she became the first licensee of the Albion.[3] By the 1890s it belonged to the Norwich brewers Steward and Patteson.

The Albion was the meeting place from 1855 of one of Cromer's FRIENDLY SOCIETIES, the Loyal Albion Lodge of the Norfolk and Norwich Unity Independent Order of Oddfellows.

Alder carr. *See* OSIER BED.

Alex Club (Cabbell Road). Licensed social club operating in the ground floor of what had once been the Elmhurst Hotel. The property was converted into

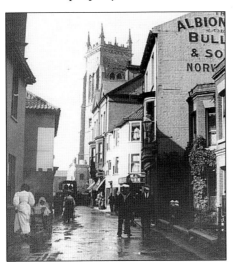

A wet day in Cromer, with the Albion on the right.

flats at the beginning of the 21st century as Alexandra Court.

Alexandra Road. Named after the *Alexandra* lifeboat which served Cromer in the 1930s.

Alfred Road. Part of the Cromer Hall estate, bought by a Mr Macdonald and sold on by him in 65 lots in 1890 as the Macdonald Estate.[1] Made up in 1896. ⌸ The architecture of this road is described in A. D. Boyce, *Pretty Villas & Capacious Hotels* (Cromer Preservation Society, 2006), pp. 17-18.

Almshouses. In 1459 Richard Chylde left money in his will to the poor in the almshouse; this, or its successor, is probably to be identified with a cottage at the west end of town described in 1723 as containing two dwellers.[1] What became of this cottage is not known; there seemed a need to provide cottages for poor widows in 1850, and an appeal was launched which attracted promises of at least £72 for building them; it is not clear what happened after that,[2] but the 1861 census refers to four poor houses.

Amber. *See* JEWELLERS.

Ambulances. The first Norfolk Division of the St John Ambulance was formed in Cromer in 1901, after Robert L. Randall had attended evening classes in first aid and become enthusiastic

Robert Randall (back left) and the Cromer Division of the St John Ambulance Brigade. The stretcher on the ground in front of them is a reminder that ambulance services in the early days rarely involved vehicles at all.

enough to form a class. Eighteen members of this class formed the Division, with schoolmaster Frank Emms as Superintendent; Alfred Salter helped form the Division and his son (of the same name) was its first Secretary.[1] They had a wickerwork stretcher on wheels, which provided the only means of transporting patients, and they supplied night orderlies for auxiliary military hospitals in the area during World War I. A motor ambulance was given by Miss Layland-Barratt in 1915 in connection with the use of the RED HOUSE as a war hospital.[2] The premises in Bond Street were acquired in 1950, converted into a meeting hall and officially opened in 1952.

See also BATHING MACHINES.

Anglia Court Hotel (Runton Road). Part of the former WEST PARADE HOTEL. Closed 2009.

Aquarium (New Street). In 1973 brothers Gordon and Michael Jessop converted part of their garage into an aquarium displaying local fish, shellfish and marine flora, as well as local fossils and dinosaur models. There was an attached art gallery.

Arbor Court (Court Drive). Flats taking their name from the hill adjacent.

Arbor Hill. 'Arborowe hill' is mentioned in a document of 1627;[1] it is called 'Harbour Hill' in manorial documents of the 18th century.[2]

Archery. *See* BUTTS.

Armorial bearings. In 1500 there were more than a dozen family coats of arms displayed in Cromer church, including those of Plantagenet, Heydon, Berney, 'Bacon Stanhow' (which was 'over the roode loft in painted cloth'), Drayton, Felbrigg and Erpingham.[1]

The Town Hall displays the arms of Robert Crowmer, an important figure in Ipswich and Yarmouth history whose family may have originated in Cromer. Many Cromer souvenirs have used them as Cromer's own.

The Town Hall bears the arms of notable families living in the neighbourhood, including Weyland, Reed, Bacon, Harbord, Windham and Buxton, though these were designed merely in carved brickwork and had to wait another hundred years before they were painted with the appropriate colours. The Grand Hotel had stained-glass coats of arms above the windows of the dining room, drawing room and smoking room.[2]

Many SOUVENIRS in the 19th and 20th centuries displayed arms purporting to be those of Cromer itself, the heraldic description being 'Or (*or* ar.) a chev. engr. sa. between three ravens (or crows) ppr.'[3]

❡ Overstrand church in the 16th century had 14 coats of arms, including those of Barney, Mautebie, Winter, Felbrigg and Erpingham, and, in the chancel window, Reymes, Calthorpe and Hastings.[4]

The Battersea arms are elaborately carved in stone over the entrance of the PLEASAUNCE.

Artists. Cromer has attracted artists at various periods.

Robert Dixon (1780–1815) visited the area from Norwich and drew a number of pencil sketches of Cromer, Overstrand and the surrounding area; these were published as separate etchings in 1810 and in book form in 1811.

Joseph Clover (1779–1853) made pencil sketches of Cromer in 1813; he also drew the cliffs at Overstrand in 1825 when work was beginning on a Morgan's slip to enable boats to land their cargoes more conveniently. (The slip was never completed.)

John Sell Cotman (1782–1842) spent the summer holiday of 1807 in Cromer, painting beach scenes and meeting his future wife, daughter of a Felbrigg farmer; **John Thirtle** (1777–1839) painted a watercolour in 1813 showing Cotman's sister-in-law walking on Cromer beach.[1] Cotman also paid two brief visits to Cromer in the year before his death, drawing the lighthouse and a 'Storm off Cromer'.[2]

James Stark (1794–1859) painted a view of Cromer from the west cliff in 1830.[3] Stark's friend **William Collins** (1788–1847) stayed in the town and frequently exhibited Cromer views in London. Other national figures such as

A beach scene at Cromer by Robert Dixon.

CROMER CHARACTERS
CATHERINE BUXTON

One of the notable amateur artists of Cromer was Lady Catherine Buxton. Born Catherine Gurney in 1814, she married her first cousin Edward North Buxton. A number of her watercolours of the scenery of Cromer and its surroundings are held in Cromer Museum. The Buxtons took over Colne House in 1838 and had 12 children. At the time of this photograph she was 90 years of age; ten of her children were still living, 53 grandchildren and 40 great grandchildren. She died in 1911 aged 96.

John Varley (1778–1842) produced views which have become well known as published engravings.

The early 19th century also saw amateurs sketching in the area, some of them extremely gifted. **Catherine Buxton** painted watercolours in the locality, and **Ellen Buxton**'s journal of 1860–64 (with many little informal sketches) has been published.[4] London ship and insurance broker **Robert Marten**, who visited Cromer in 1825, is an example of someone who made sketches in his journal just as later visitors would take photographs. Other albums that survive are anonymous.

Later in the 19th century, local clergyman **R. J. Simpson** drew many sketches in the area and published several little volumes of them. **Edward Pocock** (c. 1844–1905?), an artist on the staff of the *Illustrated London News,* was sent to sketch the railway collision at Thorpe outside Norwich. He later lived at Ipswich and then Norwich, illustrating Mark Knights' book *Peeps at the Past.*[5] Cromer Museum has a number of his watercolours purporting to show old buildings of Cromer but, with the possible exception of one or two which depict buildings standing in his own day, they seem to be entirely the product of his own imagination.

Cromer inspired a series of etchings by **Francis Sydney Unwin** in 1923 and drypoint prints by **Muirhead Bone** in 1935 and 1939 – each characteristic of the period and of the artist's own style.

From the end of the 20th century a fresh wave of artists found Cromer a congenial place to live and work; several galleries opened in shops around the town and the Town Council collaborated with other groups to issue a leaflet advertising them.

See also PHOTOGRAPHERS.

Four styles of art: ABOVE: *Cromer, 1803, from a sketchbook of Gen. George Whitcomb. (Gloucestershire Archives)* BELOW: *Watercolour by A. J. Ambrose, 1930. (Author's collection)*

ABOVE: *Drawing by Thomas Lound (1802–61).* BELOW: *'Cromer, No. 3' etching by F. S. Unwin, 1923. (Both in the British Museum)*

Assembly rooms. Usually refers to the one built at the back of the RED LION in 1887, but earlier references (e.g. to a ball held in 1828[1]) imply the Subscription Room which became the BATH HOUSE, or the Fishermen's READING ROOM which was erected in 1842 and demolished in 1882.[2]

See also PARISH HALL.

Athletics. A sports day was held in 1867 on Colne House field; Rye (*Cromer Past and Present*, pp. 146-7) quotes the published report in full.

About the year 1905 Sergeant Instructor Alfred William Batterby of the Norfolk Regiment ran gymnastics classes under the vicar's aegis. It is clear from surviving photographs that these were attended by boys who a hundred years later would have been keenly training at the High School's Sports Centre, probably as footballers!

Auction rooms. Auctions are recorded as taking place in the Red Lion Assembly Room (built in 1887), and in the LECTURE HALL.[1] In 1962 Allman's made auction rooms out of the former livery stables in Brook Street, which later became a snooker club. Auctions were held in the former Rollerdrome in Garden Street from 1978.[2]

Avon House School. Miss Rust and Miss Rayner had a school for young ladies in Miss Rust's house in the High Street in 1877; it was moved to Avon

Sgt Batterby's gym club. The lady in the middle is their pianist, Maggie Payne. For identification of all the others, see the Norfolk Museums website.

ASSEMBLY ROOMS – BANDS

House, West Street, at the corner with Louden Road, where it was known in 1889 as 'Miss Smith's School'.[1] (The LECTURE HALL was used for physical training.[2]) In 1901 it was at 6 Cabbell Road where its principal employed two governesses and two servants; most of the nine boarders (girls aged 9 to 17) came from Norfolk or Lincolnshire. In 1913 the school was at 8 Church Street.[3]

B

Back Lane. Name given to Louden Road in the plans drawn up for the sale of the Cromer Hall estate in 1852.

Back Road. Name given on the tithe map of 1840 to the road which later became Vicarage Road/Colne Road/The Croft.

Bailey Road. Part of the estate built off Roughton Road by the national building firm of Barratt in the 1980s.[1] Named after the four *H. F. Bailey* lifeboats which served at Cromer between 1923 and 1945. Henry Francis Bailey (died 1917) was a benefactor of the Royal National Lifeboat Institution.

Balcony House (Mount Street) – also known as Gallery House. Built for Herbert Mace, on a corner portion of the garden of the LORD NELSON COFFEE

TAVERN. Mace was a photographer, and had large studio windows put on the top floor of the building, though by the beginning of World War I he had let the building to a tailor who used that top room as a work room. The ground floor was later used as a restaurant and then an art gallery; and after the owner's retirement the building was sold in 2007 for conversion to flats.

See also ROYALTY.

Band of Hope. Temperance organisation which was formed at a meeting at James Mayes' house in 1875.[1] For the first couple of years they used the Fishermen's Reading Room for their meetings, but this was in a poor state of repair and it was a question whether the landlord (Mr Cabbell) would continue to let them use it.[2]

See also FRIENDLY SOCIETIES; LECTURE HALL.

Bands. As early as 1853, subscriptions were being canvassed for paying a band to play on the jetty each evening and at intervals during the morning; this was a band of six German musicians.[1]

An account from the first few years of the 20th century describes how every afternoon and evening there were performances by 'the Blue Hungarian Band, which is Cromer's nearest approach to dissipation. A very good band it is, with a violinist as its conductor, and a vocalist generally adds variety to the programme.'[2]

The band was actually the 'Blue Viennese Band', whose musical director Moritz Wurm conducted at the opening ceremony of the pier in 1901, but the Cromer band's regular conductor was Fernand Hervouet. The Hervouet family spoke perfect French, so the 1903 poster describing him as 'Herr Hervouet' was doing so simply because German and Austrian culture was still fashionable. (Cf. the Blue Danube Café.) Hervouet's library of music is still held by the Northampton Light Orchestra.[3]

During the 1911 season the pier band, conducted by Signor Gaetano Calamari, played 735 different pieces.

See also ROYAL LINKS PAVILION.

Bandstands. A bandstand on the breastwork below the Hotel de Paris was erected in 1895 but construction work damaged the cliff wall[1] and the bandstand had to be removed, being superseded by the one at the end of the new pier.

The bandstand in North Lodge Park was erected in 1956.[2]

Banks. Some of Cromer's early merchants may have offered informal banking facilities,[1] but even important local traders had to rely for their finance on personal contacts until well into the 19th century. For payments and receipts they had to use banks in London and Norwich. Even the most limited private savings facility was not introduced until 1824 (*see* SAVINGS BANK).

Cromer had a branch of Harvey and Hudson's Crown Bank from 1864; the local manager was J. W. Rust, who lived in Tucker Street at the WHITE HOUSE which is still Barclays Bank. The Crown

A cheque drawn on Barclays Bank, Cromer, by Walter J. Churchyard in 1904. The printed wording makes it clear that the bank of Gurneys, Birkbecks, Barclay & Buxton (all names with strong Norfolk connections) had only recently been incorporated into Barclays.

Bank collapsed in 1870, when Gurneys bought its premises and goodwill.[2] B. Rust was their local agent from at least 1876. Gurneys, Birkbecks, Barclay and Buxton formed the leading part of the amalgamation which led to the formation of Barclays Bank in 1896. All four of the original partners had Cromer connections and were related by marriage.[3]

Lacons Yarmouth, Norfolk & Suffolk Bank had a branch in Cromer between 1889 and 1901, when they were taken over by the Capital & Counties Bank (becoming part of Lloyds in 1921).[4] Lloyds moved from the High Street to Church Street in 1921–22, closing their premises in 2000 after merging with the TSB, and in 2002 the *Eastern Daily Press* and *North Norfolk News* opened an office in the building, now known as Old Bank House.

Midland and NatWest banks both opened branches later on (Midland later becoming HSBC), and the TSB opened its Cromer branch at 1 West Street in the mid-1970s.[5] ⸿ Overstrand had a part-time branch of Barclays Bank (listed in the 1908 and 1916 directories).

Baptist Church. Built 1900–01 by Girling & Smith on the site of Claremont House. It was originally a General Baptist church, becoming part of the Baptist Union, but later became independent.[1]

Barclay Mews. Housing development built at the rear of HERNE CLOSE (the house owned by the Barclay family) in the early years of the 21st century.

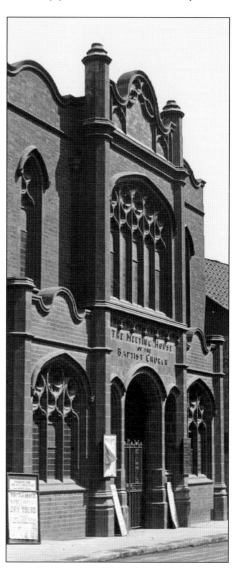

'The Meeting House of the Baptist Church', as it is named with theological precision in the brickwork over the door.

Barkers Herne. Originally a field name,[1] this site on the Holt Road was used for Council offices until the end of the 1980s, after which the Orbit Housing Association built a block of sheltered housing which opened in 1993.

Bath House. The present building was erected by Simeon Simons in 1836 (replacing a similar building built in 1814[1] which had been erected as a subscription reading room but was washed away by a storm). It was extended in 1872 after Simons' death and became a licensed hotel from 1874 (continuing to offer hot and cold sea-water baths, and billiards in the new extension). It belonged to the Trunch Brewery from 1879 to 1952, when that brewery was bought by Morgan's – later becoming part of the Norwich Brewery – and became a free house in the 1980s. After closure in the later 1990s the building was extensively renovated by Bullen's and became once again a private house.

Many people say they have seen the ghost of an unidentified woman here; also, the sounds of running footsteps and of heavy furniture being moved across wooden floorboards have often been heard, presumably relating to the attempt to save furniture when the original building was destroyed, one man losing his life in the attempt.[2]

Bathing, and bathing machines. The first bathing machine was introduced to Cromer in 1779 by Pearson and Dr Terry[1] 'for the Convenience of Gentle-

A busy scene on the beach, seen in a lithograph by J. M. Johnson dating from about 1831. The Bath House and Thomas Randell's bath house on stilts on the beach can both be seen, as can the jetty built in 1821–22.

men, Ladies and others' who could be 'conveyed into and out of the Water with the greatest Ease, Safety and Expedition.'[1] People came from far off to avail themselves of the sea water: in 1796 J. Green wrote from Covent Garden that 'Jermy and I are preparing for Norfolk, he has been Ill for some months of a Jaundice and Doctor Pitcairne has ordered him to the Sea and

In 1814, Simon Wilkin drew this scene of Cromer beach. The boat houses on the left are near the bottom of the Gangway; above them in the picture can be seen the subscription reading room (forerunner of the Bath House) which had just been built on the cliff falls. Thomas Randell has not yet built his bath house on the beach. A small sailing boat is drawn up and what is probably a crab boat is just by the boat sheds. One family group, it seems, is looking out to sea, whilst another (with a parasol) approaches one of the bathing ma-chines, having perhaps just walked down the sloping pathway from the top of the cliff. The whole mass of cliff beyond the reading room was swept away in storms in the 1820s and in February 1836, as were many of the buildings shown, including the Bath House.

See yon machines at work! what varied aim!
The infant's scream, and the loud youth's acclaim;
There the bold swimmer strikes the opposing wave,
And gains fresh vigour from the stroke he gave;
There the young female, with a softer grace,
Shakes her long locks, and strokes her dripping face.
Hail! purest exercise! by which we bind
Strength to the nerve, and firmness to the mind;
Bid loftier thoughts and nobler views engage,
And stamp on childhood all the sense of age.

H. S., 'Cromer' (1816)

This painting shows the pier of 1821–22 and the sea wall of 1838 protecting the rebuilt Bath House and other sea-front property.

he thinks of Cromer.'² A Mr Salmon in September 1804 wrote that 'he was going to Cromer to Bathe as the Baths at Yarmouth were so crowded that it made it very inconvenient to him to use them'.³ Bath houses were opened in Cromer by Thomas Randell (early 1820s?) and Simeon Simons (1828?) and in 1830 Cromer was advertised as 'the most romantic part of the Norfolk coast, and at present one of the best frequented and fashionable bathing places

in England.'⁴ Wealthy people acquired holiday homes in the disrict in order to bathe: Pigot's 1839 directory mentions 'several very handsome houses in the neighbourhood, occupied only during the bathing season'.

There were seven or eight machines in the 1820s.⁵ Josh Jacob (of 6 Jetty Street) had a bathing machine business which was inherited by Mrs Lucy Maria Miller on his death in 1870 and later sold to John James Davies; these lasted

Before the Davies family took it on, the Miller family held the concession for operating bathing machines, which were moved into the water using horses. The machines were gradually replaced by beach huts and tents as it became acceptable to walk up and down the beach in a bathing costume.

until World War 2. A photograph of the 1880s shows 28 machines lined up on the east beach.

It is said that ambulances from the Crimean War were reused as bathing machines in and around Cromer; one, from Overstrand, was turned to further service as the first 'terminal building' for the airstrip at Northrepps.[6]

Battery. *See* FORTIFICATIONS; MILITIA.

Bay House. Cromer's first tea-room, in Garden Street, built of traditional brick, flint and tile with a bay window on the first floor; delicately curved shop windows were added later. Demolished 1999 and rebuilt in the same style but

with a recessed ground floor window – known as Breakers Café.

Beach House (Promenade). Original name of MARINE VIEW.

Beach huts. The first huts were erected in 1912 by the Council, who felt the bathing machines rather out of date.[1]

Beach missions. The Children's Special Service Mission (CSSM – later part of the Scripture Union) started running beach missions in Cromer during the summer holidays in the 1880s.[1] Students came in their blazers from Oxford and Cambridge to help, and the preacher's pulpit was a sandcastle.

Photo by H. H. Tansley of a beach mission in the early to mid-20th century.

By 1890, attendances on the sands were at least 250 each morning; then the Local Board forbade the use of the beach for preaching and the meetings were held on the cliff top (in a field behind Cliff House, the residence of Major Pelham Burn who was sympathetic to the mission) or on the Lighthouse Hills. But mostly the mission has been held on the east beach, at the bottom of the Doctor's Steps.

¶ The Overstrand beach mission began in 1924.

📖 For a comprehensive account of the mission, which sets it in its local, national and theological context, see Philip Bligh, *A History of Cromer Beach Mission 1883–2007: Glimpses into the Spiritual Life of North Norfolk* (Lulu, 2008).

Beach Road. Road leading towards the sea from Cromer Beach station. It was originally to be called Station Road (the name 'Beach Road' having been used to refer to the Gangway[1]). The houses were designed by Rowland Carter in 1901–2.[2]

¶ Beach Road in Overstrand, a cul-de-sac leading off Paul's Lane, has the curious distinction of not leading to the beach at all, being situated along the top of the cliff with no direct access to the beach.

Beach Terrace. Name used in the 1841 census for the Promenade.

¶ **Beck Hythe.** Original name of Overstrand Court Hotel.

¶ **Beckhythe.** The name (recorded as early as 1297) of a fishing station on the beach at Overstrand; it is also sometimes used to refer to Overstrand itself, or the eastern part of the parish.[1]

¶ **Beckhythe Manor.** Built in the early years of the twentieth century, when it was owned by Herbert Garnett of Bournemouth but occupied as a holiday residence by the Rt Hon. Lady Mary Murray,[1] whose husband Gilbert Murray was Professor of Greek at Oxford.

Becks. *See* Gangway.

Beef Meadow. Field opposite Cromer Hall. It is named 'The Beef Close' on a map of the first half of the 18th century,[1] which takes it back to a time when cattle were called 'beef' even before they reached the butcher. Indeed, the first animals to be pastured both here and on what is now called The Meadow and car park, and to feed on the hay produced here, would have been the medieval oxen which pulled the plough in the spring.

See also Cricket; Football.

¶ **Belfry School.** Built in 1830 by Anna Gurney and Sarah Buxton (of Northrepps Cottage), and so called because they had begun the school by giving lessons to a small group of children in the belfry which was the only part of the old church still standing at that date. New buildings were erected at the rear of the site early in the 21st century, and from 2009 the original building became an arts centre with studios, meeting room, gallery and performance area.

Mrs S. A. Betts ran an Infants School in East Terrace, listed in Jarrold's 1889 directory but not in the 1893 edition.

Belle Vue. Opened in 1848 as a hotel next door to the HOTEL DE PARIS. In the middle of the 19th century Bingham's coach left the Belle Vue every morning on its way to Norwich, in time for the trains to London and elsewhere. Henry Soame Jarvis bought the Belle Vue in 1873, and it was absorbed into the Hotel de Paris from 1895. Up to the 1970s or 80s it formed a corner bar for the hotel; thereafter the ground floor was used as a shop or sandwich bar.

The Duchess of Marlborough stayed in the Belle Vue, occupying the room with the oriel window on the corner.[1]

Bells. In the late 15th and early 16th centuries, church bells would have been rung on many occasions, such as after dark on All Saints Day (1 November), to comfort departed souls in purgatory; Cromer church had five bells in 1552. Then the Reformation dispensed with most of the ritual which called for church bells; by the 1650s, Gunpowder Treason Day was about the only regular occasion they were rung.[1] Cromer church needed money to pay for repairs to the building, so four of its

bells were sold in 1767, leaving only the middle one. (The same thing had happened at Hempstead church near Holt, where permission had been obtained in 1743 to sell two bells to raise money for repairs to the church tower;[2] and at Hargham, a tiny community south of Attleborough where the church bells were sold in 1753 to pay for repairs to the church, of which the roof and parts of the walls had collapsed.[3]) Cromer's bells are supposed to have been sold to Bow church, and to have been carried to London by water, the captain of the ship that took them being one Tom Artis; no one seems able to find any

Cromer's oldest bell, made in the latter part of the 15th century. It bears the inscription 'Missus Vero Pie Gabriel Fert Leta Marie' (Now Gabriel, being sent, bears joyful tidings to Holy Mary).

documentary evidence to support this tradition, but it is quite likely to be at least partly true – maybe the bells were destined to be melted down or recast at the Whitechapel bell foundry.[4]

A man was still paid to ring the one remaining bell – in the 1871 census, Robert Payne (62 and partially blind) describes himself as 'bell ringer &c.'

The other bells now in the church were given by Thomas Fowell Buxton in memory of his mother, the Dowager Lady Buxton, who died in 1872.[5]

In 1913 it was arranged that the church bells should be rung whenever there was need in the town to summon the fire brigade.[6]

In 1933 the church bells were rung to celebrate the rescue by the lifeboat of the crew of the wrecked *Sepoy*. In 1976 they were rung to mark the digging of the first turf for the new Allies ward at the HOSPITAL – as vicar Derek Osborne pointed out, there had always been strong links between church, Christian faith and hospitals.[7]

See also TOWN CRIERS.

◀ Overstrand church in 1552 had two steeple bells' and one 'clapper'. In the 19th century the old church had one bell dated 1605.[8]

Belmont Hotel (Prince of Wales Road, at the corner of Cadogan Road). Once extended in the early years of the 20th century, it could accommodate 90 guests, and had private sitting rooms, dining room, drawing room, smok-ing, reading and billiard rooms. The hotel backed onto what became known as Evington Lawns, and was able to advertise tennis courts and croquet lawns; by 1910 it could also boast an 'up-to-date Motor Garage'.[1] The building was later converted for use as 'Hoggy' Churchyard's dental surgery and as offices ('Belmont') and flats ('Hazelwood House').

Benjamin Court. *See* FLETCHER HOSPITAL.

Bernard Road. Created as part of the 1890 Cromer Hall estate sale;[1] the 1901 census calls it St Bernard Road. It was made up *c.* 1901.[2] Norwich architect George Skipper was responsible for several of the houses.

📖 The architecture of this road is described in A. D. Boyce, *Pretty Villas & Capacious Hotels* (Cromer Preservation Society, 2006), pp. 19-20.

Bible Society. *See* CROMER LADIES' BIBLE ASSOCIATION.

Billiards. Billiard rooms were available in the 19th century at a number of hotels etc.: Mr Hogg's house (on the site of the later MELBOURNE HOUSE) from *c.* 1821,[1] TUCKER'S HOTEL (in a building at the cliff edge overlooking the Promenade) from the early 1840s, the RED LION by 1845 etc.

Billiards constituted one of the attractions of the BATH HOUSE in the 1830s, Lord Walpole being among its clients; but there was a feeling that billiards were incompatible with proprietor Simeon Simons' other profession as schoolmaster, so he sold the table in 1841.[2] When the Bath House became a hotel in the 1870s, a new extension was built as a billiard room.

The Grand Hotel was built with a billiard room, though by the 1920s this had been converted for use as a private function room.[3]

See also SNOOKER CLUB.

Bishop's Manor. One of the medieval manors of Shipden, which belonged to the Bishop of Thetford before 1066 and was given to the new see of Norwich by William Beaufoy, Bishop of Thetford. In the 13th century it was held by the family known as 'de Egmere', and in the reign of Elizabeth I it was leased to John Blowfeld, who paid for work to be done on the pier in the 1590s.[1] Although some references seem to connect this manor with the 19th-century Cromer Hall estate, it is hard to disentangle the various medieval manors or to know which land belonged to each one.[2]

Bittern Rise. Development of houses on part of the North Norfolk Mushroom farm site in Sandy Lane. Built in the early years of the 21st century, its name denotes not the presence of bitterns in Cromer but the proximity of the Norwich–Sheringham railway line which had been christened the Bittern Line by the railway operating company

a few years earlier (responding to public interest in conservation of the rare breeding bird of the Norfolk Broads).

Blackberry Grove. Developed in the late 1990s at the end of Sandy Lane, on land which had once been part of the mushroom farm.

Blacksmiths. Early records are fragmentary; thus we know of a Cromer blacksmith called John Birde whose will was proved in 1558/59, and then a Robert Wilson who became a licensed victualler in 1651[1] (being a blacksmith was thirsty work!).

At a time when metal goods were routinely made to order or repaired rather than bought cheaply from shops and national distributors, it is clear that there were opportunities for several craft smiths to work in Cromer, mostly setting up their forges on the outskirts of the built-up area but one or two even working in the town centre (where, of course, they would be close at hand for merchants and fishermen who needed boat repairs done). In the 19th century Joseph Curtis operated as a general blacksmith from Imperial House in the High Street at least as early as 1830,[2] and had a forge in the Loke, at the junction with Louden Road, while William Curtis was a smith and farrier in New Street.[3] James Francis had a forge in Bond Street, behind where the Post Office was later built.[4] There were two blacksmiths operating in West Street – Sewell (and later William) Burton, and (in a smithy in the yard of the White Horse[5]) William Watts. Dowsing Forster is listed in 1864 as a blacksmith in Red Lion Street.[6]

At the beginning of the 20th century the smithy in Corner Street was run by shoeing smiths Charles Wiseman and his son William[7]; then it was owned by John Pollock,[8] and later by Walter Burgess; when the *H. F. Bailey* lifeboat arrived in Cromer in 1935 he had to shorten its funnel, which was too tall for the boat to go in the boathouse![9] Mr Dugdale had the smithy in the Holt Road.[10] There was another smithy on the Runton Road near Shipden Avenue.[11]

Blazer's. Licensed social club, previously called the Crescent Club, occupying the ground floor of Surrey House until the owner lost his licence in 2008 after complaints from neighbours about noise and disturbance late at night. The first club to occupy the same premises was the Cromer & District Labour Club (incorporated in 1920), which bought Surrey House from Alice Sarah Cross for £500.[1]

Blue Danube café. Established before 1930 in the old stables in North Lodge Park (later the North Lodge Park Tea Rooms); the fig tree growing in it proved a worthwhile source of fruit for the Women's Institute during World

The interior of the Blue Danube café, North Lodge Park, in 1930.

War 2 – the Council received £1. 2s. 6d. for the fruit obtained in 1941.[1] The café later moved to the new development in Tucker Street, on the site of Tucker's Hotel.

Boating lake. Constructed on Evington Lawns (Runton Road) in 1963.[1]

Bomb damage. Cromer suffered bomb damage in World War 2 before London experienced the Blitz.

1940

July 11 A Dornier 217 dropped a stick of bombs from Hans Place to Joyce's café at the bottom of the Gangway.

November 17 A stick of bombs was dropped from Central Road to Suffield Park

December 6 Two high explosive bombs landed in Stevens Road

1941

April 11 Six bombs dropped, three of them hitting Lyndhurst in Alfred Road

1942

July 22/23 In an air raid at midnight a single Dornier 217 aircraft dropped four bombs on Cromer, killing 11 people. Bombs were also dropped on Cromer on 19 October 1942.[1] The following buildings were destroyed:

◻ property on the west side of Garden Street

◻ Rounce & Wortley's shop (corner of High Street and Church Street) – its space was used to allow Church Street to be widened

◻ Thurgarton Dairy (next door to Rounce & Wortley)

Bomb damage in the centre of Cromer, 1942.

¤ Mickelburgh House (next door to the Thurgarton Dairy)

¤ East House (next to the eastern end of the churchyard)

A heavy old ledger from the Thurgarton Dairy was blown to the top of the church tower; dating from 1904–06, it can still be seen in the Norfolk Record Office.[2]

There was also damage to Tucker's Hotel. The church suffered blast damage and services were held in the Methodist Church for 11 months; complete restoration took 26 years.

October 19 Bombs destroyed two properties:

¤ Swinton House (Dr Vaughan's house, 2 Norwich Road) – rebuilt 1947/50 and since known as Knighton Court.

¤ Dunrobin (corner of Vicarage Road and Norwich Road – not rebuilt) and Swinton House.

❧ Air raids were given as the reason for closing the voluntary hospital facilities in Overstrand in 1916.[3]

Bond Street. Created as part of the 1890 development by the CROMER HALL estate,[1] it took its name from Benjamin Bond Cabbell. The road was made up by 1899.[2]

Bowls clubs. Cromer Bowls Club was founded in 1761, probably using the bowling green in front of Webb's house, property of the Red Lion.

Cromer Bowling Club was founded in 1898 and by 1920 had nearly 80 members;[1] the green was at the corner of Norwich Road and Overstrand Road.

Photo opportunity, 1900: the opening of the bowling green at the foot of the Norwich Road.

Cromer and District Bowls Club was formed in 1936 by four members of the former Cromer Private Club to play EBA bowls; the green on the marrams at Runton Road was built by Cromer UDC in 1937–38 (the putting green being added in 1947).

Suffield Park Bowling Club was formed to play on a corner of FEARN'S FIELD.

¶ **Bracken Avenue.** Built on the line of the old railway: the Gurney family had sold the land to the railway companies in the early 1900s; in 1961, after the line had been closed, the land was bought by Sidney William Wallace and Eva Wallace who had plans drawn up for a building estate, using the Norwich firm of Harry Pointer Ltd.

Bracondale. Built as a pair of houses adjoining the much older LONG HOUSE on the Overstrand Road, and presumably so named in reference to the hamlet of Bracondale (on the edge of Norwich) which was the main home of Robert Herring (died 1814), whose family owned the property for many years. The owners of the older house are said to have objected to the Hoare family spoiling their view by building a stable block opposite CLIFF HOUSE; Bracondale was built to retaliate by impairing the Hoares' view from Cliff House and was hence nicknamed 'Spite Row'.[1] One of the houses was occupied by Stuart Knill, a former Lord Mayor of

Bracondale as a hotel.

London.[2] Before long the houses were converted into a hotel, then briefly Bracondale School until this was moved into GRANGE COURT. In World War 2 the property became a dormitory for SUTHERLAND HOUSE SCHOOL; it was afterwards converted into flats.

Breaker's Lane. An old name for Mill Lane.[1] Probably connected with the name 'Braky Close' given on a map of 1717 for the field where the modern Junior School stands.[2]

Breeze's Farm. On the west side of Garden Street in the 19th century. Its land was used for Corner Street.

Breeze's Yard. Off Brook Street.

Brethren. *See* GOSPEL HALL.

Brewing. An early reference to brewing in Cromer comes from the 1430s, when Joan Maryot is described as a brewer; her mariner husband, William, had been lost at sea and she and her son John, also a mariner, had to sell a manor to pay the debts William had left. Was Joan brewing while her husband was at sea, or did she take up the business to make some money after she was widowed? We do not know, but it is clear that for all their financial difficulties these were not poor people: they had owned a manor, and were prepared to take expensive legal action in London.[1]

COLNE HOUSE plans of the 1820s and 1830s show it with a substantial brewhouse of its own, in the tradition of large houses brewing their own beer for their staff.

The *Norwich Mercury* of 29 March 1828 advertised for sale a 'small but complete Brewing Plant of Mr. G. Young, who is leaving Cromer'. It was nearly new and included a three-barrel copper. John Brown, a maltster in the 1820s, had a yard at the bottom of Norwich Road, behind the original Upton House, where there were several good wells.

See also ALBION; CROWN & ANCHOR; MALTINGS; TUCKER'S HOTEL; WELLINGTON.

Brickfields. The 1838 Ordnance Survey map shows a 'Brick Ground' on the Roughton Road, and the 1886 map shows these brickworks but not Brickfields Cottages, which appear to have been built shortly afterwards.[1] The brickworks were run by John Youngs & Son,[2] the firm of Norwich builders who were responsible for the Grand, Imperial and Metropole Hotels as well as houses in Clare Road, Connaught Road and Crawford Road. (Long after the brickworks closed, the land was used for the Amazona ZOO.)

A piece of land on Overstrand Road west of CLIFF HOUSE – corresponding to the eastern half of the present North Lodge Park, and also known as Newman's Close (Newman is found as a name in Cromer from the 16th centuries) – was leased by Matthew Pank in 1796 as a brickfield.[3] The Pank family in the early 19th century were builders of many Cromer houses and also (with Samuel Simons) erected the new school in the Overstrand Road. The ambitious young schoolmaster Simeon Simons was, however, slightly alarmed and hoped none of Mr Pank's bricks would be used. 'They are only half burnt, & are also totally unfit for any outside part of the building,' he wrote to the Goldsmiths' Company. 'You know Sir what sort of Bricks they are – please to think of this – because 'tis not a Building on speculation.'[4]

¶ The 1838 map also shows a brick kiln on the north side of the Overstrand Road, just beyond the plot later to be occupied by the Cromer Sea Scouts' hut.

Brickfields Cottages (formerly simply called **Brickfields**). Row of single-storey cottages on the Roughton Road, briefly (around 1889) graced with the name of Ivy Cottages.[1]

Brook Street. Edward Brook(e) was an 18th-century gentleman and surgeon of North Walsham; he married Elizabeth Ellis, whose family owned the land on which this street is found, though the couple and their daughter Susannah lived in Stalham Hall.

The council wanted to widen the road in 1887, but rebuilding of the Red Lion was already too far advanced so

they had to abandon the idea.[1] The road was made up in 1894.[2]

Brown's Yard. *See* BREWING; WATER SUPPLY.

Brownshill. Brown's Hill is so named on the 1838 Ordnance Survey map. The modern development of housing was granted planning permission in 1986.[1]

Brunswick House (overlooking the Gangway). The Prince of Wales married a princess of Brunswick in 1795, which gives a likely date for the original building here. The house was altered in 1880.

Brunswick Street. One of several old names for SURREY STREET.[1]

Brunswick Terrace (overlooking the Gangway). Five two-storey houses built by Jeremiah Cross on the site of one

Brunswick Terrace (on the left) and Brunswick House.

of his coal-yards in 1868, increased to three storeys in 1870. The bays were added later, in 1880.

Buddies. Name (from the end of 2009) of the pub occupying the former station building built in 1887 for Cromer Beach station. The original bar and refreshment rooms were controlled by Rust's wine department. The station building was closed in 1966 and leased to Travis & Arnold for the storage of building materials, then sold with the disused railway goods yard to Safeway for their new supermarket. Their plans to use the site of the station building for a petrol station were turned down by the council, and the building was restored and reopened as Buffers bar and restaurant in 1998. Under subsequent tenants the name was changed in 2007 to the Station House, and in 2009 to Buddies bar and lounge.

Buffers. *See* BUDDIES.

Builders. In each age there has been a leading man, or firm, responsible for key developments in Cromer. Some we shall never know by name – even when the work is as notable as the CHURCHES – but others can be identified.

Samuel Simons (*c.* 1756–1830), a carpenter from Cranworth, married Elizabeth Webb in Cromer in 1790 and settled here. He became a leading figure in the town, involving himself with the militia and taking his turn as over-

seer of the poor. He built the Grammar School in Overstrand Road (together with Matthew Pank) in 1821, and the cottages/shops at nos. 25–27 Church Street, as well as other properties. His son of the same name (*c.* 1790–1875 – Samuel and Elizabeth had ten children, all of them being given names beginning with S) was a master builder who suffered a badly crushed leg whilst in charge of the pile driving for the last wooden jetty in 1846; he continued as a cabinet maker, eventually retiring to Yarmouth.

The *Pank family* supplied Cromer with building, bricklaying and surveying skills over three generations. John, a bricklayer, married in 1767. Matthew, a bricklayer by 1785, built the schoolroom (later to become a Methodist chapel) in 1790, and leased a brickfield from Lord Suffield in 1796; rating records show him in receipt of rents from at least ten tenants. Other names in the family include Francis (two generations), John and George; records do not always make it clear which Pank is being referred to, but the family were responsible for building the school on the Overstrand Road and for acting as letting agents, property auctioneers and map makers.

John Newman (1820–98), son of bricklayer and master builder William Newman, lived in Jetty Street and later in Vicarage Road. He was involved with repair work on the church, built and rented many Cromer properties and was clerk of works on the Town Hall.

George Riches (1829-1900), the son of a master bricklayer, was already at the age of 22 a master-carpenter employing five men (possibly the same five men as his father employed). He was responsible for building MELBOURNE HOUSE and for much of the 1880s building in Cromer. (The firm had its own brickworks at Felbrigg as well as a sawmill in Aylmerton.) The business was continued by his son of the same name, who worked on Overstrand Hall, The Pleasaunce at Overstrand and Gresham's School at Holt. George Riches junior was also chairman of the UDC at the beginning of the 20th century, but after a serious operation in 1909 he sold the business in 1911 and in 1913 he went to live in Provost, Alberta, Canada, where he had a son. He died in 1916.

Girling & Smith were cabinet makers who expanded into building work with the building boom of the 1890s; they had their builder's yard in Cross Street, just next to the Lecture Hall.

Henry Bullen, a son of the head gardener at Cromer Hall,[1] set up in business as a builder, the firm of H. Bullen & Son being founded in 1895 and becoming part of the R. G. Carter construction group in 1935. Over the years the firm was entrusted with sensitive work on historic buildings, including the church tower (1950) and the Bath House (1990s/2000s).

📖 A vast amount of detail on Cromer's building styles and materials, and the builders themselves, is to be found in A. D. Boyce, *Aspects of Design in Cromer: Building Materials & Features of Cromer's Historic Architecture from the 18th to the Begining of the 20th Century* (Cromer: North Norfolk District Council, 2007).

Bulls Row. Row of six cottages off New Street.[1] Mr Bull owned the land here in the middle of the 18th century.[2]

Burnt Hills. An 18th-century map names a field here as 'The Burnt Hill Eight Acres', and the name in its present form (along with Burnt Hills Wood, immediately north of where Roughton Road station was created) appears on the 1838 Ordnance Survey map.[1] The bungalows were built in the 1960s.

Bus services. By 1891, the two railway companies had arranged a horse-drawn bus service and 'the whole journey through Poppyland to Mundesley [was] daily made by numbers of visitors'.[1] After World War 1, United Automobile Services started the bus station in Cromer, running buses converted from army lorries. (At first, by 1919, they were just running a summer continuation to Cromer of the bus service from Norwich to Aylsham.[2]) Eastern Counties (partly owned by the railway companies) took over the country routes in 1931, at which time buses ran from Cromer to Norwich (*via* Aylsham and Roughton; also *via* Coltishall

Horse buses conveyed passengers into town from the railway station at the top of the Norwich Road. The photograph on the LEFT *was taken around 1896.* BELOW: *Eastern Counties buses at the Central Road depot.*

and North Walsham; and *via* Oulton, Gresham and Aylmerton), to Holt (*via* Sheringham; also *via* Aylmerton and Gresham), to Mundesley, and along the coast road to Hunstanton.[3]

In 1990 the bus depot in Central Road was sold to Bullen's as their builders' yard, leaving only the simple bus station at the corner of Prince of Wales Road and Cadogan Road; this in turn was closed in 2006, when First

Eastern Counties buses said they no longer needed it; but there was a public outcry over the lack of facilities and over disruption to traffic in Cadogan Road when buses were using the street bus stop, and in 2008 the local councils agreed to buy the site and reestablish the bus station there.[4]

Butts. In the days when archery was actively encouraged as part of the national defence system, Cromer like other towns had its archery ground or butts. They are mentioned in a will of 1648,[1] but no clue is given to the location.

Part of an enclosure called Butt Pightle was leased by Henry Samuel Partridge to John Juler Pank in 1824.[2]

C

Cabbell Park (Mill Road). *See* CRICKET; FOOTBALL.

Cabbell Road. The land was sold by the Cromer Hall estate in 1891, and the road made up in 1900.[1] It takes its name from the Cabbell family, owners of Cromer Hall.

Cadogan Road. Part of the Cromer Hall estate development. The road was made up in 1900.[1] Many of the roads created in Cromer at the time were named after aristocratic titles (such as the Earl of Cadogan), without necessarily implying any connection with Cromer on the part of the holders of those titles, but at the time this road was created the fifth Earl Cadogan was in the cabinet in Lord Salisbury's third administration; a major landowner in Chelsea and with an estate in Suffolk, he supported the Wyndham Land Bill of 1902.[2] His daughter Edith was to marry Lord

Hillingdon's son in 1916.[3]

Cambridge Street. Made up by 1899.[1] The row of cottages on the eastern side was built for coastguard officers. On the other side of the street. there used to be a Labour Exchange.

The Duke of Cambridge, Commander-in-Chief of the British army from 1856 to 1895, used the services of Mace Brothers photographers in Garden Street.[2]

Camera obscura. Herbert Mace ran a camera obscura on the beach near the foot of the Gangway in the 1880s. Visitors would pay to enter a darkened tent with an arrangement of lens and mirrors which projected an image of the surrounding scene onto a table.

Camping Close. *See* FOOTBALL.

Canada Road. Mentioned by name in the UDC minutes of 1893.

Cannon. A pair of cannon are seen in an old photograph of Ditchell's barn in Tucker Street. They had been removed there from the nearby bluff which had collapsed in a storm.[1] There seems to be no knowledge of the origin of the third cannon, seen in the ground of Ditchell's house next door, or of the cannon which has led a long and peaceful existence as a bollard at the top of the Gangway. *See also* FORTIFICATIONS.

Cannon point out to sea from the grounds of Ditchell's house and barn in Tucker Street.

Carlton Terrace. Name for nos. 3–13 Hans Place, owned before World War I by Thomas Sidle of Colchester.

Carlyle Road. Proposed name of a turning off Cromwell Road; in the event it became merely a gravel drive leading to the new Vicarage numbered 42 Cromwell Road.[1]

Carnivals. Cromer's medieval fair (*see under* MARKETS) degenerated over the centuries into a Whit-Monday regatta,[1] and the first carnivals so called took place in the late 19th and early 20th centuries.[2] After a gap of a few years in the 1960s, a new series was begun by a group of business and community-minded people led by garage proprietor Gordon Jessop and hotelier Edna Lycett. They followed much the same pattern of fancy dress, competitions, entertainments and a parade, as seen in the carnivals of the 1920s and in those organised by Alfie Howard in the 1950s and 60s. Peter Stibbons was asked to front the various events for the first two years but when work took him away from the town the role was taken over by Tony Shipp, who was rewarded for his contribution with an MBE.

The carnival grew rapidly and by the 1990s the parade was reputed to be the largest in the country apart from Notting Hill; its activity was conducted through a limited company, Cromer

CROMER CHARACTERS
ALFIE HOWARD

In the 1950s, Cromer Town Council employed Londoner Alfie Howard as town crier and summer entertainer. He provided a very successful series of events throughout the summer, with many young people taking part. Sunday evening concerts filled the tennis courts in North Lodge Park (the bandstand and stage being built for the purpose) and Alfie took the lead in running the carnival.

Not everyone appreciated some aspects of Alfie's activities, however: the events were generally sponsored by breweries, and the local temperance society made their objections known to the council, who consequently decided not to make further use of Alfie's services.

Many of the activities initiated by Alfie nevertheless continued, including the waiters' and waitresses' race which he began as an event around Church Square.

Voluntary Entertainments Organisation Ltd., whilst remaining essentially reliant on local people investing time in attracting both local people and holiday-makers to a wide range of fun activities.

¶ **Carr Lane.** Occupants of Ivy Farm (called Ivy House on the late-19th-century Ordnance Survey map), the northernmost property in the parish of Northrepps, could go through the patch of woodland called The Carrs and join this road leading right up the hill, continuing as Madam's Lane, past the cottages known as Bull's Row and into the centre of Northrepps village with its iron foundry and parish church. The tithe map shows that this road was already established by the 1830s, and as the path to Northrepps church it is probably very much older. The unmade sections of the road (signed 'unsuitable for motor vehicles' in the 21st century) give a good impression of what the whole of this and many other roads would have been like until the end of the 19th century.

Carrington Road. Made up in 1896,[1] but not built on till the 1920s.

The third Lord Carrington (1843–1928) was Liberal MP for High Wycombe, and later President of the Board of Agriculture & Fisheries and Lord Privy Seal. In 1878 he married Lord Suffield's eldest daughter. He was a foundation member of the Royal Cromer Golf Club in 1888. Lord and Lady Carrington of Wycombe Abbey stayed at the Hotel de Paris in 1891.[2]

Carrington Villas. Original name of HARBORD HOUSE; though built as a pair of villas, it seems to have been occupied as a single dwelling by 1899.[1]

❡ **Carrwood House** (Carr Lane). Built in 1910 as a retirement home for H. H. Fowler, who as Viscount Wolverhampton was the first Methodist peer.[1] Takes its name from the woodland which extended on both sides of the road, called The Carrs.[2]

Cavendish Road. Proposed name of a turning off Cromwell Road.[1]

Cemeteries. In order to accommodate burials after the churchyard was full up, the Old Cemetery on the Holt Road (next to the junction with Sandy Lane) was created in 1860 on land given by Benjamin Bond Cabbell; there was a private path to it from CROMER HALL. One quarter of the cemetery was set aside for Dissenters. The cemetery was closed in 1908.

The council agreed in 1900 to buy a ten-acre field from R. W. Ketton for a new cemetery at the top of the Holt Road, next to the junction with Greens Lane; this land was previously farmed by Henry Durrant, who in 1904 was the first to be buried in the cemetery; his grave lies just inside the gate. The land had been part of Felbrigg parish, so the parish boundaries were altered to bring it into Cromer parish.[1] The chapel, caretaker's house and entrance gates were built by W. Porter of Cromer in 1902.[2]

Censuses. *See* POPULATION.

Central Road. Created in 1902.[1] By no stretch of the imagination could it ever have been regarded as central to Cromer, or even to the new development of the Cromer Hall estate land, so its name presumably alludes to the adjacent railway bringing holidaymakers from the Midlands.

Chapel Street. Originally Pump Street (after the pump which stood at the fiveways junction with Church Street), but renamed after the Methodist church was opened on the eastern side of the street (*see* METHODIST CHAPELS). The road was given footpaths each side in 1895, the Council noting that it could be made a one-way street if necessary.[1]

Chaplains. In medieval times there were generally two chaplains, one of them described as 'parish chaplain' and another who was paid for singing masses for the souls of those departed who had left money under their wills for such services. Several chaplains are known to us from their wills:

◻ Lawrence Draper (died 1382), the son of Lady Alice de Crowmere and probably related to the Gosselyn family
◻ John Hermere, chaplain in 1384, who later became Vicar
◻ Simon Chylde, 'parish chaplain' (will 1391) and John Grym (will 1396), who both expressed the wish to be buried in the churchyard
◻ William Mannysfeld (will proved 1424), who wanted to be buried in the church itself
◻ Richard Rudde (will 1452, proved 1453), who left bequests showing him to have been reasonably well off
◻ Sir Thomas Bryning (a legatee under Richard Rudde's will)[1]

Charities. Before the invention of a state system of social security, the parish had to help its own poor. In addition to a collecting box in the church (required by legislation of Henry VIII and mentioned in Cromer as early as 1551[1]), there were various pieces of land (totalling about eight acres in the parish plus more land in Northrepps) which were used to provide an income for the aid of the poor, and in the 1650s Robert Baxter left £25 to Cromer inhabitants to increase the stock of the poor.[2]

In the early 20th century the income from 14 acres in Northrepps was still being distributed annually to poor widows not already in receipt of parish help, and 19th-century charities under the wills of John Howes of Norwich (1863) and George Webb Collison of Cromer (1893) provided an endowment for coals and clothing to be distributed to the aged poor each Christmas.[3]

❡ Overstrand parish acquired a piece of land in the parish of Cromer (apparently in 1644), approximately three acres in extent, sometimes referred to as the 'town land'. This was let to farmers, and the rent (paid in kind until at least 1716, but later commuted to a money rent) was distributed to the poor of Overstrand.[4]

See also ALMSHOUSES.

Chesterfield Cottages. Built in 1878. Also known as North Row.

Chesterfield Hall (Cabbell Road). The original corrugated iron building was erected in 1898 and used to store goods coming to the shops by railway; it became two cottages, which in 1952 were converted to form a meeting place for the pentecostal Church of God, which had met in The Upper Room behind Garden Street since 1894.[1] Demolished in 2000 and a new hall built of brick on the same site.

Chesterfield Villas and Lodge. Built on the site of the town's last MALT-

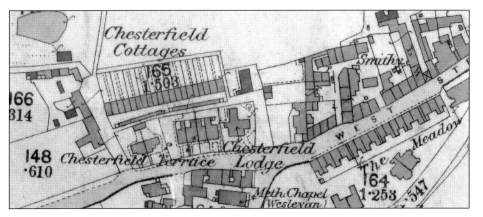

Ordnance Survey plan showing Meadow Cottages and Chesterfield Cottages (here called Chesterfield Terrace) soon after they were built. The irregular shape in the top left is the Sheep's Pit; *there are numerous cottages in Golden Square, and a blacksmith still operates in the yard behind the White Horse. The Wesleyan Methodist chapel has yet to be rebuilt.*

ings in 1878–79 (the architect probably David Brandon), and named after John Bond Cabbell's London home address (1 Chesterfield Gardens).

The future Prime Minister Winston Churchill (1874-1965) stayed at Chesterfield Lodge as a child in 1885; whilst there, he threw an inkpot at his nurse who had to see a doctor at Hamilton House; the doctor administered corporal punishment upon the young boy.[1]

⁋ **Christ Church, Overstrand.** Built in 1867[1] to replace St Martin's parish church, which was then in ruins except for the tower. It could seat 200 people,[2] but this was regarded as insufficient when Overstrand came to be rapidly developed at the beginning of the 20th century, so St Martin's was rebuilt (1911–

14) and Christ Church later demolished.

⁋ **Church Close.** Created in the 1960s.

Church House. Medieval house believed to have been in the vicinity of Cromer church; some have speculated it was on the site later occupied by Hanover House.

Church Lane. *See* Loke.

Church Rock. Name given by fishermen to remains of medieval masonry near the end of the pier, which they believed to be the remains of the original church of St Peter, Shipden juxta Mare. Once as much as 6 to 9 feet (nearly 3m) above the sea bed, it was struck by the *Victoria* steamer in 1888, as she set out for Yarmouth, and was thereafter

One of the earliest known photographs of Church Street, about 1860. It may well have been taken by Daniel Savin whose shop was nearby on the left. The cottage on the corner is Mr Randell's ironmongery shop; the building was later extended to three storeys. The cottages at the further end of the row were replaced by taller buildings later in the century.

blown up with explosives, though enough remained to be visible above water during an exceptionally low tide in 1929.[1] The site was investigated in an underwater dive by Martin Warren (of Cromer Museum) and David Pope, who found flint masonry which could be from the old church; a sample is in the museum.

Church Street. The land to the south of the church remained open until the late eighteenth century, and the fields immediately opposite the church were not built on for another hundred years after that. However, the road pattern included two important routes into Cromer, West Street and EAST STREET, and Church Street gradually, almost as it were reluctantly, established itself as a link between the two. At first the cottages were small and close together, so that a series of widenings became necessary as the town developed and through traffic increased. The road was widened near the Post Office in 1890,[1] and in the vicinity of the old LORD NELSON COFFEE TAVERN in 1892,[2] and by 12 feet at the expense of the churchyard in the 20th century. The widening of The NARROWS was the last phase of this process.

Churches. [*These paragraphs relate to the parish churches of Cromer. For other places of worship and congregations, see* BAPTIST CHURCH; CHESTERFIELD HALL; CONGREGATIONAL CHURCH; GOSPEL HALL; JEHOVAH'S WITNESSES; METHODIST CHURCHES; NEW WINE CHURCH; ROMAN CATHOLIC CHURCH; ST MARTIN'S CHURCH.]

Medieval SHIPDEN had two churches: St Peter's, which was just east of the present pier head and was washed away by the sea in the 14th century; and St Paul's, on the site of the present parish church. St Paul's seems to have had a square tower about 70 feet high. The two livings were held by the same incumbent. When in 1337 the sea began to wash away the churchyard of St Peter's and the church itself was in evident danger, the rector applied for permission to demolish St Paul's and replace it with a building big enough for the needs of both the older churches. Work was not begun straightaway; probably there was not the money to spare until

after the Black Death of 1349-50 had reduced the population and increased personal wealth; but building seems to have begun about 1377. The church was conveyed (together with other property) by the king to the Carthusian prior and convent of London in 1382, and a piece of land 20 by 60 feet, adjoining the nearby Rectory, was also granted to the Carthusians in 1393.

The size of the new building suggests rich patrons, but we do not know whether they derived their money from fishing and trading or from other sources. The height of the tower would have made it a landmark for shipping, which may have appealed to prospective donors who had made their money through maritime trade, but, most importantly of all, money was bequeathed by people who expected a return in the form of prayers to be said and masses sung for their souls. There were four chapels within the building where such masses would have been celebrated. Building work was completed by 1437, and details of the west porch suggest that the mason in the 1430s was the same as one who worked at Wiveton, Blakeney, Wymondham and half a dozen other churches in the county.[1]

In the church's pre-Reformation glory, candles burned perpetually before the image of the Holy Trinity and in devotion to St Peter and the Blessed Mary and to the Saviour; and there was a 'plough light' maintained by collections on Plough Monday.[2] Chaplains wearing rich vestments said masses every day in the side chapels, and festivals would have been celebrated with processions, bells and polyphonic organ music and singing – a tradition which was very strong at the time both in Norwich cathedral and in the Low Countries where Cromer merchants would have been trading.[3]

Lights and images did not survive the Reformation – royal injunctions issued in 1538 ordered the abolition of some of them, and threatened the rest with action later.

In 1681 Thomas Gill, rector of Ingworth, obtained permission from the bishop to demolish the vestries and chancel (upkeep of which was the rec-

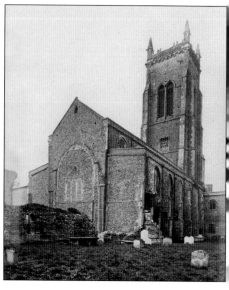

An unusual view of Cromer church, seen from the north-east corner of the churchyard before the chancel was rebuilt.

HARRY YAXLEY'S HOLE

The door leading to the top of the stair tower came to be known as 'Harry Yaxley's hole' after the said boy had a narrow escape there. As Rye recounts the story (Cromer Past and Present, pp. 102–3):

It seems he induced a schoolmate to hold him over the edge by the heels, while he harried a 'caddus's nist' [*a jackdaw's nest*] some little way beneath. His friend while holding him suspended, insisted on having more than his share of the young birds. 'Shahnut hev them,' said Yaxley. 'Then'll drawp thee,' replied the other. 'Drawp away,' retorted Yaxley, which his amiable friend accordingly did. Yaxley fell a distance of 70 feet, but (how no earthly power can tell) came to no harm, was soon well enough to punch his friend's head, and afterwards went away as a man-of-war's man, returning after an eventful life to die quietly within sight of the tower he had fallen from.

If this is the Henry Hagen Yaxley who was buried on 1 January 1852 at the age of 76, this story must date from the early 1780s.

tor's responsibility and had devolved upon Gill as lessee of the rectorial tithes). It was blown up with gunpowder, and the east wall of the aisles and nave walled up; the chancel stood in ruins for two centuries.

The roof of the nave itself soon became ruinous, and the congregation retreated to the tower – a common enough story in churches in the 18th and early 19th centuries. In 1767 permission was given to sell bells, and lead and timber from the old roof, and so raise money for repairs to make the body of the building usable again.

In 1840 the west gallery was rebuilt, and new ones added over the aisles, increasing the seating by 540 places; the architect was William Ollet.[4] Unfortunately it was soon found that the new children's seats were 'useless' as the low gallery above them prevented the occupants from hearing the clergyman.[5]

In 1857 an architect reported on the state of the fabric;[6] restoration was begun in 1863[7] (architect: John H. Brown of Norwich), with much encouragement and support from the local landowners; the galleries were demolished and the roof and windows restored. In a second phase of restoration in 1887–89 (architect: Sir Arthur Blomfield), two bays were added to the eastern end of the aisles, the tower and west porch restored and the chancel rebuilt. In Cromer's Edwardian heyday, church congregations in the summer could be more than 1,500 strong.[8]

See also BELLS; ORGANS. *For a list of incumbents, see* VICARS OF CROMER.

For fuller details see Walter Rye, *Cromer Past and Present* (Norwich: Jarrold, 1889) and S. K. Clarke's unpublished typescript *Some Notes Concerning Cromer Churches* in Cromer Library.

Churchyard. In 1843 the churchyard covered 1.175 acres.[1] On the south side it lost 12 feet to the widening of Church Street in 1895-96;[2] on the west side it has lost some ground to the widening of the High Street; on the east, foundations have been found of the original churchyard wall in the yard of a house in Brook Street;[3] on the north, in addition to losing 6 feet in 1896 to the widening of TUCKER STREET, it must once have stretched a good deal further, for originally it is said to have covered four acres.[4]

Gravestones from the parts lost to road widening in 1896 were carefully recorded before being moved close the church walls.[5]

The iron railings were removed in 1942 to contribute to the war effort – against the protests of the Parochial Church Council, whose argument that the railings had 'artistic merit' was overruled.[6] They were of no great antiquity, having been installed less than 50 years previously when the churchyard wall was rebuilt.[7]

Cinemas. Before the invention of motion pictures, lectures and entertainments were enlivened by use of the magic lantern, conducted from *c.* 1880 to *c.* 1920 by A. E. Salter and Robert Randall; the Lecture Hall in Cross Street was built with a lantern room for the purpose.

From 1901 travelling showmen brought cinematograph displays to Cromer periodically; some were shown in the pier pavilion (though the electricity company were unable to supply power there in 1912 and suggested that the operators should bring their own generator), and in 1914 the Town Hall was modified to include a film room, operating room and basement motor room,[1] enabling it to put on cinema shows in summer seasons into the 1930s. The Olympia cinema ran from 1934 to 1939 in Garden Street (later becoming a roller skating rink).

The Cromer Theatre of Varieties was opened in Hans Place in 1914 by Edward Trollor the Church Street greengrocer and C. J. Parker the butcher. They put on live shows, boxing and films; it later became the Regal cinema (and, in the early years of the 21st century, the Movieplex). The original company (whose shareholders were almost exclusively local people) was dissolved in 1930, the year in which talkies arrived – the first time they had come to the area.[2] After suffering from the general decline in audiences the cinema was due to close in 1976, but unlike the cinemas in Sheringham, Holt and North Walsham managed to stage a recovery,

being refurbished in 1986[3] and becoming a thriving multiscreen cinema in the 1990s.

Clare Road. Plans for the road were submitted to the council by John Youngs (who had been the building contractor for the Grand Hotel[1]) and passed in 1903.[2]

The road name matches those of many other roads developed in the area at this time in referring to an aristocratic title (the Earl of Clare; the Earl of Rosebery; the Duke of Connaught; etc.).[3]

Clarence Mews (Brook Street). Development of cottages built *c.* 2006–08 on the site of the Clarence riding establishment. The frontage incorporates the 1893 archway of the building (architect: A. F. Scott) erected on the site of COSSEY'S YARD for jobmaster R. W. Palmer.[1] The building became Allman's auction rooms in 1962 and then a SNOOKER CLUB.

Clement Scott Mews (Overstrand Road). Built on the site of the Royal Links Hotel's dance pavilion, which had burnt down in 1978.[1] The cottages were intended as holiday homes but became permanent homes instead.

Cliff Avenue. One of the most fashionable parts of Cromer when it was built at the end of the 19th century: here were houses occupied by doctors, professional men and members of royal families. They had a club house where they could socialise and a bowling green just around the corner. *See* GRANGE COURT; MORDEN HOUSE; PRIOR BANK; TUDOR HOUSE; VIRGINIA COURT HOTEL; WOOD-DENE SCHOOL.

Cliff Drive. Built on land previously let to fishermen as allotments.

The ilex trees, originally planted by the Hoare family in the garden of Cliff House, are descended from trees grown at Holkham from acorns which the first Lord Leicester had brought back from his Grand Tour in Italy.[1]

Cliff House (Overstrand Road). A house is marked here on a map of 1717.[1] From *c.* 1772 it belonged to Dr Sidney Terry, who let part of it as lodgings; it had 10 bedrooms, two parlours and 'a well proportioned tea room' 22 ft by 18 ft (5.6 by 4.6m).[2] In 1801, after Terry's death, the house was bought by Samuel Hoare.[3] Elizabeth Fry stayed here in 1842. During the course of the century the Hoare family enlarged the building considerably.[4]

From 1924 to 1999 the building was a hotel; after this it was divided into apartments.

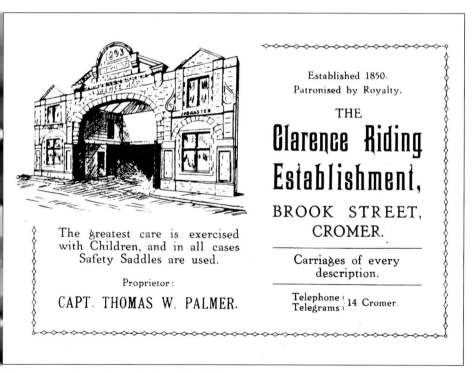

The greatest care is exercised with Children, and in all cases Safety Saddles are used.

Proprietor:

CAPT. THOMAS W. PALMER.

Established 1850.
Patronised by Royalty.

THE

Clarence Riding Establishment,

BROOK STREET,
CROMER.

Carriages of every description.

Telephone ˥ 14 Cromer.
Telegrams ˩

Front cover of a brochure for the original Clarence Mews.

57

Cliff Lane. Leading from the Overstrand Road to the open land atop the cliffs, this was once known as the Driftway, suggesting that livestock (presumably sheep) were driven this way between the clifftop pastures and the lusher meadows beside the beck on the other side of the road.

Cliff Lane Cottage. Occupied by Sherman Cutler Ransom from 1800 to 1811. Seen in a drawing of 1840.[1] The building had been converted into flats by 1962.

Cliff Road. The terrace of houses has an 1892 datestone; the road was made up in 1896.[1]

Cliffside. Name for the house adjoining Newstead House, on the corner of Surrey Street and the Gangway.

❡ Cliffside in Overstrand High Street was a home for Edward Boardman (1833–1910), architect of the Overstrand Hotel; his widow was still there during World War 1. The house was later bought by Louis Meyer Van Moppes, whose company dealt in industrial diamonds.[1] The house was acquired by the Sisters of the Sacred Heart of Mary and used as a school; after the school closed, it continued to be used under the name of the Julian House (a reference to the 14th/15th-century mystic Julian of Norwich) until 2001, when it became a

The Cliftonville Hotel in 1896 – Mr Churchyard's house has been extended into a hotel, though Skipper's enlargement has not yet taken place. In front of the hotel, the marrams are quite untamed; on the horizon, the bulk of the Royal Links Hotel.

private residence again under the name of Cliffside House.

Clifton Park. Development of the 1960s, on land belonging to a Mr Clifton; it was a cul-de-sac until Howards Hill West was built in the 1970s, and the 'No Through Road' sign was still there at the beginning of the 21st century!

¶ **Clifton Way.** Development of bungalows off the Coast Road in Overstrand. On the other side of the road there occurred a massive landslip in the 1990s, after which the cliff had to be stabilised by sinking boreholes to draw off the underground water which was making the land unstable.

Cliftonville Hotel (Runton Road). In 1894-95 William Churchyard (owner of the West Street Stores and a boarding house in West Street[1]) had a house built on Runton Road, designed by A. F. Scott. A couple of years later Churchyard began to turn it into a hotel, adding first of all the block on the corner of Alfred Road and then in 1898-99 an embattled entrance bay and the dining room with cupola on the north-west corner (architect: George Skipper; builder: J. S. Smith of Norwich).[2] In this part of the building much original stained glass survives, reminiscent of the Royal Arcade in Norwich which was built for the same architect. The façade remained entirely of red-brown brick and stone until it was given a weatherproof facelift in 1998-99. A modern 1960s dining-room extension was demolished in the 1990s to make space for car parking.

Clocks. Cromer church tower's one-handed clock was sold to Alby church in 1863 for £10 and replaced at the expense of J. Gurney Barclay and members of the Gurney and Birkbeck families.[1] The new clock was made by T. Cooke & Sons of York, with the wooden hands for which this firm was noted; the same firm was responsible for the clock installed in Fakenham church the following year.[2] Tom Mack of 21 Church Street was the first winder of the new clock, being succeeded in 1897 by the family firm of Randall, still undertaking the job more than a century later.

¶ **Close, The.** *See* GLENDON HOUSE.

Clubs. *For social clubs, see* ALEX CLUB; BLAZER'S; CONSERVATIVE CLUB; CROMER SOCIAL CLUB; FISHERMEN'S AND WORKING MEN'S CLUB; PIT; SHIPDEN CLUB; SNOOKER CLUB; VIRGINIA COURT HOTEL. *For sports clubs, see under the name of the sport. For medieval times, see* GUILDS.

Coaches. The *Diligence* coach was plying between Cromer and Norwich by the early 1790s, starting out at the King's Arms Hotel (later known as the CROWN AND ANCHOR). In the 19th century the *Express* coach office was at Tucker's Hotel. The mail coach left here at 2.20

p.m. going to Norwich; there was also a coach going *via* North Walsham on Tuesdays and Thursdays at 11 a.m. and on Saturdays at 7 a.m.[1]

The *Enterprise* left the Hotel de Paris going to Norwich *via* Aylsham on Tuesdays, Wednesdays, Thursdays and Saturdays at 2.15 pm.[2]

Robert Marten in 1825 described 'the Coach with four inside & 16 out-side & with plenty of Baskets – Game – Trunks – Bags, etc etc.' His journey from Cromer to Norwich took 3¾ hours.[3] 'It is true they were slow, owing to the inordinate quantity of luggage they had to take; but they were danger-ous enough to please the adventurous,' says Walter Rye, referring to an occa-sion when one coach is said to have gone over the parapet of the Ingworth bridge and landed all its passengers and luggage in the river! 'The depar-ture and arrival of the coaches were the events of the day, and "Church Square" was always in a bustle then. Some of us used (we were young then) to walk out to Runton [*presumably Roughton?*] and run the coach in.'[4]

The horses which had pulled T. A. Cook's coach between Norwich and Cromer were sold in 1909.[5]

Robert Walpole Palmer of CLARENCE MEWS ran afternoon trips leaving Church Square each day, using a chara banc drawn by four horses.[6]

After World War I, motor coaches took over from horse-drawn vehicles the task of taking visitors to see the sights of the neighbourhood. By the 1940s the East Coast Motor Co. offered

The Lobster *coach outside the Grand Hotel. There is quite a sense of occasion here!*

six different day trips and ten different half-day trips to various Norfolk destinations 'subject to weather',[7] and after World War 2 Babbage's 'Green and Grey' coaches were a common sight.

See also Bus services.

Coal-yards. From at least the 14th century onwards there was an important coastal trade bringing coal from Tyneside, the ships returning with grain from Norfolk. After the failure of Cromer's Pier to withstand the sea in the mid-18th century, vessels had to land their cargo on the beach and it would be brought up to coal-yards near the top of the Gangway in carts drawn by horses or mules.

As soon as the railway arrived in 1877, coal came in by train instead of by ship; there were coal-yards at both railway stations.

¶ Coast Road. The original route of the main road through Overstrand from Cromer to Mundesley. It was diverted in 1927 when erosion threatened the road.

Coastguard cottages. The coast guard was originally established not (as nowadays) to save lives but to prevent smuggling. There was a policy of moving officers around the country so that they did not have local connections which might hinder their law-enforcing duties, so accommodation had to be provided for the men. **1.** In 1833 the Admiralty, finding it hard to procure lodgings at reasonable rents[1] for the Cromer officers, leased five cottages in Ellis Newstead's former granary (at the top of the Gangway), together with the adjacent house for the Chief Officer.[2]

2. In 1899 a plot of land was bought on the east side of Cambridge Street for £422 and a row of cottages erected at a cost of about £2,700; the Chief Officer's house was at the corner, fronting onto Mount Street.[3] The equipment was kept just around the corner in Cross Street (*see* Rocket House).

Coastguard station. The Cromer station came under the port of Cley, and required premises where a boat could be kept and from which to keep watch.

1. The original Cromer station was based on the east cliff at Webb's house (later rebuilt as the Watch House). In 1895 the Cromer Hall estate terminated the lease on the Watch House, and provided the coastguards with a plot of land on the newly developing Cross Street. A Rocket Apparatus House to accommodate cart and life-saving apparatus was duly built the following year at no. 10 (architect A. F. Scott; builder James White).

2. A new lookout building was built on the marrams.[1]

3. For a time the top floor of what had been the lower annexe of Tucker's Hotel was used; this was converted into a private residence known as the Old Look-Out.

4. The last lookout building was the former World War 2 gun emplacement built of concrete on the east cliff near the top of Cliff Drive. A 24-hour watch was kept until 1979, a daytime watch thereafter; the building was sold in 1999 with planning permission for use as a holiday home, and the coastguard thereafter based in an office block in Yarmouth.

Coats of arms. *See* ARMORIAL BEARINGS.

Colne Cottage. In the Croft, opposite the Meadow. Thomas Fowell Buxton III and Lady Victoria Buxton moved into the Cottage when Colne House became a hospital for wounded soldiers of World War I; Fowell died here in 1915 and his widow in 1916.[1] In 1930 it was bought by Norfolk County Council and became a children's home; after the war it was a home for abused and emotionally disturbed children (1949–83). Sold to Derbypark in 1984 and converted into private housing.[2]

Colne House. Built about 1791 for Henry Partridge, a London barrister who became Deputy Lieutenant of Norfolk;[1] he bought the land from Gerard Levinge van Heythuysen in the 1780s.[2] The earliest representation of the house seems to be a pencil drawing in Cromer Museum, on paper watermarked 1809. In 1820, after the death of Partridge's widow, the house was occupied by Rev. Thomas Clowes. It was put on the market in 1831.[3] Samuel Gurney bought it, but sold it again in 1838, after which it was associated with the Buxton family. (It is said to be named after Earls Colne,

Colne House in 1831, before the addition of the bay-windowed drawing room.

Colne Lodge is seen in this engraving – drawn at slightly the wrong angle.

in Essex, where the first Thomas Fowell Buxton spent his childhood.[4]) During World War I it was used as a 40-bed auxiliary hospital, run by Mrs Maude Barclay of The Warren with Katherine Marshall as sister-in-charge; by the time this closed, early in 1919, it had admitted 634 patients.[5]

The house was sold to a speculator in 1922, and in 1923 was bought by J. C. Dowding, who turned it into a hotel. In the 1980s it was turned into private flats and cottages by Derbypark developers of Beeston Regis, who demolished the winter gardens and ballroom to make way for four town houses, and converted the stable block into three homes.[6]

Colne Lodge (Louden Road). Part of the Colne House estate. Sold in 1922

and used as Co-op offices and shop; demolished in 1936 to make way for the telephone exchange.

Colne Road. First projected in 1925, when houses were built on the southern part of The Croft.

Compit Hills. Named on a map from the first half of the 18th century;[1] in medieval Latin the word *compita* meant a boundary, and the land lies at the edge of the parish of Cromer where it meets the parish of Roughton. In the 19th century the Buxton family used this as part of their shooting estate; bungalows were built on it in the 1970s to 1990s.

Congregational Church. Congregationalists used to meet for worship at the LECTURE HALL attached to the Lord Nelson Coffee House in the 1880s.[1] ¶ An Independent congregation was meeting in Overstrand in 1672 – Christopher Amyraut, son of an Irish puritan minister, was licensed as its teacher in that year.[2]

Connaught Road. Plans for the road (originally to be called Caistor Road) were submitted to the council by John Youngs and passed in 1903.[1] The Duke of Connaught was a son of Queen Victoria and had played golf at Cromer. The council houses were built in the 1930s.

Conservative Club. The Cromer and District Conservative and Unionist Working Men's Club was formed in 1906[1] and had premises in Church Street, opposite Read's dairy, until it was bombed in World War 2. The club later moved to the former hospital on Louden Road. It closed in 2005.

Convent of the Faithful Virgin. *See* GRANGE COURT.

Corner Street. Plans were approved by the council in 1895 for the contruction of this road 'on the site of Breese's premises' and by enlarging the back passages to Garden Street, Hamilton Road and Prince of Wales Road. (The smithy is shown on the 1887 Ordnance Survey map, before any of the houses were built.) Made up in 1901.[1]

Cossey's Yard. Yard of cottages off Brook Street, a fisherman whose parrot was kept out in the yard and formed an attraction for local children. Trevor Medland later used the site of the yard for the extension to his cycle shop; this in turn was demolished *c.* 2007 as part of the development of CLARENCE MEWS.

Cottage (Louden Road). Public house created in 2005 in the former bar and function room of the Conservative Club.[1] The building was Cromer's first purpose-built hospital and the nameplate survives (with the words 'Cromer Cottage' picked out in white but the

next word, 'Hospital', left in obscurity).

Cottage Hospital. *See* HOSPITAL; WEST COTTAGE.

Council. Cromer had a Local Board from 1884,[1] replaced by Cromer Urban District Council in 1894. From 1974 this was replaced by the North Norfolk District Council, though the town continued to have a Town Council. At the time of the reorganisation, local hotelier and businessman Tom Bolton had been on the UDC for three years, and he served as chairman of the NNDC until 1978.[2]

Council offices. The Urban District Council used FOUNTAIN HOUSE as offices 1902–28,[2] then NORTH LODGE from 1928. The North Norfolk District Council offices at the top of the Holt road were built in 1988–90, replacing both North Lodge and a rabbit-warren of offices at Barker's Herne. North Lodge then became home to the Town Council.

Court Drive. Built in the grounds of NEWHAVEN COURT. Named on the Ordnance Survey map surveyed in 1969, but the only buildings at that date were the Newhaven Court flats.

Craigside (St Mary's Road). **1.** Boarding house, built 1901–02.[1] **2.** Flats built on its site; the cylindrical corner entrance mimics that of the original house.

CROMER CHARACTERS
THE 5TH LORD SUFFIELD

*Charles Harbord, 5th Baron Suffield
(1830–1914), was responsible for much
of the development of Cromer at the
end of the 19th century – the railway
first came to Cromer over his land,
and he sold building plots in its vicinity
(see* SUFFIELD PARK*). He later claimed
that 'the Cromer Urban Council . . .
resented my removing posts they had
put up without my permission on my
own ground, although it is entirely
owing to me that Cromer is big enough
to have a Council of any description'.[1]*

*He is here depicted by Roland
L'Estrange (1869–1919), who signed
himself 'Ao' (apparently short for
'Armadillo'); the cartoon appeared in*
Vanity Fair *in 1907.*

Crawford Road. Plans for the road were submitted to the council by John Youngs, and for six houses by Mr J. Atherton, and passed in 1903.[1]

Crescent, The. The land on which the Crescent stands was advertised for sale in 1821 as 'calculated for the erection of Lodging-houses or an Hotel, as its situation cannot be excelled on any part of the coast, and is the only eligible piece of ground to be procured in this fashionable and much admired watering place'.[1] A crescent of plain, two-storey houses was built, to which bays and balconies and a third storey were added later.[2]

Crescent Club. *See* BLAZER'S.

Cricket. J. S. Mannings in 1806 describes 'the manly game of cricket' played in Cromer; it is clearly played on grass, not on the beach, but the pitch is not identifiable.[1]

The first known cricket ground was

A ladies' cricket match being played in the grounds of Cliff House in the 1880s. The umpire is Samuel Hoare; the players are drawn from the leading Quaker families holidaying here.

on the field between what is now St Margaret's Road and Vicarage Road; it was laid out (probably in 1860[2]) by John William ('Brindy') Baker, who ran his livery business from the stables behind Upton House before moving to Ditchell's house and barn in Tucker Street in 1879.[3] By that time the original ground had already been lost to the development of St Margaret's Terrace and the Shipbourne Hotel.

A Cromer United Cricket Club (did it unite more than one earlier club?) was restricted to members of the Working Men's READING ROOM and played from 1880 on BEEF MEADOW by permission of Mr Cabbell.[4] The club won the Norfolk Junior Cup in 1891.

Colne House had a cricket field 82 yards square. 'It was surrounded with buildings, walls and a kitchen garden;

the number of cricket balls which were damaged when hit against walls was considerable.'[5] During World War I this ground was used for training new recruits for a Field Ambulance Unit.[6]

After World War I the club was re-established and played at CABBELL PARK. The first match at the Norton Warnes ground on Overstrand Road was played in 1957, the club having a lease on the ground from the R. G. Carter building group until 2011 (later extended to 2021).[7] ¶ Cricket facilities were introduced to Overstrand by Lord Battersea in the grounds of THE PLEASAUNCE.[8] This was his own private sports ground, which the village later bought from his estate.

Croft, The. In a map of *c.* 1868 the road now known by this name is simply called 'path to Lady Buxtons'; the name The Croft referred to the field on the eastern side of it.[1] In medieval times a croft was an enclosed piece of ground lying between a house and the open fields, and may have been large enough to be worth ploughing; in later medieval times crofts often became gardens or paddocks, or were simply taken into the open fields.[2] Three maps from the first half of the 18th century all show divisions within The Croft suggesting that it may have been ploughed in strips. (*See* FIELD SYSTEM.)

The part of the modern road nearest to Arbor Road was created in 1925.

See also COLNE COTTAGE; COLNE HOUSE; COLNE LODGE.

Cromer. The name appears in old documents as 'Crowmere' and occurs in a will dated 1262; earlier references are to SHIPDEN. Cromer seems to be the same as the inland part of the settlement ('Shipden-juxta-Felbrigg', as opposed to the seaside 'Shipden-juxta-Mare'). The form 'Shipden by Cromer' occurs in a document of 1425, but from about 1452 the prevailing form (used in legal documents as late as the 19th century) is 'Shipden alias Cromer'.[1] The Gough map of Britain in the Bodleian Library dates from *c.* 1360 and calls the place Cromer.

The first element of the name seems reasonably to mean 'crow', though why crows should be particularly associated with the place is a mystery; the second element is usually taken to mean 'lake'

or 'pond', but could also refer to the sea (as in the placenames Margate and Mersea).[2]

Cromer & District Labour Club. Social club which occupied the ground floor of SURREY HOUSE.

Cromer Christian Fellowship Society. *See* FISHERMEN'S AND WORKING MEN'S CLUB.

Cromer Convention. A series of Christian conferences was held at NEWHAVEN COURT by the liberal-minded Anglican Evangelical Group Movement from 1928.[1]

Cromer Country Club. Built on the footings of the ROYAL LINKS HOTEL.

Cromer Hall. The old Cromer Hall was the manor house of UFFORD'S MANOR and home of the Windham family from the 1660s. It seems that they rebuilt or remodelled a possibly Tudor house, giving it the fashionable crow-stepped gables of the late 17th century. Legend has it that one attic chamber was walled up,

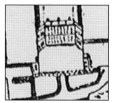 

Tiny details from two 18th-century maps showing the old Cromer Hall in semi-diagrammatic form.

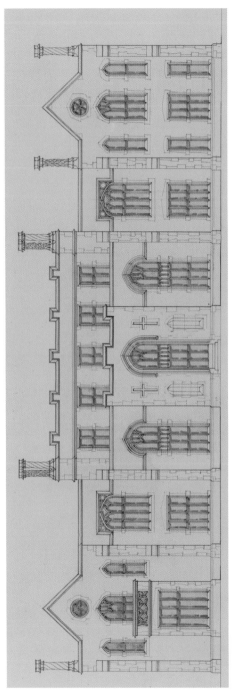

with no entrance save through the window, and that at various times large pits were discovered under the floor and in the thickness of the walls, and were imagined to have been used by smugglers.[1]

Thomas Fowell Buxton lived here with his family 1820–28.

The Hall was completely rebuilt in 1828–29 at a cost of over £12,000, the architect being W. J. Donthorn, who had recently reconstructed the interior of Felbrigg Hall and designed the East Wing and stable block there;[2] but on the night of 23 November 1829 fire gutted the centre and south wing of the completed (but not yet furnished) building. It was insured for only £2,500, but building work was quickly resumed.[3]

The Hall was the birthplace in 1841 of Evelyn, son of Henry Baring MP (a member of the banking family of Barings); he became Governor-General of Egypt and was created 1st Earl Cromer. His sister became Lady Suffield.

In 1852 the Hall was sold with the entire estate to Benjamin Bond Cabbell, who immediately set about a programme of further property acquisitions and development.[4] After his death in 1874, the property passed to his cousin John Cabbell (1808?–78), a barrister with experience in the West Indies and in Glasgow. He changed his name to Bond-Cabbell. He had the lodges built,

< *Cromer Hall as erected in 1829.*

and the battlemented porch with its turret (1875; architect David Brandon). He bequeathed his property to his widow Margaret for life, and then to his son Benjamin Bond Bond-Cabbell (1857–92).[5] After the latter's death, 974 acres of the remaining estate were sold to numerous buyers, leaving only the Hall and its home farm.

For the summer of 1902 the Hall

CROMER CHARACTERS
BENJAMIN BOND CABBELL

Benjamin Bond Cabbell (1781–1874) was a London barrister and philanthropist. He was interested in science (being elected a Fellow of the Royal Society and a Vice-President of the Royal Institution and of the Zoological Society), music, literature and the arts, and supported a large number of organisations, especially schools, hospitals and benefit and pension societies.

After several abortive attempts to enter Parliament, he became Conservative MP for St Albans 1846–47 and for Boston 1847–57.[1] In 1852, already over 70 years old, he paid more than £64,000 for the Cromer Hall estate, comprising (as the newspapers reported, with some exaggeration) 'the whole of the town of Cromer, with the exception of two houses, and about 12,000 acres of land. The property was lately possesssed by the Misses Windham, two old ladies, who were much averse to improvements and alterations. To the inhabitants of Cromer the change of proprietorship is likely to be most beneficial, as the hon. gentleman has already given orders for most extensive alterations, the laying out of new streets, &c.'

Cabbell was still active in London politics when he bought Cromer Hall, but now started building up his Norfolk interests: in 1854 he served as Sheriff of Norfolk, and in 1857 he bought the east wing of the Assembly House in Norwich, which became a meeting place for freemasons and to which he added other Norwich property. He was himself a leading freemason, succeeding the Lord Suffield as Provincial Grand Master in 1856, and a Lodge was named after him in 1860.[2]

He never married and under his will (dated 21 February 1866, proved 23 December 1874) all his personal estate went to his cousin John Cabbell.[3]

was rented by Sir John Aird (1833–1911), a contracting engineer who had moved the Crystal Palace to Sydenham and had gone on to specialise in gas and water works, notably the Aswan dam. At Cromer he entertained the editor and contributors of *Punch* magazine.[6]

The estate descended through the female line to the Cabbell-Manners family.

📖 Further details are in *Cromer Hall: Seat of the Cabbell Family* (Norwich: Paragraph Publishing, 2007).

Cromer Ladies' Bible Association. Founded in November 1827 'when our friend, Mr. J. J. Gurney, . . . first called us together'. Its first object was to enable poor people to buy Bibles and Testaments cheaply for themselves and relatives, by monthly subscription; and afterwards to furnish Bibles abroad. Visiting was carried out in the nearby parishes, and notes kept of the visitors' reception in each household. Over the first 11 years £914 15s. 10½d. was collected from the ladies of most of Cromer's professional and merchant classes.[1]

Cromer Mutual Improvement Society. Met fortnightly through the winter in a galvanised iron building in Cross Street for discussions and lantern slide lectures. Some meetings also took place in the Red Lion Assembly Room, as when T. Victor Buxton spoke of his reminiscences of India. Newspaper reports suggest that it was formed in 1890.[1]

Cromer Preservation Society. Formed in 2000 to help protect the built and natural heritage of the town. The Society has published a number of useful booklets on buildings and streets in the public eye, and members have presented the case for preservation when planning applications have threatened the traditional appearance of the town.

Cromer Protection Commissioners. Set up by Act of Parliament in 1845 to be responsible for the defences against further erosion of the cliffs. The first commissioners included the big landowners and Henry Sandford, M. B. Ransom and J. W. Rust (whose property on the cliff top had suffered in the storm of 1837). The Commissioners continued in being, alongside the Urban District Council, until the two bodies were merged after World War 2.

Cromer Social Club. Formerly the Ex-Servicemen's Club (name changed in the 1990s). Occupies former dairy premises in The Croft, adjacent to Colne Cottage.

Cromer Theatre of Varieties. *See* CINEMAS.

Cromwell Close. Turning off Cromwell Road.

Cromwell Road. Laid out in 1891,[1] but

The Crossways in 1963, before the widening of the Church Street Narrows.

possibly not named until the tercentenary of Oliver Cromwell's birth in 1899.

See also CARLYLE ROAD; CAVENDISH ROAD.

Cross Street. Developed from the mid-1890s, and made up by 1899.[1] It is named after Jeremiah Cross (1826–78), a coal merchant with coal-yards overlooking the Gangway in Cromer (Brunswick Terrace is built on the site).

¶ Cross lived at Overstrand Old Hall, and was churchwarden there, presenting the church with a silver paten.

John Cross, owner of five cottages in Brook Street in 1827, is described as 'of Northrepps'.

Crossway House. See UPTON HOUSE.

Crossways. Name for the junction of Church Street, Chapel Street, West Street and Garden Street.

¶ Also the name for a development of housing for retired people, built on the site of Holly Cottage in Overstrand.

Crown. 1. Name of a messuage (presumably an inn) bequeathed by Richard Fenne to his wife Katherine in his will dated 1787.[1]

2. Name given in the 1861 census to the SHIP INN.

Crown and Anchor (Garden Street). Also known as Goat's House (John Goat was a landowner in the early 18th century, and *c.* 1792 Thomas Goat was a shopkeeper who also let lodgings). In

1767 it was known as the King's Arms, and Isaac Alsop was paying rates on it; he was still licensee in 1790, almost certainly being supplied by Hardy's brewery of Letheringsett.[1] Petty Sessions were held here for the hiring of servants. In 1768, 340 gallons of gin were auctioned here. Alsop evidently ran into financial difficulties with his landlord, for William Windham's diary for 19 July 1790 reports that 'Poor Alsop has spared me all difficulty and delicacy with respect to him, by finding it necessary to abscond. Such a reduction at the close of life is very melancholy.' Commissioners of Bankruptcy met later that year.

The property was advertised for sale in 1828 with a small brewery 'contiguous', and by 1836 had changed its name to The Pig and Whistle.

By 1839 Charles Loynes had taken over, brewing his own beer; by 1845 he had turned it into a licensed hotel called The Crown and Anchor.

After Watneys closed the pub in 1970, the site became well known as Maryjane's fish and chip shop and restaurant.

Cuckoo Lane. Name given (e.g. in Bryant's 1826 map of Norfolk) to what is now known as Holt Road. Three adjacent fields are marked on a map as 'The Cucow Closes'.[1] The name is recorded in the 1490s in the form 'Guckehowgh'[2] (a 'how(e)' or 'hough' was a hill[3]), and is presumably the origin of the name Swacking Cuckoo (swacking = large, 'whopping') for woodland on the borders of Cromer and Felbrigg at the top of the present Holt Road next to the railway line.

D

Dairy Farm[1] or **Dairy House**[2]. Older name for Home Farm, to the south of Cromer Hall; in the 1840s J. Cross was the tenant there. Dairying on the Cromer Hall estate is believed to have ceased around the middle of the 20th century.

Dancing. Balls are known to have been held at the Reading Room on the cliff and at Tucker's Hotel in the first half of the 19th century. A diarist in 1821 mentions sailors dancing on the pier in the evening.[1] Later the big hotels made provision for dancing, and there was dancing in the roller skating rink on the pier in the 1930s.

¶ **Danish Pavilion** (Paul's Lane). Bought by Sir George Henry Lewis at a Paris exhibition and erected at Overstrand at the beginning of the 20th century (it is shown in the 1901 census as in course of construction); the four-acre plot cost him £2,363 and the house and stables £6,000.[1] Sir George was an intimate friend of Edward VII and as a solicitor was noted for his work in high-profile cases. He died in 1911. The house became a hotel, and was burnt down in 1951, being succeeded by a motel for a while. Danish House Gardens is built on the site.

¶ **Danum House** (Pauls Lane). Formerly known as 'Overstrand Cottage' or 'Corner House' or 'Dr Beverley's Cottage', the holiday home of Michael Beverley, a Norwich GP. Victoria, Countess of Yarborough, bought the property in 1906/07 and modernised it; a daughter of Maria Wyndham of Felbrigg Hall, Victoria had married the champion jockey Maunsell Richardson.[1] Later it became a holiday house of popular novelist Florence Barclay.[2] The name Danum House seems to have been given to the property around 1950 when it was bought by people from Doncaster, where the Roman fort was called Danum.

Detail from a painting of 1809 or shortly thereafter, showing Ditchell's barn with its ramp for hauling goods up from the shore. The boat house next to that ramp may be the building used from 1814 as a reading room, later becoming the Bath House.

Dentists. Edmund Bartell jnr, a surgeon living in Cromer in the 1790s, also pulled teeth, but Dr Dent[1] recalled that when he arrived in Cromer in 1889 'the town did not even possess a qualified dentist, and deputising for the galaxy of talent which Cromer now possesses, was a wonderful old man who combined great power in teeth extraction, with side lines of occupation as blacksmith, gardener and ventriloquist.'

By 1932 R. Churchyard was practising as a dentist in Cadogan Road.[2]

De Vere Court (Tucker Street). Built in 1985 on the site of the Metropole Hotel, and incorporating some architectural features reminiscent of the hotel.

Ditchell's house and barn (Tucker Street). House and granary of an 18th-century merchant. There was a crane and an inclined ramp from the back of the barn to the beach next to the Bath House, for unloading small ships at high tide.[1] The buildings were demolished in 1893[2] to make way for the Metropole Hotel. DE VERE COURT now stands on the site.

Dixon Road. Part of the estate built by the national building firm of Barratt in the 1980s. Named after the Harriot Dixon lifeboat which served as the No. 2 lifeboat in Cromer, operating from the boathouse at the bottom of the Gangway.

Doctors. Several doctors have played prominent roles in the town's history.

Edmund Bartell jnr, surgeon, lived in Cromer in the 1790s and wrote the first of the town's GUIDEBOOKS..

Sidney Terry (1732/3–96) lived in CLIFF HOUSE during the bathing season[1] and built the DOCTOR'S STEPS. Son of Christopher Terry, he was apprenticed 1751–54 to a surgeon called John Hunt, who was then practising in Framlingham but later moved to Norwich.[2] Dr Terry seems to have done quite well out of his share of the bathing machine business, and from letting out part of his house to visitors, but was most particular that his funeral should be of the humblest kind.[3]

CROMER CHARACTERS
W. H. RANSOM

One notable doctor who was born in Cromer but never practised here was William Henry Ransom (1824–1907), son of a well known family in the town. Educated by Simeon Simons at the Free School, Ransom went on to excel in his medical studies and was physician of the Nottingham General Hospital from 1854 to 1890. In 1870 he invented a gas-fired disinfecting stove for sterilising clothing, and this was widely used till steam methods were introduced. (Indeed, when Cromer's new hospital was built in 1932 gas was still being used as steam was not available.) He published papers on embryology, and became a Fellow of the Royal Society. He was an enthusiastic supporter of the volunteer movement, serving for 15 years in the 1st Notts rifle corps. Perhaps under the influence of Simeon Simons, he was interested in geology and later was active in educational matters, helping to found University College, Nottingham.[1]

Dr *McKelvie* lived at HOLLY COTTAGE and had his surgery in a cottage in the grounds.[4]

The building on the corner of Mount Street (number 2) was designed by Albert Green for Dr *R. C. M. Colvin Smith*, chief medical officer to the Urban District Council; it had a doctor's surgery and waiting room on the ground floor.[5]

Dr *Arthur Burton* had been an army surgeon in the Boer War and in Cairo before meeting his future wife in Cromer. He settled here and practised surgery in the cottage hospital.[6]

Dr *Fenner* started practice in 1884 in Hamilton House, Church Street; later he moved to St Margaret's Terrace.

Dr *H. C. Dent* played a leading role in Cromer in the early years of the 20th century, enjoying the company of the gentry and publishing some memoirs which touch on many aspects of Cromer life.

Dr *Paul Barclay* was a general practitioner in Cromer from 1946 to 1979, having his surgery for many years in the former Goldsmiths School in Overstrand Road and living in Rede's House next door. (A new purpose-built surgery was opened in Warnes Close in 1969.) Dr Barclay was secretary for ten years of the local lifeboat branch, followed by a term as its president; he was awarded the RNLI's Bronze Medal for Gallantry in 1974 after going with the lifeboat to attend an injured seaman in very rough seas.[7]

Dr *Donald Vaughan* also served as president of the RNLI branch. He had been a pilot in the RFC and a prisoner of war.

Donald Vaughan

Among other physicians who have been connected with Cromer is *Edward Bach* (1880–1936), the medical practitioner who abandoned conventional medicine to develop his system of flower remedies. He wrote *Heal Thyself* while staying in Cromer at 4 Brunswick Terrace, and gathered flowers from the nearby cliffs for some of his first recipes.[8]

See also the panel on John Henry Earle, under FRIENDLY SOCIETIES.

Doctor's Steps. Access to the beach from the path leading down from CLIFF HOUSE; the name remains, even though the steps were converted to a slope as long ago as 1894.[1] The doctor was Dr Terry, who lived in Cliff House at the end of the 18th century and introduced bathing to Cromer – the original steps were described in 1806 as 'a staircase built up the cliff for the accommodation of bathers, and called the Ladder'.[2] The path leading to the steps from the

Overstrand Road originally started in Terry's front drive and went close to the western wall of Cliff House.[3]

Dolphin (West Cliff). Previously known as the Regency Hotel, and before that the West Cliff Hotel (1948–). It was built *c.* 1800 by J. W. Rust (the local historian Crawford Holden said it was built on the site of an inn, but gave no evidence; Bellard's 1747 map shows a two-storey building). In the 1840s it consisted of dwelling houses known as West Cliff Terrace; part of the property succumbed to a cliff fall and was bought by the Cromer Protection Commissioners as part of the sea defence programme which saw the building of a sea wall and the creation of the present slope up from the esplanade in 1846. The sea frontage of the building therefore dates only from this time.

A tunnel from the eastern side of the cellars was discovered (partly col-

lapsed) in the late 1940s or early 1950s, apparently leading up the High Street; this was blocked off again.

Dolphin post. Post erected on the shore to mark the boundary between the manor of Cromer Gunners (to the east) and that of Ufford's Hall (to the west). The name seems to use the word 'dolphin' in the sense of a mooring post or bollard.[1] The post seen in the drawing was erected for Humphrey Rant (the lord of Cromer Gunners manor) by James Howes in 1764, 300 yards from the east beck, but there must have been an older boundary post, for in a dispute in 1768 John Jewell, who was then 68, said he remembered the old boundary post when a boy.[2]

Domesday Book. Cromer is not mentioned by name in the Domesday survey of 1086, but the settlement is called SHIPDEN. Difficulties which attend the

The Dolphin Post, drawn by Robert Dixon in 1832.

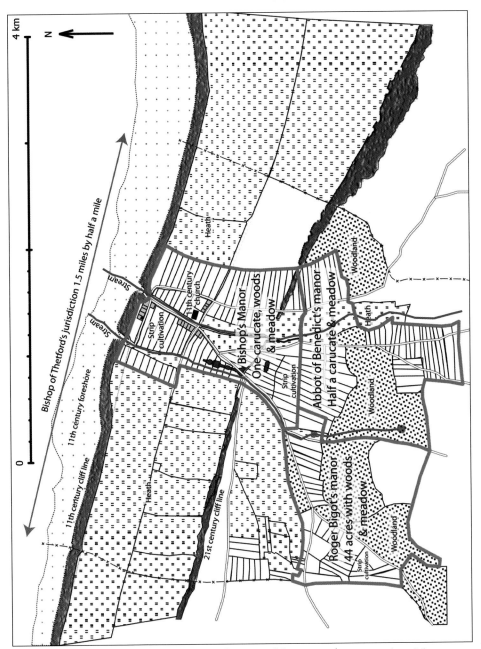

Map of Shipden as it may have looked at the time of the Domesday survey in 1086.

interpretation of the information given in Domesday include uncertainty over the size of the units of land measurement and over the precise location of the coastline. POPULATION figures have to be calculated from survey figures which did not include seamen, and although Shipden had limited land resources and appears poorer than other coastal settlements further east along the coast, this may be deceptive.

Donkeys. Before the days of motor vehicles, donkeys were commonly used for pulling carts; evidence from the 1830s and 1840s shows Cromer children leaving school to drive donkeys – clearly regarded by parents as a suitable first job after leaving school. Even children not yet in their teens could manage the animals.[1]

Donkeys as well as pony carts gave rides on the sands to visitors at least as early as 1821.[2] (In the 1860s, Mr Amis kept his donkeys in the field opposite the church.[3]) One carriage was made of basketwork by the Aylsham basketmaker William Starling, and bought by a Cromer horse dealer called Kettle together with two large Spanish donkeys; this equipage gave rides to visitors for many years.[4] Donkey rides continued to be offered on the beach (except during World War 2) until 1947, after which only ponies were used.[5] The old donkey stables in Bond Street, once home to 40 animals, were acquired in 1950 by the local St John Ambulance Division and

Going for a drive on the beach: a mule or donkey carriage, about the year 1875.

converted into a meeting hall.[6]

Donkey rides were reintroduced to the beach in 2010. The District Council (responsible for licensing beach traders) at first refused a licence because 'we feel, as a council, that this does not fit with what we are offering in Cromer. This is the decision we have made, and that decision is final.'[7] There was an outcry in the press and from the Town Council, and within days the decision was found to be not final at all, permission was granted and donkeys Ivan and Barry began carrying happy children on the east beach.

Driftway. Old name for Cliff Lane.[1]

Drying ground. Field later used for the cottage hospital. It is not clear whether its name implied somewhere to hang out the washing, or to dry fishing nets, or for the use of Weavers. Land between the eastern beck and the Gangway was also used as a drying ground.

Durrant's Farm. Converted to houses as nos. 78 and 80 Norwich Road. T. Durrant in 1941 lived in Bernard Road but had 13 acres on Norwich Road where he kept 35 pigs and some poultry.[1]

Dutch influence. The main instance of Dutch influence in Cromer architecture is the rear of Hanover House (the name itself is indicative of the period in which it was restyled); it had a shaped gable during the 18th and 19th centuries, but in 1963 was returned to its plain medieval shape – even the tell-tale name has been lost since becoming known as Shipden House. It seems also that Cromer Hall had crow-stepped gables before it was rebuilt in a completely different style in 1828.

'Secondhand' Dutch and Flemish influence appeared in the late 19th and early 20th centuries as architects followed the Queen Anne revival style used in London suburbs. Shaped gables were used on the 1936 telephone exchange on Louden Road and the much later development in The Croft behind Colne House; crow-stepped gables also appear on a number of early-20th-century buildings.

E

East Cottages. Row of cottages at the east end of the churchyard, bought by the Urban District Council for £1,000 in 1968. They were partly renovated as dwellings, part made into the new Museum.[1]

East Grove. Bungalows built in the 1930s on land formerly used as allotment gardens.

East House (Church Street). House built in the 18th century by Sherman Cutler at the east end of the church-

East House in 1805. Not long after this, a shop window was inserted in the middle.

yard. It later became the home of the Leak family. Destroyed by bombing in World War 2.

East Street. Old name for the part of Church Street east of the church.

¶ **East Terrace.** Row of cottages between Sea Marge and the White Horse,

Overstrand. Mrs S. A. Betts ran an infants school here in the 1880s.

Ebenezer Cottage. Tucked away behind 34 Church Street, this curious late-18th-century cottage has just three rooms, one on top of the other. A lantern in the roof (removed during renovation in the late 20th century) would have commanded a view of the sea until the Red Lion was rebuilt in the 1880s; legend says it was used as a smugglers' look-out, and there is evidence that the building may have been connected to the network of secret TUNNELS.[1]

Edinburgh House (Tucker Street). Built in 1867 on the cliff at the end of Brook Street (in the eighteenth century, Brook Street had extended further

Overstrand beach approach. It is salutary to note that, since this postcard was used in 1907, virtually all of the cliff masses seen here have succumbed to erosion.

north but much land was lost to the sea). A hotel by 1906,[1] the building was converted into flats in 1978. The upper part of the building was gutted by fire in 2000.[2]

Electric lighting. Before the days of street lighting, nights could be so dark that a calm sea would reflect not only the moonlight but also the red light of the lighthouse's oil lamps and even the light of a bright planet: 'The reflection of Jupiter,' wrote a visitor in 1821, had the same appearance on the sea as that of the moon, but the light was much fainter.'[1]

The Urban District Council took over the supply of electricity at the end of 1898,[2] buying an acre of land (in Central Road) from the Cromer Hall Trustees for an 'Electric Lighting Station and Storeyard'.[3] In 1902 they put up £25,000 capital to install electric lighting in the town and engaged Edmundsons as contractors.[4] The works, built by Girling & Smith, were adjacent to Cromer Beach station, and in 1903 a siding was put in, with a spur to the coal bunkers, so that coal could be delivered for the generators.[5]

At a UDC meeting in 1903, 'a letter . . . from Mr W. Nicholson, Bernard Road, was read stating he had wired his house for electric light and would be glad if the Council would give permission for the necessary connection to be made so that he might be enabled to use the light. It was Resolved that Mr.

Nicholson be informed the Council were unable to give their consent to the extensions in Bernard Road being made at present.'[5]

Because of continual demands for capital, the whole venture was turned over to the contractors in 1913.

Elizabeth Fry Walk. Path through woods off the Overstrand Road, near Happy Valley; named by the council in the 1990s. *See* QUAKERS.

Ellenhill. Development off the Overstrand Road, built from 1978 onwards by Reggie Medler and named after his mother-in-law.[1]

Elmhurst Hotel. *See* ALEX CLUB.

Erosion. Erosion was a constant feature of the Cromer coastline until the building of effective SEA WALLS in the 19th century, and continues on either side of the town. The original church of St Peter, Shipden-juxta-Mare, was destroyed by erosion between 1317 and 1350, its remains lying a little to the east of the present pier.

In 1551 the Privy Council was told that the sea had 'swallowed uppe & drowned' many houses in Cromer, and there are reports of significant loss of land to the sea in 1611 – indeed, in the century from 1565 to 1664 the number of households in Cromer fell from 117 to a mere 66.[1] Then, according to Hewitt's *Essay on the Encroachment of the*

German Ocean (1844), 'in the winter of 1799, the light house cliffs, projecting from beach three hundred and twenty feet, made several remarkably large shoots, one of which brought with it half an acre of ground, and extended into the sea beyond low water mark. On January 15th, 1825, another large mass of earth was detached from the light-house hills, and fell with great force on the beach, extending in breadth above three hundred yards from the cliffs, covering an area of twelve acres, and containing, it was supposed, not less than half a million of cubic yards of earth. . . . A large stream of water issued from the bank immediately after its fall, and discharged itself down upon the beach with great noise and vio-lence. Early in the morning of August 19th, another large shoot of the cliffs occurred near the light-house,' which prompted the hasty erection of a new lighthouse further inland.

A cliff fall in 1931 was estimated at 100,000 tons of soil, reducing the space between Happy Valley and the sea.

Cliff falls in 1962 took away a large part of the golf course's 17th fairway.

See also FOULNESS.

Esplanade. *See* PROMENADE.

Ex-Servicemen's Club. *See* CROMER SOCIAL CLUB.

F

Factories. In the 1920s Cromer had two mineral water manufacturers: William Everett at 11 Bond Street (built in 1903)[1] and 'Miss Spencer & Co.' in Prince of Wales Road.[2] Ginger beer bottles with their names embossed are occasionally found at auction sales.

In 1932 the Arrosa Products Co. Ltd was packing baking powder at 23–25 Cabbell Road.[3]

Pye built on the Runton Road a factory making televisions, which em-ployed many local people in the 1950s and 1960s, but by 1975 there was an application to turn the building into a sports centre and in 1976 to make it a milk distribution depot – both refused by the council, who did however allow it to become a warehouse for Jewson's timber merchants.[4] In due course Jews-on's moved to the industrial estate on the Holt Road, where Carter Concrete had a factory, and the Runton Road building was occupied by Structureflex, making specialist containers etc. out of flexible sheeting. When they moved to Melton Constable the factory remained empty for several years before being de-molished in 2010.

Shawco Industries set up a small furniture factory in 1952, starting with one man in a workshop in Corner Street growing within a few months to employ nine men in the old stables of

Cliff House on the Overstrand Road.[5] Kendalls shop, in Fern House in the 1960s, had a small factory at the back making umbrellas.

The Cromer Crab Company (known universally as 'the crab factory') began in 1979 with local entrepreneur John Williams and restaurateur Reg Parkin selling crabs in local pubs. In the 1980s they took a unit on the light industrial estate at the top of the Norwich Road, processing and freezing crabs and other shellfish (local and imported). The business expanded and in 1993 was sold to the Perkins Group; products were successfully marketed to shops internationally, and following a management buy-out in 1995 the Sheringham-based Norfolk Shellfish was acquired in 1999. A new factory for the combined operation, employing 135 people, was built on the Holt Road in 2000 to process more than one and a half million crabs a year.[6]

Fairs. In 1285 (and again in 1426) the king renewed permission for Shipden to hold a week-long fair once a year. Fishermen were allowed to sell at the fair whatever they had not sold to royal and noble agents or to city merchants. (*See also* MARKETS.)

In 1802 the fair was still listed as 'for petty chapmen',[1] though by this time it was restricted to Whit Monday. In the next few years it developed into a Whit Monday and Tuesday pleasure fair, largely on the sea and hence known as the Regatta.

Faldonside (corner of Cliff Avenue and Norwich Road). In the early 20th century this was a favourite holiday retreat of the Countess Dowager of Albemarle and other members of the Keppel family.[1]

Falls, The. 1. Deep ravine next to the GANGWAY, crossed at first by a wooden footbridge (still in existence in 1839[1]) and then by a brick arch before being filled in with rubble towards the end of the 19th century. The name may suggest that the beck which created the cleft formed a waterfall in its descent to the sea here.

2. Term used for any land which was once part of the cliff but has fallen to the beach. The Bath House, for example, was built on the 'falls' below Peele House.

Wooden footbridge over the ravine next to the Gangway, drawn in 1830 or 1835.

Fearns Close. Small group of houses built on part of the land which Charles Fearn had bought from the Suffield estate (*see* FEARNS FIELD).

Fearns Field. Charles E. Fearn bought nearly all of the land on the eastern side of Station Road in 1879; number 2 Suffield Park (i.e. one of the Park Road villas) was occupied by George Fearn[1] and later by Susan Fearn.[2] The field was at first held in trust for the use of the houses facing it; part of it was used for tennis courts. The trust lapsed,[3] the land reverting to Lord Suffield, and in 1951 it was sold to Cromer Urban District Council,[4] subsequently passing to the North Norfolk District Council.

Fern House (Church Street). House opposite the end of Brook Street occupied by James Sidle, who had his tailor's shop at the back. Apartments were let: John Lord the schoolmaster lived here when he first came to Cromer.

The original Fern House was demolished in 1889; the ground floor of the replacement building was used as a restaurant until 1922, then as G. W. Wilkin's bakery and restaurant, then as Kendalls umbrella shop (with small factory at the back).[1] After a while it was taken over by the Bennetts electrical goods chain.

Festival of Music, Drama and Dance. The first music and drama festival was a three-day festival held in 1948 for local amateur performers, especially from schools. It took place in the ballroom of Newhaven Court hotel and the adjudicator was Herbert Howells. Later festivals mostly used the Town Hall (until it was sold in 1963), the Women's Institute Hall in Garden Street and the Parish Hall. Dance was introduced in 1992, and in search of better stage facilities moved first to Sheringham High School and then, in 1999, to the new Auden Theatre at Gresham's School, Holt.[1]

Field system. The medieval system of agriculture, with people having widely scattered strips of land in different open fields around the parish, continued until the enclosures of the 16th to 18th centuries. Cromer and the villages to its west were described in 1667 as 'an open corn country except a little enclosure about the villages',[1] and in 18th-century Cromer there were still remnants of the strip system in the CROFT and to the west of the Norwich Road.[2]

See also the indications of strip farming in the map on page 77.

Finch Close. Development of bungalows off Ridge Way, built by Garden Link Homes of Norwich in the 1990s.

Fire brigade. Cromer, like Holt and other Norfolk towns, suffered major losses by fire before the days of fire brigades. We hear of a fire in the time of Henry VIII which destroyed

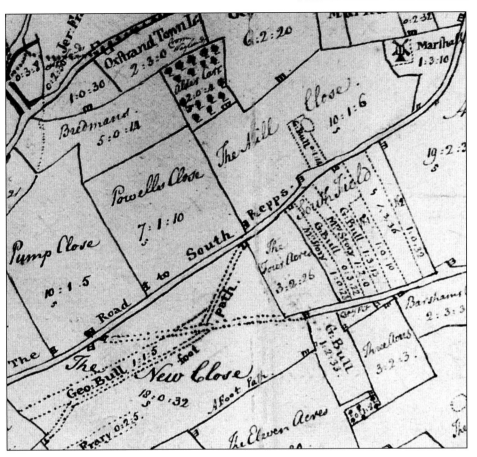

Remnants of strip farming, in parcels of around an acre each, seen in an 18th-century map of the lands bordering Norwich Road ('The Road to South Repps'). The name 'The New Close' suggests that this was the last piece of land in Cromer to be enclosed, probably in the late 17th century. The field marked 'Marshall' in the top right hand corner, with the windmill, was to become the site of Cromer's first railway station, and later still High View Park. The strips in the South Field were to become allotment gardens before being developed as Greenfield Close, Mayfield Drive and Francis Close.

a whole street of thatched houses; William Windham in his accounts for 1677 refers to a house he owned in Cromer being burnt down with 'about halfe the towne'.[1] In 1738 John Kirby's house (roughly the site either of Rust's/ Budgen's or of Barclays Bank) was burnt down,[2] and Syderstone parish sent 1s. 6d. to Cromer after (the same?) loss by fire on 11 January 1740.[3]

A fire brigade was established in 1880/1881, 'under the management of a Committee appointed by the Vestry, and supported by voluntary subscriptions assisted by sums voted from the Poor Rate'.[4] Edward Raven Priest was its Secretary and Treasurer, and it was carefully organised with a hierarchy of uniformed firemen working under rules and regulations.

The Local Board took over control of the fire brigade in 1885[5] and ordered a Merryweather steam fire engine the following year (it lasted until 1921, when it became uneconomical to repair and was replaced by a secondhand engine, again from Merryweather).[6] This was housed at first in a yard partitioned off from W. G. Sandford's premises,[7] and transferred in 1890 to a garage built

for it at the back of the Town Hall and leased from F. W. Rogers.[8] (Adjoining land was bought from Henry Marjoram in 1898.[9]) A fire escape was purchased in 1896,[10] but it was designed to run in a vertical position and was very liable to snag on overhead wires; moreover, it was not easy to move rapidly, so a new 50-foot, four-wheel escape was bought in 1908 and the old one converted into a horse-drawn hose cart.[11]

It is said that if your cart or carriage was passing near the fire station when the alarm went, your horse was liable to be pressed into immediate service to draw the engine! It was not until 1928 that the brigade tried to find lorries to pull the engine. H. H. Flaxman's vehicles appear to have been unsuitable; East Coast Garage Co. were asked if they

The fire station in Canada Road when first built. It served as Cromer's fire station from 1905 to 1971.

Fishing boats at the bottom of the Gangway, drawn by Robert Dixon about 1810.

would allow their lorry to be left in the Council's storeyard 'when not in use'. (Presumably if the lorry was in use the engine would still have had to be pulled by horse.) It was eventually decided to purchase a 'self propelling motor fire engine' from Dennis Bros. This was soon put to use at fires at Wolterton Hall and Trimingham, which was the furthest the brigade had ever been able to go.[12]

In 1903 three plots on the opposite side of the road from the Town Hall were bought from W. Porter, giving a site for a new fire station with a frontage of 54 feet; it was built in 1904/05 by W. J. Hannant of Norwich.[13] Accommodation was provided for a resident fireman in the building in 1923, but his accommodation was required for office, telephone room etc. when the government took responsibility for organising a national fire service in 1941 and Cromer became the centre of

a Sub-Division.[14]

From 1924 the football club in Mill Road provided storage for equipment, in case of fire breaking out in Suffield Park.[15]

The building became an ambulance station when the modern fire station was built further up Canada Road. ☐ For further accounts see *Cromer Fire Brigade 1881–2006* by Jamie Edghill and Keith Entwistle (Cromer: Poppyland Publishing, 2006).

Fish houses. *See* SMOKE HOUSES.

Fishermen's and Working Men's Club of Cromer. Founded 1888 as the Cromer Christian Fellowship Society, which bought the Methodist chapel in Chapel Street in 1890.

Fishing. Cromer fishermen in 1383 were using vessels of 10 or 12 tons (with a few of 18 tons) called doggers to go fishing on the coasts of Denmark and Norway.[1]

In the early 15th century Bromholm Priory (Bacton) was buying Cromer red herrings, halibut and salt fish including cod and ling.[2] Later in the century the receiver general of St Giles's hospital in Norwich paid regular visits to the north Norfolk coast, buying fish at Cromer pier for the inhabitants of the hospital.[3]

In the 1660s there were about 20 small fishing boats, and the fish they caught ended up as far away as Cambridge and Newmarket.[4]

At the end of the 18th century the fishing was for lobsters, crabs, whiting, cod and herring. In or about 1813, Robert Dixon drew pictures of both crab boats and mackerel boats at Cromer. A visitor in 1821 noted that 'crabs and lobsters are frequently caught on this coast but of other fish there is a great scarcity. Cromer is chiefly supplied with fish from Yarmouth.' Nevertheless, he saw two or three French fishing boats, who came to fish off Cromer from time to time, presumably for lobsters.[5]

In 1913 there was 25 crab boats operating from Cromer beach; a century later, about a dozen.

The first commercial glass-fibre boat, commissioned by Richard Davies, was based on a mould taken from a traditional wooden boat,[6] still with the same pointed ends fore and aft that had characterised Viking boats, but it was also the Davies family who later branched out by using a twin-hulled boat which could go further out to sea.

See also WHALING.

Fletcher Hospital. The Fletcher Convalescent Home owed its origin to Benjamin E. Fletcher, a Norwich printer who gave to the Norfolk & Norwich Hospital some land and the building for a convalescent home. The Earl of Leicester gave an endowment fund, and it was opened at Cromer in 1893 (architect: Edward Boardman[1]) and by the time of the 1901 census had 23 patients. Local doctors supervised the nursing. In 1900 patients were admitted who had been in the South African war. A children's wing was built in 1936. It was later known as the Fletcher Hospital and used largely for geriatric nursing. In the 1990s it was replaced by Benjamin Court, a purpose-built complex including rehabilitation beds, day centre and sheltered housing.

Fletcher Way. Name given to the driveway to Benjamin Court after two private houses were built in the grounds.

Flint House (1 Church Street). Built for John Chadwick in 1814. The upper storeys were added later. Became a library after 1875. *See also* JEWELLERS.

Football. An early form of football,

camping', was played on a field in the vicinity of Colne House, still known in 1741 as the Camping Close.[1]

In the 1890s, a football club used a field between Garden Street and Prince of Wales Road. 'It was a rough game then,' recalled Savin, 'with no off-side, goal nets, etc.'[2]

Beef Meadow, opposite Cromer Hall, was leased as a football ground from 1896 to 1921. In 1896–97 footballer W. N. Cobbold ('the Prince of Dribble') brought his school pupils to Cromer and matches were arranged between them and Cromer Football Club.[3] On the outbreak of war in 1914, the club abandoned all further plans for games, urging 'as many as possible of the friends of Cromer football' to enlist

in the army.[4] The pavilion, which had cost just £70 to erect, was burnt down in 1915.[5]

Cabbell Park (in Mill Road) was given as a replacement football ground and the first match played there in September 1922.

Cromer Youth Football Club was founded in 1982 with a committee of enthusiastic parents. A single under-12s team played on Fearns Field, and the club grew until by the early years of the 21st century there were so many teams (including girls) that they had to move to a playing field next to Northrepps Village Hall.

¶ Football facilities were introduced at Overstrand by Lord Battersea.[6] There was a pitch where Beach Close is now.

Cromer Football Club, 1904.

The Napoleonic fortifications overlooking the Gangway, drawn in or shortly after 1809. On the clifftop, at the left, the Watch House; at the right, the Red Lion; at the foot of the cliff, sheds or boathouses just west of the Gangway.

Foresters, Ancient Order of. *See* FRIENDLY SOCIETIES.

Forges. *See* BLACKSMITHS.

Fortifications. Cromer suffered the attentions of hostile ships for centuries. In 1450 Margaret Paston wrote: 'There been many enemies against Yarmouth and Cromer, and have done much harm and taken many Englishmen and put them in great distress and greatly ransomed them,' and in 1458 (when 60 French ships had been sighted off the Sussex coast) someone reported that 'he heard of a soldier of Calais how Cromer and Blakeney is much spoken of amongst Frenchmen'.[1]

In 1588, with the specific threat of the Spanish Armada, instructions were received that the cliffs at Sheringham and Cromer were to be cut sloping and access to the beach walled up. Parapets were to be built on top of the cliffs, and nearby heathland trenched.[2]

A pair of small (6-pounder) guns was kept; Bellard's 1747 map shows them pointing out to sea from where the Hotel de Paris was later built.

When France, Spain and Holland entered the War of American Independence, England was once more threatened from the east, and a battery was sited on the marrams to the west of Cromer (roughly opposite the end of the present Beach Road)[3] with four 18-pound guns to protect shipping from privateers. In 1803 Thomas Mickelburgh paid tribute to these guns, writing to the government that 'in the

World War 2 fortifications:
LEFT: *Pillbox on Howards Hill.*
BELOW: *Gun emplacement on the beach.*

last War we saved a great Deal of Property by the Guns now here'; in this year, with the new threat of invasion by Napoleon, they were replaced by 24-pound guns (*see also under* MILITIA) and the fort was supplemented by two half-moon batteries, each with two 24-pound carronades. One of these batteries was sited overlooking the pier; the other is described[4] as 'about 400 Yards the east of the Town', which would mean at the DOCTOR'S STEPS if measured from the old jetty or a little further east (at the point where the World War 2 battery was sited) if measured from the Gangway. The Gangway itself was blocked with a carefully constructed barricade of thorn bushes, and if an invasion took place fishing boats were to form a further obstacle, arranged on their sides and held in position by being filled with sand.[5] The fortifications were largely dismantled in 1813, but the battery on the marrams remained in existence[6] and fired a salute at the opening of the new pier in 1846.

In World War 1 two 4.7-inch guns were sited at Cromer.[7]

After the fall of France in 1940 a battery was installed on the east cliff at Cromer to guard the approaches to potential landing places, as part of a big expansion in coastal defences. It had two 6-inch guns (dated 1906 and 1912 – following normal practice they had been stripped from HMS *Africa* and HMS *Dublin*); a tunnel made by cut and cover led from each gun to a small complex of rooms for the gun crews and there was a vertical access shaft. Erosion of the cliff required a new observation post to be moved back to the edge of Warren Woods in 1942, but the perceived need for the battery decreased and for its last few months it was manned only by the Home Guard.[8] It was closed in 1944; part of the original infrastructure is a raised hump in the garden of 'Cliff Nook', in Cliff Drive, plus a brick building in the garden of a bungalow in The Warren which was the engine room for the searchlights sited on the promenade;[9] the gun emplacement became a coastguard lookout. A Bofors anti-aircraft gun was positioned on the Watch House site.[10] A heavy machine-gun pillbox was erected on Howard's Hill, with a spigot mortar base and infantry section pillbox; there were pillboxes at Runton Road, Hall Road and the Gangway. Loopholes can still be seen in the retaining wall of the path below the Crescent, and in the old telephone exchange in Louden Road.[11]

Foulness. The promontory immediately to the east of Cromer, lying in the parish of Overstrand. Here was built the first LIGHTHOUSE. The landslips of the 19th century, one of which took the derelict lighthouse with it, were just the latest in a series of slips which had already destroyed most of the 'ness' and severely reduced the size of Overstrand parish;[1] consequently Foulness is now the name of the shallows just off shore.

The *-ness* element of the name is the same as in Orford Ness or Dungeness, cognate with the modern French *nez* 'nose'; the *foul* is equivalent to the modern word *fowl*, though in medieval times this word applied to any bird, not just domestic ones, so there is a parallel with the reference to crows in the name of CROMER.

Fountain House. In the angle of Chapel Street and West Street, this acquired its name from overlooking a drinking fountain (which replaced one of the two town pumps in 1894[1]). It was occupied by Daniel Neave, a plumber and glazier, between 1854 and 1889.[2] Cromer Urban District Council bought it in 1900[3] to use as offices, with caretaker's rooms over;[4] this lasted until 1928, after

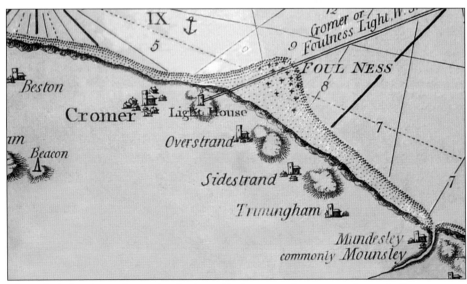

This Admiralty chart of 1790 clearly shows Foulness as a large area of very shallow water where the cliff has slumped into the sea.

Fountain House at the time it was being used as District Council offices.

which the building was converted to a shop by Henry Bullen the builder, occupied by Randall's from *c.* 1930 to *c.* 1968–70,[5] and remained a shop until the Trustee Savings Bank took it over (becoming Lloyds TSB from 1999).

Francis Close. Bungalows built off the Roughton Road by Francis Parker Developments. The land had previously been used as allotment gardens.

Friendly societies. Friendly societies were formed in the 19th century to help people protect themselves against hardship. Belonging to a friendly society was a way to ensure that in times of need a member received financial help. Known societies in Cromer are (in order of date of foundation):

1848 Manchester Unity Independent Order of Oddfellows Loyal Baring Lodge (met at the Red Lion; 584 members by 1906)

1855 Norfolk and Norwich Unity Independent Order of Oddfellows Loyal Albion Lodge (met at the Albion; 227 members in 1895)

1884 Independent Order of Rechabites (a temperance organisation which met in the Vicarage Room, later moving to the Lecture Hall; had a Juvenile branch, the BAND OF HOPE, which by 1914 had 12 boys and 10 girls in its membership)

1895 Ancient Order of Foresters Court Loyal Lord Battersea

CROMER CHARACTERS
JOHN HENRY EARLE

The relationship between a friendly society and its doctor was mutually important. The society provided a regular income for the doctor; members of the society knew they could consult the doctor without fear of his fee. In addition, it was necessary for a society to appoint a medical officer who would 'safeguard its funds by his vigilance over claims for sick pay', and whose ministrations would help members recover quickly, keeping sick pay to the minimum.[1]

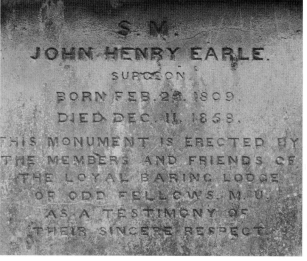

The considerable respect of the members of the Manchester Unity Independent Order of Oddfellows Loyal Baring Lodge is apparent in the substantial memorial erected to their surgeon, John Henry Earle, which stands in the north-east corner of the parish churchyard, just a few yards from where he had lived in EAST HOUSE.

A Labourers and Mechanics Provident Institution was formed in 1859 as a provident society, but it seems not to have been successful, perhaps because it was organised by the gentry and the clergy rather than being a self-help society run by the members. Its sole and final member, on dissolution in 1859, was Ann Goose.

Fulcher Avenue. Developed in the 1990s by Norfolk Homes, part of the site having previously been used for allotments. Named after William Fulcher, a long-serving member of Cromer Urban District Council (and its chairman from 1952) who had also been booking clerk at the nearby Cromer Beach station.[1]

Furze Hill. In the 19th century the hill was known as Storey's Hill.[1] The houses were built 1962–64.

G

Gallery House. *See* BALCONY HOUSE.

Gangway, The. This was the larger of two places in Cromer where small streams (or 'becks' – from the Old Danish *bekr*) entered the sea; the western 'beckway' is to the west of the present pier, the beck coming down through what we now know as The Meadow and being channelled through an underground pipe for most of its length, emerging close to the pier. The eastern beck comes past the back of the hospital in Mill Road, is visible where it crosses the bottom of Mill Road and Cromwell Road, and is now buried where it crosses under the Overstrand Road near the junction with Norwich Road. Bellard's map of 1747 shows it flowing through the middle of an orchard which occupied the site bounded by Overstrand Road, Church Street and the Gangway. There was a deep ravine, the FALLS, where small boats were pulled up out of reach of storms.

The land between the beck and the Gangway was used as a drying ground (for sails?), and it was so convenient for storing goods brought by coastal

shipping that Henry Sandford (and his father before him, from 1804) rented it from the Cromer Hall estate as a COAL-YARD; it had large gates giving access to the Gangway. With the coming of the railways, coastal trade ceased and the yard was bought by a builder, George Riches. The ravine was filled in during the 1860s with rubble from building sites, and the coal-yard became a builder's yard, with various workshops and stores built on it.

The Gangway itself was given a macadamised surface in 1882, given the name 'Beach Road',[1] and paved with

Sketch map of the Gangway made about 1863 (NRO: Rye 134). The lifeboat has been moved to the new lifeboat house provided by Benjamin Bond Cabbell, leaving the Fishermen's Reading Room in the old building. Daniel Savin's photographic studio is shown, and there are boats pulled up quite close to the footbridge. Compare this with the picture on page 83.

Two photographs of the Gangway taken in the 1870s or early 1880s. ABOVE: *Taken from the footbridge at the top of the Gangway. Three coal ships unload on the beach. Notice the beck running across the sands having descended the eastern side of the Gangway across the sands to the sea.* BELOW: *Bathing machines and fishing boats at the bottom of the Gangway, which has not yet been paved.*

granite setts in 1901,[2] laid at such an angle that horses' hooves would not slip, whilst smooth granite tracks were laid for cartwheels to run on. Since colliers had now been supplanted by the railways, these Gangway improvements must have been largely for the horses which pulled bathing machines off the beach for the winter; they might also have been of some benefit to the fishermen (fish were sold on the Gangway as they were landed). The council probably had holidaymakers in mind, however, when in 1902 A. White was permitted[3] to have a stand for boot cleaning here: many Edwardian boots must have stood in need of his attention after an overdressed outing on the sands.

In 1911 Riches' yard was sold to W. J. Miller, who turned it into a motor garage; in 1919 the business was sold to Rounce & Wortley, who covered the yard (using the roof trusses from old World War I aircraft hangars[4]) and added a showroom. Trading continued for many decades under the name of East Coast Motors. Brammall's had their secondhand furniture business at the north-west corner of the site until they moved into the former Sanders coach garage in Cadogan Road in the early 1990s (later changing their name to Cromer Furniture). All buildings on the site were demolished in 1998, and housing erected under the name of Merchants Court.

On the western side of the Gangway a granary was built, probably to store the grain which the coastal ships took to London. It had been converted to cottages by 1833, when it was leased to the coastguard service;[5] more recently it has been used as holiday homes.

Gangway, New. Name given on Bellard's 1747 map to the path leading from CLIFF HOUSE to the beach.

❡ **Garden of Sleep.** In the context of Cromer and Poppyland, the Garden of Sleep is a specific reference to the graveyard around the old site of Sidestrand church, now long gone to the beach and sea. London theatre critic and travel writer Clement Scott stayed nearby at Mill House, Overstrand, in the summer of 1883, and penned a poem 'The Garden of Sleep'. The graveyard stood around the round tower which had been left standing when the rest of the church was demolished and

Sidestrand church tower presides over 'the Garden of Sleep'.

rebuilt further inland as cliff erosion threatened its future. Scott was the populist poet of his time, in particular as a contributor to *Punch*, and his poem became nationally known – and nationally parodied – and was set to music by Isidore de Lara. It continued to be sung by local singers into the 1970s.

Garden Street. Following the back of the gardens of properties in the High Street, this road also marks the course of the underground beck which flows through the Meadow. Documents of the 1760s suggest that the beck may still at that date have run overground along the side of the street, though it is not marked on Bellard's 1747 map (which shows the road as bounded by walls or fences, and just two buildings, one at the top and one at the bottom of the street on the eastern side).

Building seems to have begun with the WELLINGTON and a few adjacent cottages at the end of the 18th century; most of the development took place in the late 19th century. Plans for the redevelopment of numbers 11 to 17 as a Job Centre were approved by the council in 1976.[1]

Gardens. 1. Gardens of the gentry. In the 1830s, the gardens of Cromer Hall were notable: a directory of 1839 comments that 'the sequestered walks in the woods near it are delightful, and the grounds are ornamented by plantations'.[1] On a smaller scale, the Rust family's properties in the High Street had ornamental gardens reaching to Garden Street at the rear. Cliff House in 1914 was set in over five acres of ground and its gardener was allocated a double cottage (six bedrooms, five living rooms).[2]

❡ Lord Battersea's gardens at The PLEA-SAUNCE were laid out by the architect, Edwin Lutyens. Seven gardeners lived on the premises; Harry Naylor was head gardener for 25 years, and had a set of the 8-volume *Illustrated Dictionary of Gardening* (1901).[3] The gardens now cover about six acres, but originally extended to 48 acres.[4] The Japanese water gardens (*picture: page 10*) were a special feature.

2. Market gardens. Simeon Simons referred in 1828 to guarding his father's peas by night. Once the railways came, giving opportunity for the transport of crops and animals, market gardening became relatively important; the National Farm Survey[5] of 1941 shows many people having smallholdings, especially for poultry.

3. Municipal gardens. The land on the north side of the Runton Road (which had previously been rough marrams on the cliff top) was bought by the Council and made into public gardens 1910–39. The sunken gardens were constructed in 1953–57 as a job creation scheme. The Council also took over or created gardens in North Lodge Park and at the top of the Gangway (1935–37), and accepted responsibility for maintaining the churchyard.

4. Allotment gardens formerly existed next to Cliff House (used by fishermen); on the lighthouse hills (used by lighthouse keepers); on the Runton Road (later to be redeveloped as Westcliff Avenue); at the top of Sandy Lane (later to become the mushroom farm); between Howard's Hill and the railway (later to become Fulcher Avenue); at the top of the Norwich Road; and in Suffield Park (the site occupied by Links Avenue and also by Reeve Place). Those shown on the 1928 Ordnance Survey map add up to about 26 acres. Overstrand in 2007 had 26 allotments, established before 1941 and covering 3.28 acres owned by the land owner but administered by the parish clerk.[6]

Gas works. The Cromer Gas & Coke Co. Ltd was formed *c.* 1875, though there had been proposals from as early as 1859 to build gas works in the town.[1] Benjamin Bond Bond-Cabbell of Cromer Hall was chairman; directors included local gentry and merchants, and the engineer was Hodgson Jones.[2] Gas works were built in Mill Lane,[3] and the associated 'Gas house' remained there for many years after the gas-holders themselves had been removed to the end of Sandy Lane in 1898. Cromer's streets were still partly lit by gas in the 1950s.

The Sandy Lane site was converted to a new sewage works in the 1990s.

Giglers Croft. (Sometimes spelled **Jiglers**.) Name of a field on the north side of New Street/Runton Road,[1]

The Sandy Lane gas works viewed from Howard's Hill.

roughly where the Melbourne slope is now. It included some glebe land, but by 1709 the part belonging to the church was 'all eaten away by the sea'.[2]

Giovanni's. Licensed social club established on the first floor of the Melbourne House hotel in the 1990s, and named after the son of one of the founders.

¶ Gissing House. Early-20th-century property opposite the cricket ground in Overstrand, originally known as Midways and then as Scole Cottage. Here lived Ida Keppel, the first woman to chair Overstrand's parish council.[1]

Glebe land. The church owned a number of scattered plots of land whose produce went to support the minister. In medieval times he would have cultivated them himself to provide a subsistence, but they were later subsumed within the large manorial estates in return for some regular payment.
¶ Overstrand parish had only the one piece of glebe, on which stood the old RECTORY house in Paul's Lane.

Glebe Lane. Name shown on the 1852 sale map of the Cromer Hall estate for a lane between fields on the west side of Norwich Road. It led to glebe land on which a new vicarage was shortly to be built, so the road which superseded Glebe Lane was called Vicarage Road.

Glencoe (house in Norwich Road). Built between 1885 and 1888 by George Riches. From the second-floor balcony a lady who was staying here as a holiday visitor fell to her death; at the inquest it was recommended that the height of the balcony be increased to at least 3ft 6in.

¶ Glendon House (Carr Lane). The site was bought in 1903 by S. Cozens Hardy, who built the house and called it The Close. Sir Kenneth Kemp, a Norfolk barrister and banker, had the house on a three-year lease before World War I.[1] As Glendon House, it became a nursing home for the elderly (later specialising in Alzheimer's patients).

Goat's House. *See* CROWN & ANCHOR.

Golden Square. Cottages off West Street, just south of the White Horse. Named after Mr Golden. The 1901 census shows it as consisting of 19 houses (plus four more in 'Golden Terrace'), though most were later demolished.

Golf. The Royal Cromer Golf Club was inaugurated at the beginning of 1888, with a nine-hole course designed with the help of George Fernie, on land leased from Lord Suffield, who 25 years later recalled: 'The land now occupied by the golf links was nothing but a sandhill used for pleasure, and not very good for that, bringing in only about eighty pounds a year. I turned it into

CROMER CHARACTERS
HENRY BROADHURST

The first person to conceive the idea of a golf links near Cromer lighthouse was Henry Broadhurst (1840–1911), stonemason, trade union leader and Liberal MP. In 1890 he came to live on the Overstrand Road at Trent Cottage (later renamed Trent House – Broadhurst had been MP for Stoke-on-Trent from 1880 to 1885), and became a local magistrate and chairman of the UDC. He died here and was buried in Overstrand.

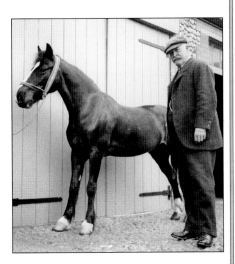

a links, and immediately an effort was made to show that it did not belong to me at all. But we went to law about it, and proved it to be included in the Overstrand property bought for a large sum by my grandfather. Now it brings in £400 a year.' (Lord Suffield clearly wishes the golf course to be thought his idea, but newspaper reports suggest that it was Henry Broadhurst who was chiefly responsible.)[1]

Compton Mackenzie recalled that golfers here wore red jackets so that they would be seen easily.[2]

Royal patronage was granted by the Prince of Wales (later Edward VII), and later by George V. The course was extended to 18 holes in 1895, with an opening-day match between J. H. Taylor (open champion) and 'Herd, the famous Huddersfield player', in which both players managed to drive a ball into the club house.[3] The course was remodelled in 1912–13 with the advice of J. H. Taylor. After the purchase in the 1970s of part of Riseborough's Field, the course was rearranged so as to avoid the parts most threatened by cliff falls.

People who played here included the Princess of Wales (later Queen Alexandra), the poet Tennyson (in 1889), prime minister H. H. Asquith, Arthur Balfour, James Barrie and Malcolm Sargent (who was inspired to write a piece of music called 'An Impression of a Windy Day' after he had hit six balls into the sea in quick succession).[4] Cromer was also the venue for the first golf match between Britain and America, when a Ladies' Open Championship was held here; Britain won.

A clubhouse was erected in Happy Valley *c.* 1890, using a prefabricated building which had previously been a butcher's shop (belonging to R. Le Neve of Hamilton Road) with the addition on each side of ornately roofed wings.[5] It was replaced in 1912–13 by a clubhouse on the present site (next to the Roman Catholic church) and extended in 1980–81. The steward's bungalow was built in 1922.

An Artisans' Section was established in 1922 and continued until 1979.

For 90 years green-keeping was the responsibility of the Clements family (three generations); the wife and daughter of the first green-keeper also ran a ginger-beer hut on the course.

Professional Ernie Plummer served the club from 1921 to 1968, retiring on his 70th birthday.

The freehold of the land was purchased from the Harbord family in 1976.

For further information, see *A Hundred Years of Royal Cromer Golf Club* (1988).

Gooseberry Lane. An old name for Surrey Street, supposedly because there was a greengrocer's shop there.

Gordon House (West Street). This house, on the corner of West Street and Meadow Road, reputed to have been at one time the home of the Cromer Hall estate manager, is shown in the 1901 census as a hotel. In 1908 the YMCA took it over as a holiday home. The upper floors were later converted to flats and the ground floor became the gas showroom (and from the 1990s a cycle shop).

Gospel Hall. A 20th-century prefabricated building at the top of the Norwich Road, with brick entrance hall added later. Built by a Brethren congregation, which had met in 'The Upper Room' in Garden Street (by the end of the 1880s) and then in the primary school. In the 1990s the membership dwindled to just a couple of families, so the Brethren assembly was closed and the hall became home to the Cromer Christian Fellowship.[1]

Granaries. *See under* DITCHELL'S HOUSE AND BARN; GANGWAY. (There were also granaries at Cromer Beach station.)

Grand Hotel (Runton Road). Built 1890–91 (architect: George Skipper; contractor: J. Youngs & Son) for Benjamin Bond Bond-Cabbell.[1] Seven Norwich subscribers formed a company in 1893 to take it over – two of Cromer's other hotel proprietors, A. E. Jarvis and F. W. Rogers, bought shares a little later, but were not directors.[2] Among its guests was Sir Francis Burnand, editor of *Punch* and correspondent and publisher of Clement Scott. Dr Dent recalled that 'the catering and comfort to be obtained ... was not remarkable, and on being asked his opinion of the

The Grand Hotel's Music Room (which was also used for private dances) in the 1920s.

hotel Burnand though the house might be re-christened the "semi-grand" with advantage'.[3] When the hotel was put on the market in 1925 it had 79 bedrooms and 9 bathrooms; there were 18 lock-up garages for motor cars and rooms for their chauffeurs.[4] The hotel was renamed the Albany Hotel in 1965, and demolished after a fire in 1969[5] had made it unsafe.

¶ **Grange, The** (Paul's Lane). Built for Sir John Hare, the actor–manager who was associated with London's Garrick Theatre. In 1910 it was bought by William Player (of the tobacco company) for £4,200.[1] It was later occupied by Sir

Jesse Boot (founder of Boots the Chemist).[2] It became a council Children's Home *c.* 1956, closed in the late 1990s and put on the market in 2000, after which it was divided into residential apartments.

¶ **Grange Avenue.** Bungalows built in the 1950s by Drury Estates of Leicestershire.[1]

Grange Court (Cliff Avenue). Built for a Mrs MacFarlane, and originally called Tigh-na-mara; among those who rented it were the nonagenarian Duke of Grafton (1912).[1] In 1923 it was bought by the Convent of the Faithful Virgin who initially used it as a rest home; then they bought Bracondale School and moved to The Grange.[2] The building subsequently became a hotel, before being converted into flats.

❡ Grangegorman (16 Coast Road). House built *c.* 1904; before World War I it was owned by Mrs Edward Lyttelton,[1] whose husband was headmaster of Eton 1905–16 and became incumbent of Sidestrand 1918–20.[2] The house was later turned into flats.

Greenfield Close. Built on land which had previously been used as allotment gardens (seen as such on the 1928 Ordnance Survey map and in 1946 aerial photographs).

Grove, The (Overstrand Road). Bought as a holiday house by Joseph Gurney (1755–1830), who added to it and called it The Grove.[1] It was later the home of Henry Birkbeck (1821–95, another banker), who added the eastern extension containing study etc. on the ground floor and bedroom, dressing room and w.c. on the first floor (designed by Edward Boardman's practice and built by George Riches in 1895).[2] He sold it to one of the Barclay family *c.* 1897 because the building of the new Links Hotel meant the garden was now overlooked.[3]

Until the boundary change which made Suffield Park part of Cromer, The Grove was the last house in Cromer before you passed into Overstrand. The house became a hotel in 1936.

Grove Farm (Overstrand Road). The 1871 census shows Richard Lambert here farming 70 acres. As late as World War I the farm ran to over 40 acres, stretching across to the Norwich Road,[1] but houses were already beginning to be built on the land.

Grove Road. Council houses built in the 1930s on land which had been part of Grove Farm.

Guidebooks. The first guide to Cromer was published in 1800 by Edmund Bartell, son of a Holt surgeon of the same name.[1] He lived in Cromer, and his work as a surveyor led him to become very familiar with the district he described. Rye's verdict was 'poor stuff, giving little or no real information', but it must have sold well enough, for a second edition appeared in 1806.

Next, in 1841, there appeared *A Guide to Cromer and its Neighbourhood, by a Visitor* (published by the Cromer bookseller Mary Leak). The 'Visitor' was Jane Alice Sargant,[2] a widow who ran a school for young ladies in Clapton Square, Hackney, and had written one or two mildly feminist books as well as a great many moral and religious books for children, almost all appearing anonymously. Her *Guide* was so popular that it appeared in several subsequent editions and formed the unacknowledged basis for

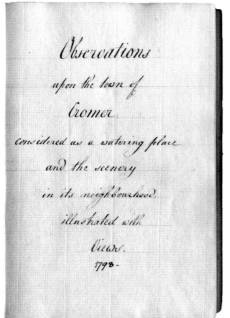
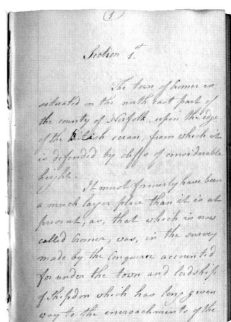

The manuscript of Bartell's guidebook.

the later illustrated guide compiled by Mark Knights and published by Jarrolds.

The UDC produced the first official guide in 1902; it had been compiled by Alex Jarvis, who was already a leading figure on the council and was to be chief organiser of all the music on the pier for over 20 years.[3]

More recently, the *Cromer Town Guide and Trade Directory* has been published by the Cromer and District Chamber of Trade and Commerce.

Guilds. In medieval times, guilds were social clubs, friendly societies, trade unions and religious organisations, based on the parish church but often including in their membership people from outside the parish.[1] In a place like Cromer, one can imagine that membership might have included sailors from elsewhere, wanting to ensure that if they died away from home their funeral would be taken care of, and natives of Cromer whose success in business had taken them to live elsewhere but who desired some form of continuing link with their home parish. From Cromer wills of the 15th century we learn of eight guilds, such as the Guild of St George and the Guild of the Holy Trinity.[2] They are likely to have held annual feasts, which would have served much the same function as a business lunch or Rotary Club dinner today.

Gun batteries. *See* FORTIFICATIONS.

Gunner's Manor. A medieval manor consisting of land in Felbrigg, Runton and Cromer (including the land between the two becks). It belonged to a John Gunnor about the early 16th century and was later in the hands of John Ynglonde (*c.* 1572), Thomas Blofeld and Thomas Baxter (*c.* 1614). Nathaniel Life acquired it in 1697, together with the manor of Overstrand, and it went down in his family to Mary, the wife of Humphrey Rant of Ipswich, in 1763. Mrs Rant died in 1781 and the estate was eventually sold to the Gunton Estate Trustees; Lord Suffield built a seaside house here (*see* HOTEL DE PARIS).[1]

Gypsies Close. Piece of land of about eight and half acres on the northern side of Cuckoo Lane (= Holt Road), so named on a map of the first half of the 18th century.[1] In the later 20th century it became the site of the Co-operative supermarket and Travis Perkins' builders' merchants' yard.

H

Hall Road. The road past Cromer Hall (named Hanworth Road on an 18th-century map) was diverted in the early 19th century so as not to pass so close to the Hall; the original line corresponds roughly to the drives of the two Victorian lodges.

In the 1860s Benjamin Bond Cabbell had the idea of diverting the road away from the Hall completely, so that it ran from the Felbrigg Road/Metton Road junction straight to the junction of the proposed Prince of Wales Road with Louden Road; or else straight across to the Roughton Road (roughly opposite where Alexandra Road is now) or to the Norwich Road (roughly where St Mary's Road is now); these plans were abandoned, probably because of objections to the increased distance people would have to travel.[1]

Halls. *See* MEETING ROOMS AND HALLS.

Halsey House (junction of Norwich Road and Cromwell Road). Built 1900–01 for Sir Francis Layland-Barratt (Liberal MP for Torquay 1900–10) and known as The Red House; architects George J. Skipper and F. W. Skipper did work on the house in 1908.[1] During World War 1 the owners at their own expense turned it into a 50-bed military hospital, genteel but with well qualified nursing staff; part of the coach house was used as a reception room, with seats (sacks of hay from the stables!) and a bath. The local paper enthused that 'a more ideal and nicely arranged place it would be difficult to imagine. From the moment of their arrival to the time of departure the twenty patients for whom accommodation is available are the guests of Sir Francis and Lady Layland-Barratt.'[2] By the time the hospital closed in December 1917 (the owners were moving to Devon early in 1918) it had admitted 734 patients.

The house later became Kingsmill School; was sold by Sir Francis Layland-Barratt's executors in 1934 to Torwood Estates Company; was requisitioned for army use in World War 2; and was bought in 1946 by the Royal British Legion, which opened it in 1948 as a nursing home named after the Legion's Eastern Area President, Sir Lionel Halsey.[3]

A later rear extension enabled it to accommodate 62 residents in single bedrooms, but new government legislation in the early 21st century called for even better facilities, and in 2006 a new block was opened (built on the front garden) to which the residents were moved whilst the rear wings were demolished and rebuilt; once completed in 2009, they offered 30 beds for nursing care and 30 for residential care, with the front block able to accommodate 16 elderly mentally infirm residents.

Hamilton Road. Made up in the 1890s and named after barrister Col. Henry Best Hans Hamilton, brother-in-law of Benjamin Bond Bond-Cabbell..

Hampshire Gardens (Cromwell Road). The converted stables of HAMPSHIRE HOUSE.

Hampshire House. Formerly a nurses' home. It was converted to apartments after it had been sold by the Norwich Health Authority in 1986/87.[1]

Hanover Court (Overstrand Road). Retirement flats built by the nationally based Hanover Housing Association.

Hanover House (High Street). The Victorian bay windows of this house opposite the west porch of the church hide interior walls of flint and thin tile courses; above the false ceiling of the ground floor shops are beams of early 16th-century type. The rear part, originally quite detached, once had a shaped gable – was it added to an existing building, or was the whole of this building erected in the Hanoverian period?

The Victorian front of Hanover House and, on the right, Warwick House.

ABOVE: *The shaped gable of Hanover House seen in an early photograph.* LEFT: *A clearer image showing the garden behind the house, but now the Victorian addition is seen built up high between the house and the church.*

Its distinctive shaped gable is seen in two 17th-century paintings and it may well be still older.[1] The name 'Hanover House' was still in use in the early 20th century for the rear part of the building, but at this period the SHIPDEN CLUB occupied the first and second floors at the front of the building, and the name on the front door opposite the church now reads Shipden House.

Hans Place. Name given to the northern section of The Loke when houses were built there; named after Col. Henry Best Hans Hamilton, a barrister and brother-in-law of Benjamin Bond

Bond Cabbell. *See also* CARLTON TERRACE. 📖 For a description of the interior of one of the houses, and mention of its connection with the Beach Mission, see Philip Bligh, *A History of Cromer Beach Mission 1883–2007: Glimpses into the Spiritual Life of North Norfolk* (Lulu, pp. 27, 29 etc.

Happy Jack. *See* WATER SUPPLY.

Happy Valley. The valley immediately below the lighthouse, once part of the golf course. (The large shelter was erected on the site of the original golf clubhouse.) It was let to the council annually from 1912–13 for recreational purposes.

In 1956 archaeological excavations were carried out here and fragments of Iron Age urns found. The site has been declared a Site of Special Scientific Interest.[1]

Harbord House (Overstrand Road). Built (as two houses, called Carrington Villas)[1] by the Norwich architect Edward Boardman[2] for the 5th Lord Suffield in 1878/79. 'Though we lived for a good many years in the house,' Lord Suffield wrote later, the place never seemed like home to me,'[3] and in 1890 his son even secured a provisional ale-house licence for it, presumably thinking to turn it into a hotel, though this idea was superseded by the idea of building the much larger ROYAL LINKS HOTEL on the hill behind it.[4] In 1898 Lord Suffield put the house at the disposal of Alexandra, Princess of Wales. Later it was occupied by his daughter Lettice, and in the later 20th century by Robert Harbord-Hamond, a son of the 11th Lord Suffield. The house was converted in the early years of the 21st century for use as apartments intended for the mentally ill.
❡ Harbord House in Overstrand is the name given to the building on the corner of Harbord Road and the High Street, once having a shop on the ground floor but latterly consisting entirely of flats.

Harbord Road. Harbord was the family name of Lord Suffield. This road was part of the original Suffield Park development plan of 1887,[1] and the houses were built during the 1890s and after. The road was made up in 1896.[2]
❡ Harbord Road in Overstrand was built on the eastern tip of the Overstrand estate belonging to Lord Suffield; the middle section between the two bends was originally to be called Suffield Road and the northern section connecting with Paul's Lane was called Sea View, or Sea View Road.[3] Lord Hillingdon, owner of Overstrand Hall, married Alice Harbord, a daughter of the 5th Baron Suffield.

After the death in 1907 of Lord Battersea (owner of The PLEASAUNCE), his widow paid for no 7 Harbord Road and nos 1 & 6 Sea View to be turned into convalescent homes.[4]

Hartington Road. Part of the original Suffield Park development plan of 1887; the road terminated at the edge of Lord Suffield's property.[1] Made up in 1901, when Mr Fearn gave the necessary land for widening it to 30 feet as far as Mr Kettle's stables.[2] At the end of the road the WHITE HOUSE was built; this was demolished in the 1990s and its grounds used by Broadland Housing for low-cost houses.

Hastings House (Tucker Street). Seaside house of the Astley family, Lords Hastings, of Melton Constable Hall.

Hastings House (top left, with bow window) seen above over the Bath House Hotel's new extension in 1875.

In 1499 Thomas Multon bequeathed a house in Cromer called 'Hastyngs', with two acres of land, to his son Bartholomew.[1]

Haverhill House (13 Bond Street). In the 1950s the ground floor was used by Thomas Walter ('Tarts') Baker as a confectionery shop; the business was later taken over by Mrs Wright, whose husband ran a taxi business (formerly and afterwards known as Blue Star Taxis) from the back room.

Heartwell Road. Part of the estate built by the national building firm of Barratt in the 1980s. The name commemorates the *Louisa Heartwell* lifeboat which served Cromer from 1902 to 1923.

Heath House (51 Church Street). One of the houses used as lodgings by the Gurney family when they first came to

Cromer in the 1790s, it belonged to Mr Heath the chemist (*see* PHARMACISTS).

Henry Blogg Road. Part of the estate built by the national building firm of Barratt in the 1980s. Named after the lifeboat which in turn had been named after Cromer's most famous lifeboat coxswain (*see* LIFEBOATS).

Heraldry. *See* ARMORIAL BEARINGS.

Herne Close. Originally a field name (a map of 1717 spells it 'Hurn Close', possibly meaning the enclosed piece of ground next to the 'hurn' or corner at the bottom of what was then Mill Lane).[1]

Herne Court. 1. The name given to a house built in Herne Close for Robert Barclay of The WARREN shortly after the 1885 Ordnance Survey map was prepared (architect: Edward May[1]). In 1959, after the death of Miss Barclay, it became part of SUTHERLAND HOUSE SCHOOL; it was converted into flats in 2000 and renamed Sutherland Court.

2. Development of flats built on land between The Warren and Herne Court after demolition of THE WARREN.

High Street. One of the oldest roads in Cromer, leading naturally up to the parish church, and indeed to the earlier church of St Paul, which was demolished in the 14th century. Both sides of the road were built up by the time of the first surviving map of Cromer in 1717.

¶ The road from Cromer to Mundesley originally followed the route of what came to be called the High Street in Overstrand, and continued along Coast Road. It was rerouted to avoid the erosion threat. The boundary between the parishes of Overstrand and Northrepps followed the middle of the road.

High View Park. Housing built on land previously occupied by Cromer High railway station.

¶ **Highfield Road.** On the outskirts of Overstrand and actually in the parish of Northrepps.

Hill Close. Built by H. Bullen & Son.

¶ **Hill Farm.** On the northern side of the road from Cromer to Overstrand, just west of Overstrand Hall; later (as a private residence) called Yeomans.

¶ **Hillingdon Park.** Named after Lord Hillingdon (owner of Overstrand Hall, and of Hillingdon Court in Uxbridge, Middlesex).

Historians. Cromer has had at least three amateur local historians whose antiquarian interests have caused much original documentary material to be preserved.

Walter Rye (1843–1929) practised as a solicitor in London from 1866 to

Walter Rye

1900, when he came to live in Norwich (of which he was Mayor in 1908). He was instrumental in saving several historic buildings there, including the Maid's Head Hotel.[1] He liked to trace his ancestry back to the Rye family of Cromer. He spent a great deal of time transcribing documents, some of them difficult medieval Latin ones, such as a prolix papal Bull 'which Bull I have copied at length, and I earnestly hope no one may ever have occasion to do so again'.[2] His sense of humour also shows through when, having transcribed the monumental inscriptions in Overstrand church where many of the Buxton family are buried, he adds: 'I have been, hitherto, unable to find any record of a bad Buxton, but should be most grateful for a reference to such an one, as he would be an immense relief from the monotony of goodness asserted by their tombstones.'[3]

Rye's 1889 book on *Cromer Past and Present*, published in aid of the church restoration fund, remains a hugely useful quarry of material on the earlier history of the town.

Alfred Collison Savin (1860–1948), the only one of the three to have been born and bred in Cromer, was the son of Daniel Savin; in their Church Street antiques shop they sold specimens of local fossils, and Savin junior published *A Short Guide to the Geology of Cromer and Neighbourhood, with Lists of Fossils* (Norwich: Fletcher, 1887). This built on the work of geological scholars such as Charles Lyell and C. Reid, presenting their work for a more popular market.

Fifty years later Savin published *Cromer in the County of Norfolk: a Modern*

C. Crawford Holden

History (Holt: Rounce & Wortley, 1937; reprinted posthumously with some additional notes in 1950), supplementing Rye's account of earlier years; it traced the successive occupants of properties in each street using documentary sources of the 19th century as well as the author's own memories.

Savin's notes on the streets of Cromer were transferred onto cards and updated by **Cyril Crawford Holden** (1902–76). Originally from London, he

A. C. Savin

had first visited Cromer in 1919 and moved to the town with his parents when they retired in 1939. Apart from being involved with the Cromer Players, and being keenly interested in the cinema, his most notable passion was for Cromer history, on which he gave frequent talks and published a booklet,

Cromer: the Cutting of the Gem (1967; rev. ed. Poppyland, 1979). His collection of newspaper cuttings, 1,500 photographs, nearly 700 slides and extensive manuscript notes was eventually to find a home in the Cromer Museum which was established after his death.

Holly Cottage (corner of Louden Road and Chapel Street). This house seems to have been built as the residence of Nathaniel Smith in 1724. It later belonged to John Juler Pank and was occupied by John's sister Mary; it was known as Pank's Lodge (the first reference to it being called Holly Cottage is in 1848).[1] The 1861 census shows a GP called James Cooper living in Louden Street with his family, possibly at Holly Cottage. Rev. Horatio Marsh, the curate, lived here in 1864.[2] Dr Robert McKelvie lived here for some years with his wife and a cook, a housemaid and a dispenser. The house had a stable, a yard and a row of three cottages (only one of which survives, the others having burnt down).

Compton Mackenzie stayed here as a child, with his sister Fay and their father, and would play around the horses stabled on the corner.[3]

There was a back way to the old schools and Parish Hall along the side of the property.

¶ Holly Cottage in Overstrand stood where the Crossways housing development was later built.

Holt Road. *See* CUCKOO LANE.

Holway Close. Development of bungalows on the Roughton Road (actually standing over the parish boundary into Roughton). They appear on the 1969 Ordnance Survey.

Home Farm (Hall Road). Formerly known as the Dairy Farm or Dairy House Farm. In 1861 the farm extended to 180 acres.

Homecolne House (Louden Road). Warden-controlled flats for older people, built in 1987 by McCarthy & Stone on land previously used for holiday chalets. All their developments had been given names beginning with 'Home', so this one became 'Homecolne House' because it was built in the grounds of Colne House.[1]

Horseshoe Pond. A natural feature on the beach a little to the west of the pier during the period between the two World Wars. Attempts were made in the 1950s and again in the 1970s to recreate the pond as a safe place for children to play, catch small fish and crabs left behind by the tide, but winter storms quickly destroyed it again.

Hospital. The original hospital was in a pair of cottages in Louden Road (they were then known as School Cottages because they were on the same plot of land as the Vicar's school on

Church Street, but they have since been called West Cottage). The first patient was received in 1866 and the hospital remained in the same premises (at first offering six beds, increasing to seven when an extension was built) until 1887.

George Webb Collison, a retired banker of solid Cromer ancestry, then gave the money to buy a larger plot of land just along the road and to build a new hospital on it. This closed in 1903 for alterations and an extension by Edward Boardman, reopening in 1904; an X-ray room was added in 1914.[1]

The hospital moved to Mill Road in 1932; the new premises were designed by Edward Boardman & Son,[2] a late example of the idea of a cottage hospital being picturesque rather than forbid-dingly institutional. The old premises were taken over by the local Conservative Party for their party offices and club. (*See also* COTTAGE, THE.)

The Allies ward, a ten-bed surgical unit (architect: Barry Hastings; builders: H. Bullen & Son), was built in 1976–78 solely as a result of voluntary fundraising and with much volunteer labour after a group of business and professional people resolved to help cut waiting times for surgery.[3]

A new operating theatre was built in 1982.[4]

In 2000 it was announced that a bequest of about ten million pounds had been left to the hospital by Mrs Sagle Bernstein,[5] an American resident of Richmond Court Gardens whose sister had enjoyed the hospital's care. A little

Aerial view of the hospital buildings in Mill Road in the 1930s.

of this bequest was spent quite quickly, on a mobile 'response unit' to attend emergencies, but there followed years of debate about the hospital's rebuilding, which would be funded largely from Mrs Bernstein's money. Rebuilding work was at last begun in 2010.

See also FLETCHER HOSPITAL; HALSEY HOUSE; ISOLATION HOSPITAL; X-RAYS.

❡ After the death of Lord Battersea in 1907, his widow paid for the conversion into convalescent homes of three houses in Overstrand (7 Harbord Road, and numbers 1 and 6 Sea View).[6]

Hotel de Paris. Built as a Marine Villa for the 3rd Lord Suffield about 1820, it was sold in 1830 and turned into a hotel by Pierre Gustavus le Francois (born in 1783, the son of Pierre Augustus, Baron del Barr, who had fled to England in 1794 to escape the French Revolution). He died in 1841 and his widow Mary continued the business with Mrs Garthon (a daughter of George Cooke Tucker of the New Inn) as manageress. Edward Seppings was licensee from 1844 (still with Mrs Garthon as manageress); in 1847 Matthias Goggs[1] became licensee; later the same year, Thomas Boulter. The hotel was sold to Henry Soame Jarvis in 1851 and extended in or shortly before 1860 (probably by adding the third floor).

Henry Jarvis's son Alex commissioned Norwich architects G. J. & F. W. Skipper to redesign the building in 1894, taking in the neighbouring Albert House and part of the Belle Vue Hotel and altering the internal layout. The builder was J. S. Smith of Norwich, who had already built the Cliftonville Hotel on the Runton Road.[2] Opening day was in 1895.

Among famous guests were Lord Tennyson (who stayed in 1877) and Lord Curzon, who stayed here just before going out to India, where he was Viceroy from 1898 to 1905.[3]

The hotel was later sold to Norwich property developer Edward Bush, who modernised the interior and reopened it in 1964; after Bush's death in 1972 it was sold to a London property company. When C. & H. Hotels Ltd collapsed in February 1975, the hotel was shut; it was then sold to Embra Investments Ltd, who reopened it in May 1976. By the 1990s, it was owned by the same group as Shearings coaches, and the majority of its visitors came in coach parties.

Hotel Street. Name given to the High Street in the tithe map of 1840 and to Tucker Street in the sale map of the Cromer Hall estate in 1852.

Howards Hill. The hill bears this name on a map of 1717.[1] Howards Hill West and Howards Hill Close were a development of the 1970s.

Hunting and shooting. Sporting opportunities were one of the main reasons wealthy men bought or built houses in the locality in the 19th century, and when Cromer Hall was to be rebuilt in 1828 the architect planned a room on the ground floor for 'guns, hats, whips &c'.[1] Compit Hills were used for shooting, and a gamekeeper's lodge was built close by, next to the brickfield between the Roughton Road and Hall Road.

The 4th Lord Suffield kept stag-hounds for two seasons from 1836, and the 5th Lord Suffield established a pack of foxhounds and was Master of the East Norfolk Foxhounds from 1856 to 1859. Col. H. A. Barclay hunted with his own harriers around the Cromer area in 1875, followed till 1887 by his brother, E. E. Barclay. Sir Fowell Buxton of Cromer was one of the landowners receiving the thanks of the Master of Fox Hounds after the 17th Lord Hastings restarted the Eastern division in 1862, but after the latter's unexpected death his horses and hounds were sold and fox-hunting declined in the area.[2]

I

Ice house. Shown on the 1st (1886) edition of the 1:2,500 Ordnance Survey map, in Hall Wood. In addition to providing ice for Cromer Hall, local tradesman Mr Breeze stocked it with ice for his use in the summer season.[1] It is not shown on the 1911 O.S. map.

Iceland. Robert Bacon (late 14th-early 15th centuries), a seaman from Cromer, is said to have discovered Iceland. The island was well known long before this, and what he probably did was to start trading directly with Iceland again after the Norwegian kings had been insisting for more than a century that all Icelandic trade should be conducted through them.[1]

Imperial Hotel (9, 11 and 11a Church Street). (In full, the Imperial Temperance Hotel and Restaurant.) Built by J. Youngs & Son. Patronised in 1913 by the Crown Prince of Jahore and his entourage.[1] Methodist church services were held here in 1909–10 while the new chapel was being built in West Street.[2] It was later converted to flats and renamed Kentford House.[3]

Imperial House. Shop at the corner of the High Street and Jetty Street. In the 19th century and the first half of the 20th it was occupied by the Curtis family, running a very mixed business as BLACKSMITHS, grocers, drapers, fruiterers and tailors. James Curtis was a leading figure in the town and Thomas Curtis was the church organist in the 1860s.

Inkpot (Bernard Road). Another name for the house officially called St Katherine's, which when newly built, with its single central chimney, caused someone to complain about the view being obstructed by 'that wretched inkpot'. The architectural style is in stark contrast to the more ornamented buildings then being erected on all sides. The architect was Walter John Tapper, the builders were Rudd & Sons of Grantham[1] and the house is first listed in the 1900 directory, occupied by S. Bentley Rudd.

Iron Age. *See* HAPPY VALLEY.

Isolation Hospital. In the 1890s there was much concern over infectious diseases such as scarlet fever. This gave impetus to the council's attack on insanitary housing through the enforcement of building regulations and, when a notifiable disease occurred, the compulsory disinfecting or destruction of anything likely to harbour germs.[1] A hospital marquee was bought so that it could be erected quickly in the event of a serious outbreak of infectious disease. Soon, two cottages on Roughton Heath were converted into an isolation hospital (two wards of two patients each, plus administrative offices).[2]

The hospital fell out of use in the 1920s/30s and was finally sold in 1952.

Ivy Cottages (between Church Street and Louden Road). Built on gardens belonging to the Cromer Hall estate. The same name was at one time given to Brickfields Cottages on the Roughton Road.

¶ **Ivy Farm.** Originally called Ivy

House, and in the parish of North-repps because the parish boundary ran down the middle of what is now called Overstrand High Street. Before World War I it was owned by the Gurney family; Lady Battersea took a 14-year lease on the house in 1909.[1] Later in the 20th century the Reynolds family opened a caravan park here.

J

Jehovah's Witnesses. The former fire and ambulance station in Canada Road was converted into a Kingdom Hall of Jehovah's Witnesses in the 1990s. Previously they had met in a building behind Church Street (east of Mount Street).

Jet. *See* JEWELLERS.

Jetty. *See* PIER.

Jetty Street. There were already houses on both sides of this street by 1717,[1] but they were enlarged at various later dates. The council took the decision to have the road made up in 1893.[2]

Jewellers. *James J. Briggs* jewellers, a business founded in Norwich in 1820, opened in Cromer's Flint House in 1894; a photograph of 1896 shows that 'E. H. Briggs, practical watchmaker and working jeweller' had set a clock on the front of the building, flush with the wall; this was later replaced with a more eye-catching clock supported on brackets which still (2010) survive, albeit clocklessly. The business moved along the road to Hamilton House in 1934, and to 38 Church Street in 1962. Male heirs of the Briggs family died out and the business was bought in 1985 by Michael Jones, who had bought Bond Street Jewellers in 1973. Briggs' shop finally closed in 2008,[1] while Mark Jones (son of Michael) continued to run the Bond Street shop.

Other jewellers in the town have included *Daniel Savin* in Church Street (from at least as early as the 1861 cen-

Flint House when occupied by Briggs.

sus), *Saul Salkind* in Bond Street and Church Street (late 19th/early 20th century) and more recently Bentons in Hamilton Road (opened in 2009 – they already had shops in North Walsham and elsewhere).

In the 19th and early 20th centuries the local jewellers sold items made from amber and jet found on the beach (*Tom Mack* proudly described himself for the 1866 directory as 'manufacturer of the original Cromer jet, and other stone trinkets, brooches, &c'.) The local amber was usually cloudy or opaque, occasionally clear wine-colour and the pieces were usually of half an ounce to two ounces in weight. Jet was usually found in seaweed after easterly gales.[2] The 1871 census shows *Gilbert Mack* in Brook Street as a jet worker, *John Fox* in Jetty Street combining jet working with his duties as postmaster, and *Robert Filby* in Church Street as a jet ornament manufacturer with his two nephews as apprentices.

Jiglers Croft. *See* GIGLERS CROFT.

Jubilee Lane. Presumably named in honour of Queen Victoria's jubilee. Made up in 1901.[1]

Jubilee Terrace. Row of cottages in Jubilee Lane, built just yards from Cromer's first railway station, to house men working on the railway.

¶ **Julian House.** *See* CLIFFSIDE HOUSE.

King's College pupils with their teacher and (on the balcony) William Vaughan and family.

K

Kennel Burn. A stream running near North Lodge; Frank Hoare used to bathe in it every day.[1] It was later channelled through an underground pipe carrying it under the promenade.

Kentford House. *See* IMPERIAL HOTEL.

King's Arms. Old name of the CROWN & ANCHOR (though sources often confuse it with the KING'S HEAD).

King's College. Private school opened by William Vaughan in St Mary's Road, opposite Craigside, in 1900.[1] The 1901 census shows him living there with his wife and baby daughter, employing two teenage girls as servants and having eight boys aged 9 to 15 as boarders; all the boarders came from Hertfordshire or London (where the Vaughans had been born). William moved on at the beginning of 1903, leaving the school in the charge of Henry Madeley Padley (the house then being known as 'Cheltenham'), but his elder sister Eleanor Vaughan went on to run a 'ladies' school' at 11 & 13 St Mary's Road, before emigrating to New Zealand in 1919.

King's Head (High Street). John Harvey paid rates here 1780–91; it was owned by the Coltishall Brewery till 1841,[1] then by the Weybourne Brewery, then by

Steward & Patteson (1897–) and thence became one of the Pubmaster chain.

Said to be connected to the network of underground TUNNELS leading to the Hotel de Paris, Rust's etc.

Kingsmill School. Private school conducted in The Red House (which became HALSEY HOUSE), during the 1930s. A field on Overstrand Road, opposite Warren Woods, was used as a playing field.[1]

Kingston House. *See* TEA-ROOMS.

L

Labourers and Mechanics Provident Institution. *See* FRIENDLY SOCIETIES.

Lancaster's Manor. One of the medieval manors of Cromer, part of the Duchy of Lancaster. It was probably part of UFFORD'S HALL. At the time of Edward I it was held by the family of de Warren, and from 1663 by the Rant family, from whom it descended to the Harbord family by 1750.[1]

Laundries. W. P. Baker of the Ship Hotel on Church Street opened a steam laundry in 1889 offering 'Family Washing on reasonable terms' – no doubt with an eye on the increasing number of holiday-makers and middle-class incomers. Known as the Ship Laundry or Central Laundry, it was described as successor to the East Cliff Model Laundry in Windham Park. Subsequently owned by R. Rodwell and then E. Edwards, it was closed and pulled down in 1926.[1]

The Cromer Steam Laundry in Cross Street was set up by half a dozen Norwich investors in 1898 and run by A. E. Salter and A. C. Savin. Its steam whistle was used during daytime for summoning firemen to emergencies from 1938.[2]

A self-service launderette operated in Mount Street during the later part of the 20th century and when it closed another was opened on Church Street (opposite the Gangway), lasting only a few years.

Lecture Hall (Cross Street). Opened in 1891 by the Band of Hope as a temperance lecture hall; the builder was Ambrose Fox, who had been the second boy in Cromer to sign the pledge. It had a projection room and a wall of Parian cement on which to project magic lantern slides; here local schoolteacher A. E. Salter used to give lectures on local history and on general subjects – one, in aid of the Wesleyan Church building fund, was entitled 'From the North Sea to the Pacific Ocean and Back' and was illustrated with over 100 lantern views.[1]

The hall could seat 250 people, and its kitchen facilities enabled the catering manager, Frederick W. Burton,

The Lecture Hall in use as a restaurant. On the projection screen is a picture of the outside of the building.

to hire it for use as a restaurant (the Victoria Restaurant' – Burton's 12-year lease allowed him to use the hall for 19 weeks a year, May to September); it was later used for dances.[2] In 1922 the auction sale was held here of the Colne House estate. From 1949 to 1994 the hall was used by the Junior School for physical education (being sold to the County Council in 1970). After the Junior School moved to its new premises on the Norwich Road the hall was redundant; it was sold in 2000 and converted into a private house.

Libraries. *(For earlier facilities, see* READING ROOMS.*)*

1. Thomas Leak started a circulating library at the end of the 18th century, consisting chiefly of a few novels'.[1]

Here were also to be found two of Greathead's books on lifeboats, for study by those who were considering the appeal for funds to establish a lifeboat in Cromer in 1804;[2] and it is probably Leak's that is alluded to in a novel of 1823 when it describes someone placing an advertisement 'at the door of the public library' and 'in the most conspicuous part of Adam's shop' offering a cottage to let.[3] The pretensions of the shop did not, however, impress everyone: the London visitor Robert Marten wrote that 'There is a shop with such wares as are usually found in what are called at watering places Libraries'.[4] After Thomas Leak's death in 1830 his widow Mary continued the business, being listed in White's 1836 directory as 'stationer, circulating library & toy warehouse' in Church Street. A diarist mentions obtaining the latest instalment of *Nicholas Nickleby* at the shop on 18 July 1839.[5] Mrs Leak was also the publisher of *A Guide to Cromer, by a Visitor* (*see* GUIDEBOOKS).

Although the church architect, John H. Brown, suggested building a room over the north porch as a library,[6] nothing seems to have come of this.

2. A printed catalogue survives from the later 19th century of the 'Cromer library', probably to be identified with the fishermen's reading room (*see* READING ROOMS 2) in Chapel Street. It was open on Mondays and Thursdays between 11 a.m. and 7 p.m. and contained 220 titles, mainly world travel, religion, history and natural history. Donations were requested, but it was made clear that 'No novel or romance will be admitted; the object of the library being to elevate the tone of mind in the readers, by combining instruction with amusement.' (The collection did, however, include *Robinson Crusoe* and *The Swiss Family Robinson*.)[7]

3. C. Munday leased 43 Church Street from 1906[8] and opened a circulating library there. He had previously worked for W. H. Smith & Son in their building in London's Strand, so the building where he opened his Cromer shop is called Strand House. The shop was later known as Hewitt's. A commercial circulating libraries was also operated by Jarrold's (run in conjunction with Mudie's).[9]

4. An adult lending library service operated from the Board school in Louden Road from the 1930s.[10] The County Library then established a branch in the Methodist schoolroom in West Street in the 1950s;[11] later the old Free Methodist chapel in Prince of Wales Road was converted for use as the library.

❧ Lord Battersea built a lending library for Overstrand, which grew to at least 1,500 volumes.

Lifeboat houses. The first lifeboats were simply kept on the beach, 'on wheels ready for an instant start to the water'.[1] A lifeboat house was built at the top of the Gangway in 1842 with a reading room above (*see* READING ROOMS 2); a new house was built lower down the Gangway in 1867 (paid for by Benjamin Bond Cabbell);[2] this in turn was replaced by a larger one in 1902. The advent of motor lifeboats demanded the building of a new shed and slipway at the end of the pier, where building was commenced in 1919 and completed in 1923.[3] The old boat-house remained in use for the no. 2 lifeboat until 1967, subsequently becoming a lifeboat museum.

The boathouse at the end of the pier was replaced by a larger shed with better facilities including a tipping launch cradle in 1998–99 and further modified to take the new class of lifeboat in 2007.

The inflatable inshore lifeboat was (from 1967) kept in the 1902 boathouse and then in an 'igloo' at the foot of the Melbourne slope, but was frequently moved back to the east beach when exposed rocks on the west beach made launching difficult. A shed was constucted for it in 1984 on the promenade a few yards east of the Gangway. This was demolished in 2004 and replaced by a new building on the site of the Rocket House café, to include both a restaurant and a new lifeboat museum; the 1902 boat-house was then restored to its original use.

Lifeboat museum. *See* MUSEUMS.

Lifeboat service. In the autumn of 1804, the gentlemen and leading citi

pectators gather on the beach and pier for the lifeboat H. F. Bailey (ON 694) to be pulled up
nto the boathouse, possibly for her arrival in 1924 or a later lifeboat day.

ens of Cromer launched an appeal to ¡und the purchase of a lifeboat for :romer; from the outset they foresaw he need not only for buying a boat but lso for housing and equipping it, and or rewarding the fishermen who would)e its crew. Their vision was for boats at 'arious points along the Norfolk coast, ¡nd they argued that such a humani-arian cause concerned not only the 'oastal communities but the whole 'ounty. Contributions came from lo- ·al landowners, merchants and clergy some of them promptly and willingly, ·thers almost certainly shamed into ac-ion by well organised publicity of how ¡nuch each of their colleagues had al-eady subscribed), and even from Kings ,ynn, and from the promoters' friends ¡nd relatives in Norwich and London.[1]

The Cromer service was the first in

Norfolk, and after the 3rd Lord Suf-field had helped on shore during a rescue in 1823 he proposed setting up a county-wide association. The Nor-folk Association for Saving the Lives of Shipwrecked Mariners (often known simply as the Norfolk Shipwreck Asso-ciation) was duly formed, the first such county association.

At the end of 1857 the Norfolk life-boat stations were all taken over by the Royal National Life-boat Institution (which had been founded in 1824).

📖 For a brief history of the Cromer lifeboat service, see R. W. Malster and P. J. R. Stibbons, *The Cromer Lifeboats 1804–1979*, 4th edn (Poppyland Publish-ing, 1994).

Lifeboats. The first lifeboat in Cromer operated from 1805 to 1830, when it was

CROMER CHARACTERS
HENRY BLOGG

One of the lifeboat service's most famous coxswains, Henry Blogg (1876–1954) was born to Ellen Blogg in a cottage whose site has since been covered by the rebuilt WELLINGTON INN. He lived at first with his grandmother and then in Chapel Street with his stepfather John James Davies, second coxswain of the lifeboat under his father James Davies. Henry attended the Goldsmiths' School, leaving at the age of eleven to follow the family trade of fishing. He joined the lifeboat crew in 1894 and was its coxswain from 1909 to 1947, being awarded the British Empire Medal, the George Cross, three RNLI gold medals and four silver ones. A new lifeboat was named after him in 1948.

Blogg married in 1901 and lived in Church Street and in Corner Street. He is commemorated

¤ by a plaque on his own house in Corner Street
¤ by a bronze bust looking out to sea from a granite pedestal in North Lodge Park (sculpted by James Woodford RA, who also made the great bronze doors for City Hall in Norwich; the bust was made in the Morris Singer foundry at Kennington in London,[1] presented by Miss E. Scales and unveiled in 1962 – it was later replaced by a cast alloy copy and the original moved into the new lifeboat house)
¤ by a large plaster-of-Paris wall plaque originally in the Ship Inn, later moved to the White Horse and finally to Cromer Museum
¤ in the Henry Blogg Lifeboat Museum on the east promenade.

A further memorial was the Henry Blogg Memorial Shelter, which stood next to the eastern end of the churchyard until refurbishment of Cromer Museum made it necessary to demolish it and replace it with a garden.

Blogg's nephew Henry 'Shrimp' Davies served on the lifeboat for 47 years, starting pulling an oar under his uncle and ending in 1976 after 28 years as coxswain; he was honoured with a television 'This is Your Life' programme.[2]

📖 See RNLI leaflet The Life of Henry George Blogg, coxswain of Cromer lifeboat; biography by Cyril Jolly, Henry Blogg of Cromer (Harrap, 1958; revised edition Poppyland Publishing, 2002).

moved to Wells. A visitor who went out in it in rough weather in 1821 reported that 'it is much more affected by the waves than any other boat, but is not so liable to be overset, as there is a great quantity of cork fastened to the sides'.[1] A model of this boat was made for the Great Exhibition of 1851 and is now in the RNLI Henry Blogg Museum at the bottom of the Gangway.

The second boat, in use from 1830 to 1858, was ordered by the Association for Preserving the Lives of Shipwrecked Mariners and built by Robson of Shields at a cost of £160. It was clinker built, with 12 oars on thole pins, an airtight deck, and a low cork belt inside; it was steered by a sweep oar. Its length was 31 feet, beam 9 feet 6 inches and depth 3 feet 9 inches. There was no regular crew, and by 1857 it is doubtful if the boat was even seaworthy. A new boat was provided by the RNLI in 1858.

The first motor lifeboat arrived in 1923, and from then on Cromer had two lifeboats. The one stationed at the bottom of the Gangway was replaced by an inflatable inshore boat in 1967. (As early as 1902 the fishermen had been keeping one of their boats at the ready for helping others: John Allen was fined for obstructing the Gangway by leaving his boat on it, but 'the Magistrates expressed the view that the Local Authorities might consider whether a position could be found for a boat so as to be readily available in case of need for assisting the fishing boats in distress'.[2]

📖 *See* C. Crawford Holden, *A History of Cromer Life-boats* (unpublished typescript in Cromer library); Nicholas Leach and Paul Russell, *Cromer Life-boats: A Pictorial History* (Ashbourne: Landmark, 2008).

Lighthouses. 1. The earliest warning light to sailors passing Cromer is traditionally said to have been a fire lit on the platform half-way up the northwest corner of the church tower. (Improbable as this may sound, providing lights for shipping had been regarded as a religious duty in pre-Reformation times, and it is akin to the abortive proposal to put a light on top of Winterton steeple in 1585 – or the actual lighthouse built at Caister about 1600, which was a wooden tower and apparently had just three candles tended by an elderly woman living some miles inland!'[1])

2. In 1674 Sir John Clayton leased a piece of land on FOULNESS from William Reymes of the manor of Overstrand, and erected a lighthouse as a private speculation – one of five such lights he built down the east coast. He hoped to get his money back by charging fees to shipping, but Trinity House proved obstructive and he had to abandon the venture in 1678; it seems that the tower on Foulness was never lit. It is thought to have succumbed to a cliff fall around the year 1700.[2]

3. In 1717 a lighthouse was built (or, if the Clayton tower was still standing, then plans were made to activate

Bowell's lighthouse depicted in about 1831.

its light) on the same headland by the Ipswich merchant and shipowner Edward Bowell (1680–1737). He and Nathaniel Life, who now owned the land, obtained a 61-year patent in 1719 from Trinity House allowing them to charge dues on shipping freight; their three-storey octagonal brick tower was first lit on 29 September 1719 by a coal fire (kept up by hand-operated bellows[3]) burning in a wrought-iron basket or grate, inside a glass lantern so that it should not be affected by the weather. Bowell bequeathed it to his nephew Thomas Bowell, the manor of Overstrand continuing to hold a half share. Trinity House extended the lease to 1822, by which time the venture was showing net annual profits of between two and three thousand pounds.

In 1793 the light was equipped with 15 oil lamps with 36-inch silver-plated copper reflectors and a mechanism with a weight like a grandfather clock to make them rotate, giving the effect of one flash of light every minute. This was leading-edge technology: the only other lighthouse that had a light identifiable by its flash was in the Isles of Scilly. The lighthouse keepers of Cromer had to light the lamps every day at sunset and wind the clockwork every 5½ hours. Oil consumption during the longest nights was 3 gallons.[4]

4. The cliff edge drew closer and closer to Bowell's structure: in the winter of 1812–13 an acre and a half directly in front of it fell into the sea,[5] and

after a further major landslip in 1832 it was finally decided to build a new lighthouse further inland. Built hurriedly in 1833, the building may have been prefabricated for another site but shipped to Cromer because of the need to replace the existing threatened structure (which in fact only collapsed into the sea in 1866).[6] The new octagonal white stone tower 38 feet high shone a light 274 feet above high water level;[7] the original lantern had 30 oil lamps, together burning some 1,000 gallons of oil a year. The lamps required trimming every three hours,[8] a job which was undertaken by two keepers (Ellis Field and his sister are shown as light keepers in the 1871 census). The light was converted to gas in 1905 (using two sets of seven burners with a combined light of 49,000 candlepower) and to

a combination of gas and electricity in 1935. The lantern was replaced by a smaller one in 1958, using all-electric lighting with prismatic lenses in place of the old reflectors. (It had been the last surviving English lighthouse to use reflectors). The last of East Anglia's lighthouses to be tended by round-the-clock keepers , it was finally automated in 1982, after which the keeper merely performed routine maintenance.[9]

A helipad was created in front of the lighthouse in 1977 as a base for a Trinity House helicopter to relieve offshore lights once every four weeks.[10]

A keeper's single-storey cottage was built alongside the 1833 lighthouse. (It was replaced in the following century by a pair of larger ones.)

The lighthouse keeper had a garden nearby, which was bought by the UDC and incorporated into Warren Woods.[11]

📖 By far the most informative account of the Cromer lighthouses is in *Lights of East Anglia* by Neville Long (Lavenham: Terence Dalton, 1983). The Trinity House website usefully clarifies the earlier history.

See also EROSION.

Lime kilns. Lime was used in agriculture (to improve sandy soils) and building (for making mortar, plaster and limewash). It was made by burning chalk.

A piece of land on the western side of the Gangway was called Lime Kiln Close in 1627.[1]

The 1838 Ordnance Survey map

The lighthouse in the 1920s or 1930s.

Cromer from Warren Woods, with lime kiln in the foreground.

shows a lime kiln in the grounds of Cromer Hall, near the top of Holt Road – in the 6-inch map (surveyed 1885) it is marked 'old lime kiln'.[2]

Some brickwork survives in Warren Woods which was a lime kiln in the 19th century.

Links Avenue. A development of council houses erected 1947–49, with the westernmost houses added in 1953.[1] Its eastern end was opposite the golf links and very close to Links Halt.

Links Halt. Rudimentary railway station opened in 1923 on Northrepps Road, with a single wooden platform, serving the golf links and Royal Links Hotel. *See also* Railways.

Links Hotel. *See* Royal Links Hotel.

Linkside (Park Road). Before World War 1, the building was occupied by Suffield Park Preparatory School, run by headmaster Heathcote Gordon Winter. By 1921 it had become a Holiday Fellowship hostel; it was later converted into flats.

Literary mentions. Possibly the earliest mention of Cromer in a literary work comes from *John Taylor* the 'Water-poet', an eccentric 17th-century Thames waterman who turned himself into a celebrity with his accounts of somewhat bizarre travels. He recounts (in highly undistinguished verse) how he travelled up the east coast by wherry and was forced ashore by the weather at Cromer, where at first he was treated by the locals as a pirate. The constables brought him to two local magistrates who had read some of his books and so gave him 'corn and wine and lodging'.

T. S. Norgate (1772–1859), a Norwich journalist, wrote a poem 'Madness' about the lone survivor of a shipwreck (supposedly an actual person) who paced the cliffs at Cromer with a staff made from the plank upon which he had escaped the wreck.[1]

'Verses written on the sands at Cromer, in Norfolk' by **Pratt** were included in *The Nursery Garland* (1801), p. 165. Cromer also features as the setting of an encounter related in Pratt's *Gleanings in England* (1801), justly weighed

and found distinctly wanting by Tobias Smollett (*The Critical Review*, 1801).

Cromer was the subject of a tedious poem by **J. S. Mannings**, published anonymously in 1806 – Walter Rye describes it as consisting of 'some 700 lines of the blankest verse I have ever had the luck to come across'.[2]

In 1816, the *Bury and Norwich Post* published a poem about Cromer by an author identified only as **H. S.**

The resort is mentioned briefly in **Jane Austen**'s *Emma* (1816), but there is no evidence that Jane Austen herself ever visited the place.

As part of the regeneration project of the early 21st century, a number of literary quotations referring to Cromer were embedded in the town's paving. There is obvious satisfaction at completing the paving with the Jane Austen quotation at the Crossways.

Elizabeth Gaskell's novel *North and South* (1855) features Cromer as the place where a character goes for re-cuperation, and more recently **Edwin Brock** has written a short story called 'Convalescing in Cromer'.[3]

Charles Dickens' periodical *All the Year Round* describes Cromer in 1885.[4]

The lighthouse hills are described in one of *Jean Ingelow*'s poems, 'Requies-cat in pace'; and, more readably, by **A. C. Swinburne**. A short piece by **W. H. Hudson** about a child he met 'On Cromer Beach' appeared in his book *A Traveller in Little Things* (London: Dent, 1921). **David Rees**' novel *Landslip* (1977), for teenagers, is set in and around Cromer in the late 19th century. A poem by **George Barker**[5] memorialises a narrow escape from drowning at Cromer.

See also WRITERS.

Local government. East Anglia, which had been a separate kingdom until the tenth century, was gradually integrated into the rest of England during the century or so after 917. The county of Norfolk was created during the reign of Cnut (1016-35).[1] Subdivisions of the county were from Saxon times called 'hundreds', and Cromer was in the Hundred of North Erpingham. From 1834 the significant local unit was the POOR LAW UNION. *For the development of government by council, see* COUNCIL.

Loke, The. Lane leading from the brickfields to the church (and hence called Church Lane[1]). The thorough-fare was closed to vehicular traffic at the junction with Cross Street in 1892.[2] The lower part was widened to 30 feet in 1896.[3] *See also* LOVE LANE.

London Mayors. Two natives of Cromer became Lord Mayors of London:

1. William Crowmere was elected Lord Mayor in 1413 and again in 1423.[1] He dealt with German merchants of the Hanse resident in London, help-ing them recover debts.[2] In his will he left money to pay for the rood loft in Cromer's new church.

2. Bartholomew Rede (*c.* 1457-1505) became Lord Mayor in 1502. In his will he left property to the Goldsmiths Company to be used to support a priest

---

CROMER CHARACTERS
BARTHOLOMEW REDE

Born in Cromer, Bartholomew Rede (or Read) became a wealthy goldsmith and minted the first English sover-eigns. He entertained Katharine of Aragon at his London house. It is said that 'at a banquet an Italian mer-chant showed him a jewel worth 1,000 marks and said that it was beyond the purse of the King. Rede had it ground to dust and drank it with his wine. "Speak honourably of the King of Eng-land," he said to the Italian, "for thou hast now seen one of his subjects drink 1,000 marks at a draft."'[1]

who would run a grammar school in Cromer. Rede's father is buried in the church; a Matthew Rede, possibly related, was a chaplain in Cromer in 1521.

London Road. Name used on the Ordnance Survey map of the 1880s for Norwich Road. In 1748, however, before the building of the turnpike roads, a guidebook recommended a quite different route from London to Cromer, going by way of Bawdeswell, Reepham, Aylsham and Gresham. This suggests that the roads had recently been improved, for before that time the only major road to north Norfolk had been from Brandon to Fakenham and Walsingham.[1] Travelling between London and Cromer by road before the 18th century was hard; the obvious choice was the sea route.

⁋ Londs, The. The name may be a corruption of 'the Lands', i.e. strips of land in an open field system. Thus one strip of land belonging to Joseph Gurney in 1809 is described as 'A Land (in the Field)' and lay a short distance west of the White Horse.[1]

Before World War 1 the cottages were owned by Lady Battersea.[1]

Long House, The (Overstrand Road). Original name of Old Bracondale, owned in the late 18th century by Mr Ditchell,[1] and throughout the 19th century by the Herring family – they had about seven acres of meadow and arable land[2] with it, stretching to the Norwich Road. It is said originally to have been used by Danish fishermen for their tackle: does the name of one of

Sketched by Miss A. M. Dashwood whilst staying at Chadwick's lodgings (Flint House) in 1840, this shows the Long House on the left, the lighthouse in the centre and Cliff Lane Cottage at the right. INSET: *The Long House in a 19th-century photograph.*

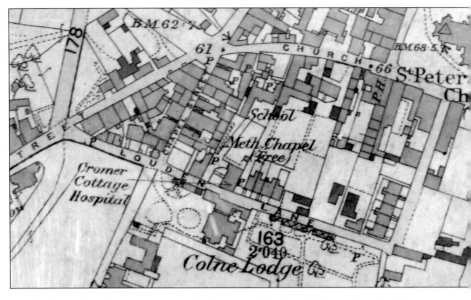

Louden 'Lane' and its surroundings in the 1880s. The hospital is still in West Cottage;
Meadow Road is planned; Mount Street has yet to be built.

the pieces of land, 'Shed Piece', reflect this, perhaps?

Lookout. See COASTGUARD STATION; OLD LOOKOUT.

Lord Nelson Coffee Tavern. Old

The Lord Nelson Coffee Tavern.

farmhouse used as a temperance tavern from 1880. The prospectus for the Cromer Coffee Tavern, Reading Rooms & Public Hall Company Limited announced its object as 'placing within reach of the Working Men of the Town and Neighbourhood a place of resort where they can have Tea, Coffee, and other Refreshments of the best description, at a reasonable price, with means and opportunities for social recreation and mental culture.'[1] A small corrugated iron lecture hall was built alongside and used for temperance lectures, musical entertainments[2] and worship of the CONGREGATIONAL CHURCH. The lease expired in 1890 and the buildings demolished to make way for Mount Street and Balcony House.

Louden Road (formerly Louden Lane). As 'Back Lane', before the creation of Mount Street, this lane led along the back of the properties facing Church Street.

Love Lane. Extension of The Loke, leading from Arbor Hill to the Brickfields cottages on the Roughton Road; the path is however at least a century and a half older than those cottages.[1]

Lower Tucker's Hotel. *See* OLD LOOKOUT.

Lynewood Close. Built in the 1970s.

Lynewood Road. A development of council houses completed in 1955-56 (nos 18–24 added in 1958).[1]

M

Macdonald Road. Part of the Cromer Hall estate was bought by a Mr Macdonald. and sold on by him in 65 lots in 1890 as the Macdonald Estate.[1] Road works were under way here in the mid-1890s,[2] and the road made up *c.* 1901.[3]

Nos 12–22 (evens) were built as council houses in 1956.[4]

Maltings. Cromer residents were buying malt from Bromholm Priory (Bacton) in the early 15th century.[1]

By the 17th century Cromer had its own malting facilities, and barley was sent here from the Felbrigg estate for malting.[2] In the 18th century Thomas Mickelburgh rented a malthouse near Rust's shop,[3] which seems to have been bought by Henry Sandford *c.* 1819-20.[4] Savin refers to John Brown as a maltster in Cromer in 1825, and he was still there when the Cromer Hall estate was sold in 1852. In 1860 the Trunch Brewery employed James Neal at this malthouse, in West Street, though the 1877 directory refers only to their maltings in North Walsham – the West Street site was then about to be used for the building of Chesterfield Villas. The arrival of the railways enabled Norfolk farmers to sell their barley more profitably to maltsters further afield.[5]

See also BREWING.

Manors. Although Domesday Book in 1086 described the country in terms of manors, these were not like parishes or modern local authority districts, but were part of a system of landholding. 'Manors were tenurial units, bundles of rights, privileges, immunities and lands, each in the possession of a single lord,' writes N. J. G. Pounds.[1] They were constantly being inherited, sold, divided, combined – and renamed after their successive owners. For those associated with Cromer, *see* BISHOP'S MANOR; GUNNER'S MANOR; LANCASTER'S MANOR; UFFORD'S HALL; SHIPDEN ABBOTS; WEYLANDS.

The name 'Manor House' on 44 Cabbell Road is misleading; built in 1891, it was originally called 'The Rest'.[2] *See also the map on page 2.*

📖 The complex history of the medieval manors of Cromer/Shipden is detailed in Walter Rye's *Cromer Past and Present.*

Marine Villas. Name for the four properties adjacent to Melbourne House in New Street.

Marine View (Promenade). Built some time between 1814 and 1831 as Beach House, a simple two-storey house, extended to three storeys in the 1850s. The lock-up shops and flatter roof were added after its purchase in 1903 by R. W. Clarke, despite the council's initial objection that 'the erection of shops on the promenade would be detrimental to the Town'.[1] A later pitched roof was blown off in a storm.

Markets. In 1285 (and again in 1426) the king renewed permission for Shipden to hold a market every Friday. In medieval times all buying and selling had to take place at approved markets; Cromer's fishermen would first sell the bulk of their catch to the king's and nobles' purveyors, and to the big city merchants; then, under royal Letters Patent of 1358, they were allowed to sell the residue of their catch in local fairs and markets.[1]

By the beginning of the 19th century the market was being held on Saturdays,[2] though it had ceased by 1836. The 1840 Tithe Map locates the 'old market-place' between Church Street and Louden Road (in what later became the back garden to Read's Dairy, and subsequently the private car park behind Woolworth's (later Iceland) and the NatWest bank), though it seems likely that the original medieval market-place would have been somewhere near St Peter's church (now inundated).

In 1895 the council considered (but abandoned) the idea of establishing a market in order to rid the streets of hawkers' barrows.[3]

In the 20th century a weekly market (on Fridays) was held on the car park between Canada Road and Cadogan Road, moving to the Meadow car park in the early 1990s.

In 2000 a Sunday market on the marrams was begun by the North Norfolk District Council (against the opposition of local traders), during the holiday season only, in an attempt to increase revenue from the car park there and provide an additional attraction for visitors.[4] It failed to attract the expected custom, and was abandoned after only the one season.

Marlborough House Hotel (Prince of Wales Road). Built in stages 1883–89, starting as a small boarding house for Mrs S. Rogers and extended by her son F. W. Rogers along with the John Smith who also owned the Red Lion and other property in Cromer. Rogers married

The marrams in the 1890s.

John Smith's daughter and they had a daughter who continued to run the hotel with her husband Arthur Gowing. It offered accommodation for 150 visitors. It was used by the army in World War 2 and demolished in the 1950s.

Marrams. Following Dutch practice, marram grass was planted along many of East Anglia's sandy beaches in the 18th and early 19th centuries in order to consolidate the dunes.[1] The word itself is of Scandinavian origin, and was the name used on the coasts of Norfolk and Suffolk from at least the early 17th century for the grass and, from the 19th century, for the sandhills.[2] Curiously, in Cromer it refers to high sandy cliffs rather than to low sand dunes.

See also MARKETS; RUNTON ROAD.

Marrams Avenue. A development of council houses completed in 1950.[1]

Meadow car park. The Meadow, a green field through which the western beck flows down to the sea, was given to the town by R. W. Clarke. A children's playground was established there; a wooden shelter in Mr Clarke's memory was later burnt down. By the early 1960s cars were parking on the northern end of the Meadow. The area was given a hard surface, then in 1983 extended to 175 places,[1] and further extended later.

See also MARKETS.

Meadow Close. Built in the 1970s on a field once known as Meeting House Piece (after the Methodist church or meeting house at its corner).

¶ **Meadow Cottage.** Acquired in 1903 by Sir Frederick Macmillan, the head of the family publishing firm of that name. Having bought the house for £2,500, he then spent some £1,800 improving it.[1] It became a guest house in 1946, and 20 years later was bought by the Elizabeth Fitzroy Trust as a home for severely handicapped people; in 2010 it was announced that this would close in favour of more modern provision.

Meadow Cottages (West Street). Terrace of 19 cottages built in 1885. Originally simply called The Meadow.

Meadow Road. Created in the 1880s to link with the new Prince of Wales Road. With houses being built on it for the middle classes, it was for a time called Park Meadows.[1]

Meeting rooms and halls. In medieval times, the only public meeting place was the church, or its vestry or porch (used for meetings which would later come to be thought of as Council meetings). It was not until the 19th century that private enterprise established an ASSEMBLY ROOM, and the Church built a PARISH HALL. In the 20th century NORTH LODGE offered a home to Council meetings. The St John Ambulance' meeting hall in Bond Street was officially opened in 1952 after being converted from disused donkey stables. The Women's Institute Hall was built in Garden Street *c.* 1958; with the decline in membership of the WI, the hall became too much for them to manage but they wanted it to remain available for community use, so in 2008 they leased it to the Town Council to promote its use generally; a charitable trust took over in 2010. MERCHANTS' PLACE offered facilities for meetings from 2005.

❡ The PARISH HALL in Overstrand was acquired by the parish council in 1938.

Melbourne House (New Street). In 1821 Mr Hogg bought a house here from a Mr Ives;[1] Celia Hogg offered letting apartments here, and had a quarter of an acre of garden on the western side of the house.[2] About 1867 Melbourne House was built on the site by George Riches and John Webb Rogers.[3] *(Picture: page 212.)*

From 1877 to 1889 George Breese lived here; he ran a confectionery shop in Brook Street and a bakery in the High Street.[4] By the time of the 1892 directory Miss Maria Comben (who appears to have been related to Breese) was offering 'private lodging houses & apartments, facing the sea' on the West Cliff, and Mrs Edith Comben was still here in 1912. Between the two World Wars it was run as Melbourne House Hotel Ltd. In later years the majority of the building became flats, with GIOVANNI'S licensed club on the first floor, the Regency fish bar on the ground floor and The PIT night club in the basement.

Melbourne slope. A slope giving access from the cliff top to the beach was formed here after the loss to the sea of GIGLERS CROFT; drawings show a rough track (with a gate half way down) where small boats could be pulled up out of reach of high tides. It was reinforced in 1884 to provide for its use by carriages,[1] then further modified as part of the esplanade works in 1900.

Merchants Court. *See* GANGWAY.

Merchants' Place. Offices, meeting rooms and other facilities opened in 2005 on the ground floor of Merchants Court as part of the REGENERATION programme.

Meteorological station. A 'climatological station' was established on Howards Hill in 1902, with a salaried observer;[1] it was later moved to the marrams.

Methodist chapels. 1. Reformed Wesleyan. The first chapel was at the corner of West Street and Hall Road (entrance on Hall Road); it had previously been used as a schoolroom but was converted into a chapel by Matthew Pank before he sold it to the church on 1 January 1813. It measured 29 by 21 feet. After alterations in 1821 it had a seating capacity of 225 people.

The chapel was rebuilt to designs by Edward Boardman[1] in 1881, with a gallery and a partition that could be moved aside to accommodate the larger summer congregations.[2] A new building was erected in 1910 (architect A. F. Scott), fronting onto West Street. Henry Broadhurst MP was one of those involved in the stone-laying ceremony in 1909, at which he used the old mallet he had used when working as a stonemason on the Houses of Parliament.[3] One of the stone corbels is carved with the face of a bearded man, reputed to depict the builder, Henry Bullen.

The extra meeting rooms on Hall Road were built in 1971.

2. Free Methodist. In Pump Street (later to be called Chapel Street) – built by William Riches, a bricklayer from East Runton, in 1856 on land bought from the Pank family. Riches occupied the ground floor himself and leased the first floor to the United Methodist Free Church. Ten years later he sold the building to the church.[4] When their new chapel in Prince of Wales Road was built in 1890 the Chapel Street building was bought by the Cromer Christian Fellowship Society; it was sold and converted into flats in 1999. ¶ The Methodist church in Overstrand was built in 1898 to a design by Edwin Lutyens; services had previously been held in the Reading Room. The design is said to be based on a lifeboat station; it was commissioned by Lord and Lady Battersea from Edwin Lutyens, and is the only nonconformist chapel he designed.[5]

Metropole Hotel (Tucker Street). Built in 1893 (contractor: J. Youngs & Son) on the site of DITCHELL'S HOUSE AND BARN. Used as a billet for troops in World War 2, semi-derelict for some years and eventually demolished in 1972;[1] the site was used for De Vere Court.

Mickelburgh House (High Street), overlooking the church, was occupied in the late 18th and early 19th centuries by Thomas Mickelburgh and at the begin-

The Wesleyan chapel built in 1881.

ning of the 20th century by Mr Limmer the estate agent.[1] It was bombed during World War 2 and the site later occupied by Ponds (later Michelle's) shoe shop.

Middle Lane. An old name for Surrey Street.

Middlebrook Way. Industrial development of the 1990s on land which had once been used by the Middlebrook mushroom farm, a venture whose 250 workers were made redundant in 1979.[1]

❦ **Midways.** *See* GISSING HOUSE.

Midwives. Miss E. L. Woodard came to Cromer as its second Parish Nurse in 1927 and retired in 1960, having delivered well over a thousand babies.[1]

Militia. The Cromer Loyal Volunteer Artillery was formed in 1797, at the time of the war with Napoleon. The unit consisted of between 40 and 60 men under the captaincy of Henry Partridge,[1] a lawyer who lived at Colne House. They manned the Cromer battery (*see* FORTIFICATIONS), and practised regularly – which was necessary: in 1799 Corporal R. Cook was nearly killed by the explosion of a cartridge.

With the renewed threat from Napoleon in 1803, fresh impetus was given to the need for defence. The volunteer infantry, under Captain Thomas Mickelburgh, consisted of lieutenant, ensign, four serjeants, four corporals, two

drummers and 73 privates; they wore blue and red clothing with yellow binding and black accoutrements. When inspected in 1803, their carbines were declared 'remarkably clean'; 'much praise' was offered to the captain for 'the soldierlike appearance of this corps'.[2]

The Cromer volunteers were the first in Norfolk, and in the mid-19th century formed the nucleus of the 3rd Norfolk Volunteer Regiment.[3]

Mill Road (originally Mill Lane). Takes its name from the windmill which was near the top of the hill. Until the boundary change which brought Suffield Park within the limits of Cromer, the centre of Mill Lane formed the boundary between Cromer and Overstrand. It also formed the main road down into Cromer (Norwich Road is newer) until at least the end of the 17th century.[1]

The portion from Station Road to St Martin's Hall is described on a map of *c.* 1843 as 'very steep and narrow – scarcely room for a single carriage – so sandy – or muddy as to be sometimes almost impassable'.[2] After the coming of the railway, it was widened on the railway side, and made up in 1901.[3]

Mills. No mill is mentioned for Shipden/Cromer in the Domesday Book of 1086, but one was included in a bequest from Sir John de Reppes, knight, to his nephew John de Plumsted in 1370/1, and Robert Swanne of Cromer was a miller in 1587.[1]

A post mill is shown on a map of 1717[2] on the site later occupied by Cromer High railway station; it was perhaps this mill that was bought by Sherman Cutler (a Cromer builder) in 1784 after Philip Terry had defaulted on his mortgage.[3] The 1838 Ordnance Survey map shows Mill House at the top of Mill Road, roughly opposite where the Suffield Park Hotel was later built, but shows no mill there, and the fact that the granary at the top of the Gangway was converted into cottages in the early 19th century implies that corn was no longer the significant export commodity it had been a hundred years earlier. Indeed, the agricultural depression was so severe that gamekeeper Larry Banville commented in 1830 that 'bread and water is chiefly their food in this town of Cromer'.[4]

Bryant's 1826 map shows another windmill near Barkers Herne, presumably operated by William Sharpen, who is listed as a miller in West Street at about this time,[5] but it had disappeared by 1841.[6] It is probably this mill that is depicted in two drawings by Robert Dixon in 1810.

❡ Overstrand had a mill at the time of the Domesday survey in 1086 (it would have been a watermill, the site since lost to the sea). A windmill was functioning when Clement Scott visited in the 1880s

Cromer mill, drawn by Robert Dixon in 1810.

and 1890s, but had ceased working by 1927; the site became in the 1950s the garden of 26 Coast Road.[7]

Mineral waters. Everett's mineral water factory was in Bond Street. *See also* WATER SUPPLY.

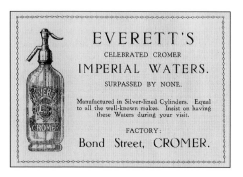

EVERETT'S

CELEBRATED CROMER

IMPERIAL WATERS.

SURPASSED BY NONE.

Manufactured in Silver-lined Cylinders. Equal to all the well-known makes. Insist on having these Waters during your visit.

FACTORY:

Bond Street, CROMER.

Morden House (Cliff Avenue). Morden is a name of Lord Suffield's family: Sir William Morden was created Baronet Suffield in 1745 and assumed the name Harbord.

Morriston House. The former name of Faldonside, on the corner of Norwich road and Cliff Avenue.

Motor garages. Henry Bullen advertised his Cromer Motor Garage in the 1908 trade directory; it seems to have been in Canada Road next to the Town Hall. By this time, also, George Wilkin had branched out from his original business as a farrier and carriage builder to run garages at several of the big hotels.

William Linford started even earlier: listed in the 1900 directory as a cycle

agent at 29 Prince of Wales Road, he had a motor garage built by William Porter at the corner of Cabbell Road and West Street in 1903 – a plot originally earmarked as suitable for a hotel (but then his wife did let apartments in the house next door in Cabbell Road). His cycle engineer George Frederick Allen took over the business in 1911 and it became known as Allen's Garage. He continued to run it until his death in 1956, when his son Victor George took over; grandson Peter joined the firm in 1966, when the premises were extended by building on the adjacent garden an office, stores and a showroom for Renault cars. The business continued in family ownership until it closed in 2007.[1]

East Coast Motors were also early in the town, with premises at the top of the GANGWAY and on Beach Road, where they operated the garages belonging to the Grand Hotel; they also acquired the Church Street garage business established in 1920 by William Hardy and George Nash.

¶ Curtis' garage in Overstrand was originally the private garage for Lord Battersea.

Mount Street. Built in the early 1890s[1] on 'the Mount', a piece of rough ground on the Cromer Hall estate, and extended in 1896.[2] Roadmaking was completed by 1899.[3]

¶ **Mundesley Road.** The part in Sidestrand parish was constucted in 1890.

A new concrete road was built in 1927 (along the course of an existing footpath) because of the erosion threat to the Overstrand part of the coast road.

Museums. As early as 1868 Thomas Fowell Buxton (of Colne House) wrote to the Norwich Museum saying that 'certain Gentlemen in Cromer are anxious to set afoot a local Museum, but it was not until 1978 that, through the initiative of Philip Sage, it proved possible to open a museum, located in East Cottages and gaining an immediate reputation because of the display design by the first curator, Jane Bagnall-Oakley, and the deposit of the extensive documentary collection of Cyril Crawford Holden (*see* HISTO-

RIANS). Curator Martin Warren (along with Alistair Murphy and a number of knowledgeable and committed volunteers) devoted much time to the task of cataloguing the material and analysing its significance.

A separate Lifeboat Museum was established in the boathouse at the bottom of the Gangway when this was vacated by the No. 2 lifeboat, and was subsequently moved into purpose-built premises when the Rocket House Café was rebuilt.

Mushroom farm. *See* MIDDLEBROOK WAY.

Music. Little evidence survives of any music-making in Cromer before the 1890s, but music certainly featured in church services, especially before the Ref-

Allen's garage in 1904. INSET: *George Frederick Allen.*

ormation – a former vicar bequeathed to the church a service book with music in 1388 – and there may well have been players of some sort at the FAIR; whether chamber music was played in the larger houses, or dance music in the barns or beerhouses, we do not know, though there must have been music for the balls which were advertised in the assembly rooms. Simeon Simons (1792–1862), Cromer's schoolmaster, played the violin, but 'in a very peculiar manner, holding the instrument between his knees, so it was strung just opposite to the ordinary player's',[1] which may suggest that he was self-taught.

Musical entertainment in Cromer in the 20th century centred on the pier and (until it was sold) the Town Hall. An article in 1904 described the pier 'with a bandstand and rows of seats sheltered by awnings at its further end. Here, afternoon and evening, plays the Blue Hungarian Band, which is Cromer's nearest approach to dissipation. A very good band it is, with a violinist as its conductor, and a vocalist generally adds variety to the programme. At the town hall a travelling concert party or a band of pierrots may be giving a performance – and that is all the evening amusement Cromer cares for.'[2]

The billiard room at the Grand Hotel was converted by 1925 to a Concert Room, and was also used for private dancing.[3]

There were those who appreciated the value of music. In World War 2, local music teacher Ethel Bennett was told to work in munitions, but the vicar, Gilbert Barclay, protested that 'to leave Cromer without a music instructor is a blow for the duration. Mrs Bennett can better serve the war effort in that capacity than filling shells. Music is an important part of a child's education.'[4]

See also BANDS; BELLS; FESTIVAL OF MUSIC, DRAMA AND DANCE; ORGANS; ROYAL LINKS PAVILION.

N

Napoleonic Wars. *See* FORTIFICATIONS; MILITIA.

Narrows, The. Name for the narrowest part of Church Street at the western

The Narrows.

'Very bare but the trees will grow up in time': Newhaven Court in the 1880s.

end (where it was only 15 feet wide). Widening in 1963 involved the demolition of cottages on the northern side of the road.

Nelson Heights. Part of the FULCHER AVENUE development, named in honour of Vice Admiral Lord Nelson, who had no particular connection with Cromer.

New Inn. *See* TUCKER'S HOTEL.

New Street. Known by this name from at least 1839,[1] and possibly much earlier. *See also* RUNTON ROAD.

New Wine church. Charismatic congregation meeting in the early years of the 21st century in the Junior School.

Newhaven Court. Built in 1884 and 'so named after King's Haven Courts

held at Cromer to deal with Admiralty matters, during the reign of Henry VIII particularly,' according to Crawford Holden, though it should be noted that Frederick Locker's wife came from Newhaven Hills, Vermont. The home of the Locker-Lampson family, who had many famous guests to stay. Kate Greenaway described how they 'used to drive long distances to nice old Houses – but then they were all belong to the Lockers friends'. In 1921 the house became the Royal Cromer Hotel ('royal' because of such guests as the King of Greece). Albert Einstein stayed here, though as it was believed his life was under threat he lived anonymously in a little wooden hut on Roughton Heath and was protected by armed guards;[1] another house guest, Kate Greenaway, illustrated its visitors' book. (In a letter of 1889, she had written: 'I dont consider the Lockers House in a nice position – it is very bare but the trees will grow up in time and inside it is a very nice House.') Other guests included Alfred Tennyson, Andrew Lang, Henry Fowler, Augustine Birrell, Ernest Shackleton, Jacob Epstein, Oscar Wilde and E. V. Lucas.

Its covered tennis courts were described as 'some of the best in England, with wonderful lighting'.[2] The house was burnt down in 1963 and the flats of the same name were built on the site within a few years.

Newhaven Drive. Built on the grounds of NEWHAVEN COURT.

Newstead House (1 Surrey Street). Built some time before 1836 at the corner of Surrey Street, adjacent to the old granary on the Gangway. Ellis Newstead was the owner of the granary (which he later turned into cottages).

Night clubs. *See* PIT, THE; BLAZER'S.

Nightingale Close. Development of bungalows off Ridge Way, built by Garden Link Homes of Norwich in the late 1990s.

Nonconformity. There appears to have been no religious nonconformity in Cromer in the 17th century. At the end of the 18th century, the Fry and other families who began resorting to the neighbourhood were mostly QUAKERS, but there was never any Quaker meeting-house in Cromer.

❡ An occasional conventicle was reported in Overstrand in 1669, and in 1676 the number of nonconformists in Overstrand was given as 23 (compared with 193 adults who attended the Church of England).[1]

See also BAPTIST CHURCH; CONGREGATIONAL CHURCH; METHODIST CHURCH.

Norfolk Hotel. *See* WELLINGTON.

Norfolk House (corner of Hamilton Road and West Street). Built by George Riches as a boarding house. The mansard roof was removed before 1964, and the upper floors were converted into offices in the 1980s.

Norman Trollor Court. Housing development opened in 2001 in the former Board School buildings. Builder Reggie Medler named it after the much-respected owner of the town's Regal Cinema and Olympia Rollerdrome, who died in 1997 at the age of 89.

North Cottage (in North Lodge Park). Built in 1873, on the land belonging to the Goldsmiths' Company, as the schoolmaster's house.[1]

North Lodge and **North Lodge Park.** The Goldsmiths' Company held land

< *Architect C. Beasley's idea for redeveloping the land belonging to the Goldsmiths' Company. In the event, all that was built was one house, North Lodge.*

North Lodge as originally built.

as part of the school's endowment, and considered various plans for developing it: in 1825 C. Beasley prepared plans for an ambitious scheme like the squares then being built at many south coast resorts, making two terraces of 16 dwellings each, though in 1834 Philip Hardwick outlined plans for letting a number of plots on 61-year building leases, which would have created 13 detached and semi-detached houses. In the event all that was built was a single lodging house, the main part of the present North Lodge, for which the original plan is dated 1838.[1] In 1857 the house became the summer residence of Joseph Hoare, eldest son of Samuel and Louisa Hoare of Cliff House. The west wing was added in 1886.

Here in 1916 died Lady Victoria Buxton, famed for her philanthropy despite a crippling spinal condition.[2]

The house remained a summer residence of the Hoare family until bought by Cromer UDC in 1928, later becoming the home of Cromer Town Council (which bought the house from the North Norfolk District Council in 2006 and licensed the Council Chamber for use for civil weddings). The gates on the Overstrand Road were erected in 1936 to commemorate King George V's silver jubilee of the previous year.[3]

North Row. Another name for CHESTERFIELD COTTAGES.[1]

Norwich Road. Named 'the Road to Southrepps' on an 18th-century map, and occasionally called LONDON ROAD. The houses near the bottom were built between 1885 and 1888.

The road was widened in 1964, at which time there was a plan to extend Vicarage Road to connect directly with the Holt Road opposite Beach Road, thus by-passing the town centre. This plan was not finally abandoned until the late 1990s.

O

Oakleigh (21 Norwich Road). Miss C. H. Pearce ran a girls' school in this house about the years 1907–13.

Oddfellows. *See* FRIENDLY SOCIETIES.

Old Coach Road. Road extending round the back of Herne Court. Though it had been subject to a road closure or-der in the early 19th century, the council decided to repair and light the road in 1902 and it was not finally closed until the 1990s when Sutherland Court Gardens was built over part of its length.

Old Lookout. Built in 1875 as an annexe to Tucker's Hotel, to which it was connected by an underground passageway. Elizabeth, Empress of Austria, stayed here in 1887. Because she lived in constant fear of being poisoned, a local farmer would lead a cow through the archway of Tucker's Hotel and milk it on the cliff top where it could be seen from the Empress' window. Bread was baked by Arnold Copsey and his family at their Russell House bakery in Jetty Street, under the scrutiny of the imperial staff, before being taken round to the hotel and down the tunnel to the annexe.

After Tucker's closed, the Salad Bowl café was here, but later this closed and the building used solely as flats.

See also COASTGUARD STATION.

Oliver Court. Development of houses built off Cromwell Road in the 1980s,[1] at the bottom of the garden of HALSEY HOUSE. The land, bought from the British Legion, had been used for pig farming.

Olympia (Garden Street). Cinema formed in 1934 after the garden of Rust's house (HANOVER HOUSE) was covered in. It ran until 1939, and hosted some concert parties after the war in 1948 it became a roller-skating rink, the 'Rollerdrome', being used also as a music venue in the late 1960s. Skating continued until 1974, after which the council approved an application for change of use of the premises to packing of herbs and spices.[1] The building was demolished in 1984 to make way for Budgen's car park.

One-way streets. Jetty Street was made one-way (northbound) during the summer months from 1889.[1] (At some point the direction of travel was changed to be southbound.) The main one-way system (eastbound traffic using Church Street and westbound traffic using Mount Street) was created in 1956.[2]

Organs.[1] A will of 1500 left money to the keeper of the small organ.[2] If this implies the existence also of a greater organ, Cromer must have been one of the earliest English churches to have great and small organs.[3] They did not survive the Reformation.

A single-manual gallery organ was opened by J. Beckwith of Norwich in 1792 (it is described in the 1841 guidebook as 'a well-toned organ'), and restored in 1855. (At this time the organist was a full time appointment held, according to the 1861 census, by Thomas A. Curtis.) After the galleries were pulled down in 1862 the organ was stored in a granary.

The vicar's sister-in-law, Miss S. Colson, raised money for a new organ in 1867. Built by Mack of Great Yarmouth, it had two manuals and 'an

octave and a half of small pedals, with a weak Bourdon'; it was opened by Mr Mann of Norwich, and remained on the north side of the church until the chancel was rebuilt, when it was moved to the present organ's position. Later it went to Saham Toney church.

In 1897, after the arrival of a new vicar, Norman & Beard built a new organ using the case and other parts (but not pipes) from Bath Abbey. It had three manuals and pedals, a fourth manual being added in 1903 and a new console in 1912. It was rebuilt and enlarged, with a new console, in 1948, and renovated with new stops in 1968.

Weekly organ recitals in the holiday season were introduced in the 1890s by the organist and composer L. Meadows White, who was serving a curacy here before becoming vicar of Potter Heigham.

Norman Cutting was master of the music from 1942 to New Year's Day 1978, maintaining a high standard of music with a choir of adults and boys.[4]

❡ Overstrand's organ, again built by the Norwich firm of Norman & Beard, was given in memory of Vera Carr, the Rector's daughter, who died in an accident in 1916 at the age of 25. An inscription records that 'She lived her joyous life in Overstrand loving and beloved in close communion with all things beautiful'. It was renovated in 1953 in memory of Lawrence Carter Carr, the village's Rector for 55 years.

Osier bed (between Mill Road and

Norwich Road). On Bellard's map of 1747 this is marked as an alder carr; the 1838 Ordnance Survey map calls it a 'withy bed'; on maps of 1886 and later it is called an osier carr. It would have provided the raw material for basket-making – James Bilham, for example, was a basket and sieve maker who moved from New Street to Ebenezer Cottage in the 1830s, and his descendants continued the same trade at 6 Hamilton Road until at least 1929.[1] In the 1960s the osier bed was absorbed into the playing field behind the new Infants School.

Our Lady of Refuge. *See* ROMAN CATHOLIC CHURCH.

❡ Overstrand. The Old English word *ofer* meant 'border, bank, sea-shore' and possibly also 'edge of a hill', giving the probable meaning of the name here as 'shore with a steep edge, narrow shore', as opposed to the 'broad shore' of Sidestrand. (The Domesday Book's spelling 'Othestrand' and some mapmakers' 'Oxtrand' are probably mere confusions, though there is some possibility that it could have been called the 'other strand' as opposed to Sidestrand.)[1]

❡ Overstrand Court Hotel. Originally called Beck Hythe, owned (along with BECKHYTHE MANOR) by Herbert Garnett of Bournemouth and occupied by Col. Garnett.[1]

❡ Overstrand Hall. The property of Caesar Life in the 18th century; it was then inherited by his aunt, Mary Rant, whose tenant was Joseph Howes.[1]

Jeremiah Cross was the tenant farmer in the mid-19th century; the 1871 census shows him employing 15 men and six boys to farm 350 acres. He made his money as a ship-owner who sent his corn to the north-east and brought coal back to Cromer, where he had coalyards next to the Granary. When the Hall was advertised to let in 1892, it was described as having four sitting rooms and 12 bedrooms.[2]

The Hall was bought by Charles William Mills, Lord Hillingdon, a partner in Glyn, Mills bank, whose other residence was Hillingdon Court, Uxbridge. He had it completely rebuilt in 1899 (architect Edwin Lutyens, builder George Riches).

During World War I it was used briefly as a 15-bed auxiliary hospital for officers, financed by Lady Hillingdon and with Lady Keppel as Commandant, but this was closed after less than three months because of the possibility of air raids.[3]

Lord Hillingdon died in 1919, Lady Hillingdon in 1932 and in 1935 the Hall was sold to Leicester Convalescent Homes; after closure in the 1990s it became a field study centre of the Kingswood Centres.

❡ Overstrand Hotel. Built 1899-1900 (architects Edward Boardman & Son;[1] builder J. S. Smith of Norwich[2]) a little to the east of Ivy Farm; bought by Norwich banker Hugh Gurney Barclay (one of the original investors[3]) in March 1905 for £7,500; it had 57 bedrooms.[4] It was planned with stables, carriage washing yard and (a sign of the times) cycle shed but, of course, no garages or car park. During World War 2 it was used as a base for the army who were mining the cliffs, and the process of clearing the mines after the war did nothing to help the stability of the cliffs; the hotel was clearly going to fall into the sea before long. The empty building was gutted by fire in 1949, and it was demolished in 1951.[5]

¶ **Overstrand Lodge** (High Street, Overstrand). Built for Thomas Ritchie about 1903 and bought by Mr & Mrs Frederick Hampshire in 1926. During World War 2 it was used by the WAAF.[1]

P

Parish Hall. Built by the Buxton family in 1902 because the church could not accommodate everyone who came to services.[1] The site had previously been used for the church-supported schools which became the Board School in Cross Street in 1896 (*see* SCHOOLS). ¶ The parish hall in The Londs, a metal building by Boulton & Paul, started life as a convalescent home for patients of the Metropolitan Hospital in London. It was given to the parish council in 1938 by Christian Endeavour Holiday Homes, owners of The Pleasaunce.

Parish registers. Cromer's parish registers survive only from 1689 (marriages from 1696). The originals and microfiche copies are in the Norfolk County Record Office, with a duplicate set of microfiche in the Norfolk Studies Library in Norwich. A typed transcript with an index of names was made by Crawford Holden; one copy is held by the church and another by Cromer Museum, with a photocopy in the Heritage Centre in Norwich's Millennium Library.

Registers of the Roman Catholic church are transcribed in Charles A. Munkman, *The Catholic Revival in North Norfolk: Centenary of Our Lady of Refuge Church in Cromer, 1896–1995* (privately printed).

¶ Overstrand parish registers survive from 1558, though with some gaps in the 17th century. Originals and microform copies are held in the Norfolk Record Office, again with a duplicate set of microform copies in the Heritage Centre.

Park Meadows. Early name for MEADOW ROAD.

Park Road. The first part of Suffield Park to be developed, so addresses given in the form '4 Suffield Park' referred to number 4 in what later became known as Park Road. The road was made up in 1896.[1] *See also* SUFFIELD PARK PREPARATORY SCHOOL.

Parsonage houses. *See* RECTORY (Overstrand); VICARAGE.

Paston family. The Pastons, famous for their many letters which have survived, owned Shipden and Ropers manors in Cromer, together with land in Overstrand, in the 1460s and 1470s, but rented them out.[1]

¶ Paul's Lane. Paul as a surname has been found in Overstrand since at least 1397. In the early 20th century, Herbert Paul lived in Gunton Terrace[1] and Mrs J. Paul in Poppy Lodge.[2] There was a John Paul living in The Londs in 1915.[3]

Peele House (Tucker Street). Late-18th- or early-19th-century house of Edmund Peele, tailor and draper who, jointly with Thomas Field, established a subscription reading room in 1814 on land which had been part of the garden of Peele House but had fallen to the beach during a storm; this was sold to Simeon Simons and became the BATH HOUSE.

After Peele's death, his house remained in the possession first of his widow and then of his daughter, who offered holiday apartments. Later it became an annexe of the Metropole Hotel next door. Susbequently it was occupied by Peele House School, an independent training establishment; it was converted into flats in 1998.

Pharmacists. *Daniel Davison* started practising as a pharmacist in 1889 in Jetty Street and continued there till his death in 1930. A prominent figure in the town, he was for many years chair-man of the Urban District Council.

Mr Heath occupied HEATH HOUSE in Church Street, and the same building was later occupied by Boots the Chemist, then when Boots moved to Rust's premises across the road in 1985 it was used by Savory & Moore (becoming Lloyds chemists in 1998).

Photographers. From at least as early as 1842 Cromer was being photographed for artistic, social and record purposes. Early subjects included the Vicar (posed talking to a parishioner in the street near the church), the lifeboat and the beach and promenade.

Daniel W. Savin described himself in the 1866 directory as a 'photographic artist', and for the 1871 census as 'artist photographer', with a shop in Church Street; he also had a photography studio in the little thatched building at the top of the Gangway as early as 1868. *John Morley* is also shown in the 1871 census as a photographer, though he combined this with work as a piano tuner. The *Mace brothers* had studios in Hunstanton and Cromer (Augustus Mace gave his occupation as photographer when his son was baptised in 1888); when Herbert Mace first came to Cromer, he set up in a caravan on the beach, where he also had a camera obscura. In partnership with Norwich photographer Thomas Mase, he had BALCONY HOUSE built, and after the death of his brother in 1898 seems to have taken over the latter's business

ABOVE: *Carte-de-visite photo-graph of an unknown man by the Mace brothers.* RIGHT: *Tom Mack, a self-portrait*

local views. One of his customers was the Empress of Austria. He also had a studio in Hamilton Road; in the same premises (known as Pretoria House), almost a hundred years after Mary Mack had lived there[2] a photographic processing shop was opened, the first Cromer business to offer facilities for printing photographs from digital files.

H. H. Tansley had his 'Burlington Studios' near Lloyds Bank in Church Street by about 1912[3] (having started his business in Sheringham in 1899) and a shop in Prince of Wales Road by 1925. He was active in photographing the people and events of his times, notably shipwrecks and wartime damage (he had a licence for photography so he was exempt from the normal restrictions on civilian photography during the war). It is estimated that

in Garden Street and moved it to the newly built shop at number 25, on the corner of Corner Street, where a glass studio at the rear of the property – possibly originally used by Tom Morley – could still be seen as late as the 1960s.[1] Mace Brothers were proud to style themselves 'Royal Photographers'.

Tom Mack, the son of a Cromer watchmaker, was taking photographs by 1862 and had a business as photographer and jeweller in Church Street, where he and his wife had a shop selling books and newspapers and he produced a range of photographic postcards and souvenir booklets of

his Cromer premises alone contained 24,000 negatives.

S. H. Wrightson was working in Cromer *c.* 1901.[4]

Philip Vicary at various times ran guest houses in Cromer and in Wales, including Westward Ho at Cromer. Whilst he was not a full-time photographer, he was skilled with the camera and kept a keen eye on developments in Cromer, with a particular interest in the lifeboats and the railways. His friend Henry Blogg gave him access to the lifeboat house; he took the best-known photos of the *Sepoy* rescue in 1933 and was able to contact his London agents, get his glass plates on the evening train and see his pictures on the front of the national dailies the next day.[5]

At the beginning of the 21st century there was a burgeoning of local photography with professional and semi-professional practitioners offering their work (mainly local scenery photographed artistically) for sale in shops such as Silver & Salts (which opened in the very same Garden Street premises that had been used by photographers at the end of Victoria's reign).

❡ Overstrand had its own photographers in Herbert S. Church (listed in the 1908 directory) and John Church (1916 directory).

Pier. The first pier was built *c.* 1391; the early piers (which were constantly being rebuilt after storm damage) were designed to protect shipping from the

Watching the waves from the wooden jetty (destroyed in 1897). One lady on the pier has come in a wheelchair.

weather and from hostile ships, and to facilitate loading and unloading. The last attempt to build a pier as a substitute for a natural harbour was *c.* 1732; this uncompleted pier was damaged by storms in 1797 and 1799, and finally washed away in a storm in 1820.

The first pier designed primarily as a promenade was built, with cast iron supports, in 1821–22 (thus predating the Brighton chain pier which is sometimes said to have been the first 'pleasure pier'). It was replaced by a simple wooden jetty in 1846 and by the present structure in 1901. The bandstand area at the end was covered to form a pavilion in 1905, and a lifeboat house added to the end in 1923.

📖 For a documentary history of the various piers and the entertainments and other activities upon them, see Christopher Pipe, *The Story of Cromer Pier* (Poppyland Publishing, 1998).

Pig & Whistle. *See* CROWN & ANCHOR.

Promenading on the new pier, 1902.

Pit, The. A night club opened in the basement of the Melbourne Hotel; under various changes of management it had a number of different official names, but the sobriquet of 'The Pit' was coined as soon as it opened and in popular usage it seems never to have been called anything else. It never aspired to great heights either in the music (invariably recorded, never a live band) or in food and drink (an early bar manager sold pies, and handed out a free indigestion tablet with each one), but for decades it remained the only place of entertainment open to young people after the pubs closed. It lost its raison d'être after BUDDIES opened in 2009 staying open on some nights till 3 a.m.

¶ The Pleasaunce. In 1888 Lord Battersea bought from the Suffield estate two adjoining properties in Overstrand

---

CROMER CHARACTERS
LORD BATTERSEA

Cyril Flower (1843–1907) was a famously handsome MP who married Constance de Rothschild (1843–1931) in 1877 and rebuilt The Pleasaunce. The son of P. W. Flower of Surrey, he was a grandson on his mother's side of Jonathan Flower, a farmer of Feltwell, Norfolk. He was created Lord Battersea in 1892.[1] After his death, his widow continued to play the role of the great lady in Overstrand for many years.

(described as 'small' seven-bedroom cottages) and engaged the architect Edwin Lutyens with instructions not to demolish them but to turn them into something larger. The result was known as The Cottage, and later as The Pleasaunce. The building contractor was George Riches. The property was sold to Christian Endeavour Holiday Homes in 1936.

Police. The Norfolk Rural Police force was formed in 1839; it was responsible at first to the local magistrates, then (from 1889) to the newly formed County Council. The 1879 directory shows the Cromer police under the charge of Sergeant Charles Parr, but as the town grew so did the need for a greater police presence, and an inspector (Frederick Woodhouse Lovick at first) was appointed.

Police station. 1 (14 Church Street). Built in 1879 (architect: John Phipson of Norwich) next to Sandford's yard south-east of the top of the Gangway. It included a magistrates' room[1] (magistrates in the 19th century had met in Tucker's New Inn and later at the Red Lion), with a judge's retiring room at the back.[2] When the premises were replaced, the main building was used during World War 2 as a Food Office and ARP Centre; after rationing ceased, the East Coast Garage stored parts in it. It became a Youth Centre in 1961 and converted to offices in the early years of the 21st century. The Inspector's house (no. 12) was purchased by solicitor P. E. Hansell in the early 1890s.

2 (Holt Road, opposite the railway station). A replacement building complex opened in 1938, including police houses and magistrates' court.

3 (top of Holt Road). A new 'operational deployment base' (without cells, since by this time anyone who needed to be detained was sent to North Walsham police station) opened in 2009 next to the council offices, to replace the stations in Cromer and Sheringham. This was the first station to be equipped for taking witness statements by computer.

Poor Law. Up to the 19th century poor people were helped by the parish, which from 1598 was empowered to levy a Poor Rate for the purposes (*see also* CHARITIES). In 1805, under Gilbert's Act of 1782, a workhouse was built opposite (Upper) Sheringham church to serve Cromer, Runton, Sheringham and half a dozen other parishes.

Under the 1834 Poor Law Amendment Act, Cromer was one of 49 parishes which joined to form the Erpingham Union, whose Board met every Monday morning at the New Inn in Tucker Street.[1] They adopted the Sheringham workhouse for the aged and infirm (100 places) and the Gimingham workhouse for others. The Sheringham house was closed in 1848 and converted into cottages, and a new workhouse was opened in 1850 at West Beckham (latterly dubbed 'Beckham Palace').[2]

In the 1840s the Trustees of the Poor in Cromer also owned a small group of cottages in New Street; the site was redeveloped later in the century.[3]

Poor Law Unions were abolished by the Local Government Act of 1929. ¶ Before 1850, Overstrand was one of nine parishes using the Gimingham workhouse.

¶ **Poppyland.** Name coined by journalist Clement Scott when he was commissioned by the railway company to write a series of articles promoting the Cromer district. The first of his articles was published in 1883 and gave rise not only to an immediate tourist boom but also to a minor industry producing Poppyland souvenirs.

See Peter Stibbons and David Cleveland, *Poppyland: Strands of Norfolk History* 3rd ed. (Poppyland Publishing, 1990); Elizabeth Jones, *Poppyland in Pictures* 2nd ed. (Poppyland Publishing, 2004).

Population. In 1066, Shipden had two freemen, four villagers and nine smallholders (increasing to 11 smallholders by 1086).[1] Allowing for people not enumerated in the survey (such as clergy, tradesmen, fishermen, women and children), this might suggest a total population of around 200 to 250 people.

In 1565 Cromer had 115 households; mariners and fishermen numbered 48.[2]

In 1603 the vicar claimed 250 communicants for the parish.[3]

In 1676, there were 68 households (implying a population of perhaps 289).[4] In 1784 there were about 100 houses;[5] in 1801 there were 140.

Census figures[6] for Cromer and Overstrand in the 19th and 20th centuries, together with the percentage change in the Cromer figure, are as follows (there was no census in 1941):

		CROMER		OVER-STRAND
1801	10 Mar	676		117
1811	27 May	848	+25%	111
1821	28 May	1,008	+19%	154
1831	30 May	1,232	+22%	178
1841	7 Jun	1,229	– 2% [a]	240
1851	30 Mar	1,306	+ 6%	260
1861	7 Apr	1,365	+ 5%	251
1871	2 Apr	1,415	+ 4%	272
1881	3 Apr	1,597	+13%	227
1891	5 Apr	2,239	+40%	443
1901	31 Mar	3,781	+69% [b]	397
1911	2 Apr	4,070	+ 8%	429
1921	19 Jun	4,011	– 1%	633
1931	26 Apr	4,171	+ 4%	473
1951	8 Apr	4,719	+ 13%	638
1961	23 Apr	4,892	+ 4%	796
1971	25 Apr	5,376	+ 10%	1,009
1981	5 Apr	6,180	+ 15%	995
1991	21 Apr	7,143	+ 16%	951
2001	29 Apr	7,749	+ 8%	952

(see notes overleaf)

Notes: **a.** The apparent decline between 1831 and 1841 is attributed by one writer to the time of year the 1841 census was taken – when there were no holiday visitors and many of the fishermen were away in Yarmouth after mackerel. One of the census enumerators, however, whilst putting the number of fishermen absent for the mackerel fishing at 28, says there were 50 visitors who had come to Cromer 'as a watering place'. **b.** The big increase between 1891 and 1901 (and the decrease in the figure for Overstrand) is partly accounted for by the boundary change which brought Suffield Park within the parish of Cromer.

By comparison, North Walsham, which had been three times the size of Cromer in 1801, was only twice its size in 1851, and had only 200 more inhabitants in 1901.

❡ Overstrand in medieval times seems to have been more populous than Cromer: Domesday Book lists five freemen, six villagers, 18 smallholders and two slaves (totalling 31). But by the 1590s there were only two men in Overstrand liable to pay the Subsidy, as compared with Cromer's 21, and in 1603 the incumbent reported only 44 communicants, rising in 1676 to just 48.[7]

Port. In medieval times Cromer ships brought in fish and timber and exported malt barley, wheat, peas and beans;[1] there was also a brisk trade with ICELAND, where the fishermen went for cod.[2]

Some idea of the relative size of the different ports can be gained from the numbers of Norfolk seamen pressed for naval service in 1599: 11 men from Cromer were pressed, which was as many as from Cley and more than the eight men from Blakeney; in north Norfolk only Wells supplied more, with 19 names. (Lynn supplied 80 men, Yarmouth 102.)[3]

For administrative purposes,[4] Cromer was at the boundary between the port of Blakeney & Cley and that of Great Yarmouth: in 1676 the limits of the port of Blakeney were said to end at 'a fall opposite to Cromer church', and a 1738 document[6] says the port of Blakeney & Cley extended 'to ffoulness Lighthouse'.

Post offices. In the 1790s mail was still being delivered and collected only three days a week,[1] but by 1830 the mail cart was leaving the Star Inn, Norwich, at 9.45 a.m. every weekday, arriving with letters for Cromer at 3.30 p.m.[2]

Cromer's post office was in Jetty Street until in 1889 the growth of the town demanded a purpose-built post office (at the corner of Church Street and Bond Street). Counter services moved to Tucker Street in the early 1990s (and to Budgens shop in 2009, though the sorting office remained at the bottom of Bond Street.

Suffield Park had a post office in Salisbury Road;[3] then it moved to the corner of Mill Road and Crawford Road until 1918. Later it was at 17 Sta tion Road, opposite Links Avenue; then in Mill Road opposite Crawford Road. ⁋ The Post Office in Overstrand was once in Beckett's shop on the corner of Harbord Road and the High Street.

Pound. Stray animals were kept in a pound at the beginning of Sandy Lane (on the site later occupied by Cheverton's printers, or at the south-eastern corner of the old cemetery).[1]

Prince of Wales Road. Projected in the 1860s – Benjamin Bond-Cabbell wanted to divert HALL ROAD to join the new road at the junction with West Street and Louden Road, but this plan was never carried through. The 1887 Ordnance Survey map still shows only a new road with no buildings on it at all, and the road was not macadamised when the Town Hall was completed in 1891.[1]

Printers. When handbills were required to attract pupils to the school in 1821, the schoolmaster had to go to Aylsham to find a printer,[1] but as Cromer began to prosper again in the 19th century several tradesmen started to provide printing services. (No doubt the school itself played a part in increasing the demand for such services, as posters could be printed in the knowledge that a growing number of local people would be able to read them.) In the late 19th and early 20th centuries, small jobbing printers included Munday the Church Street bookseller (who printed posters); Battson (picture postcards); William Bacon[2] in Canada Road (posters – succeeded by W. J. Chambers of West Street, and in the 1920s Mrs Alice Louisa Chambers[3]). The two most successful were Rounce & Wortley (with a shop opened in 1899 at the corner of Chapel Street, then at the corner of the High Street, and at one time also in Holt – the last surviving part of the business, in North Walsham, was sold to Aylsham printers Barnwells in the 1990s); and Cheverton & Son (established by T. Cheverton in 1897 in Bond Street, then moving to new premises next to the old cemetery on the Holt Road, surviving into the 21st century).

Prior Bank (Cliff Avenue). In the early 20th century this house was a favourite holiday retreat of the Countess Dowager of Albemarle and other members of the Keppel family.[1] By 1923 it was the home of solicitor E. M. Hansell.[2]

Prior Bank Orchard. Name of a small development of bungalows erected behind Cliff Avenue in the early 1990s.[1]

Promenade. The first promenade was created by the building of the first sea wall in 1838, and was of grass. It was given a hard surface later in the century, was extended from the Gangway to DOCTOR'S STEPS in 1894, and widened when the new sea wall was built in 1890-91.

The public conveniences at the foot of the Red Lion steps were built after

the council bought the land for the purpose in 1897,[1] and rebuilt in 1982.[2]
See also SEA WALLS.

Public health. *See* ISOLATION HOSPITAL.

Public houses. In 1601 Cromer had nine alehouses, and there was complaint that this was too many – in fact, it was alleged that the constables set them up purely in order to get extra rent, because they could get three or four times the rent from them as alehouses than would otherwise be possible.[1]
See also the names of individual pubs.

Pump Street. Original name of CHAPEL STREET.

Pumps. *See* WATER SUPPLY.

Q

Quakers. The Gurney family of Quakers were based mostly at Earlham (now part of the University of East Anglia on the outskirts of Norwich) and North-repps (Northrepps Hall and North-repps Cottage), and together with their friends and relatives the Buxtons, Hoares and Barclays spent much time in Cromer. Since the families were large, numerous lodging houses in Cromer used to accommodate them. Kate Greenaway, staying in Cromer

in August 1889, wrote that 'Cromer is composed of the Hoares and Gurneys and Buxtons *everywhere.*'

Members of the Hoare family of Quaker bankers lived at CLIFF HOUSE (on the Overstrand Road), at North Cottage (in North Lodge Park), at Morden House (in Cliff Avenue) and elsewhere.

Elizabeth Fry (1780–1845), the prison reformer, used to stay at The Grove, in Overstrand Road, which belonged to a branch of the Gurney family. There she would read and preach to the family. She held a Quaker meeting in a sum-merhouse in the nearby wood. She stayed in Cliff House when she was ill in 1842, and in the same year she col-laborated with J. J. Gurney to establish at the top of the Gangway a reading room for fishermen.

Amelia Opie (1769–1853) was an-other of this circle of Quakers, dividing her time mostly between Norwich and London; her last outing, however, was to her favourite resort of Cromer.[1]

Queen's Road. Council houses com-pleted in 1955,[1] a couple of years after the coronation of Queen Elizabeth II. (A similar development in Holt includes a Coronation Road, Charles Road and Elizabeth Crescent.)

Quoits. J. S. Mannings singles out cricket and quoits when describing the sports of his day (1806). He regards them both as being useful training for young men engaged in seafaring and warfare.[1]

R

Railway cottages. Four rows of cottages were built for the railway workers: **1.** eight cottages on Central Road (named Beach Cottages, or Beach Station Cottages, since they were just the other side of the goods sidings from Cromer Beach railway station); **2.** at the top of the Norwich Road, backing on to Cromer High station; **3.** in Jubilee Lane (opposite Cromer High station), with the house on the embankment opposite; **4.** near the top of Mill Road (subsequently demolished).

Railways *(see map overleaf)*. The first station in Cromer was opened in 1877 by the East Norfolk Railway at the top of Norwich Road; it was later taken over by the Great Eastern Railway. The 'Cromer Express' trains from London ran from 1897 to 1914 (called the 'Norfolk Coast Express' from 1907), with 12 to 15 coaches of varnished teak (with a restaurant car) going non-stop to North Walsham and taking only 2 hours 55 minutes to reach Cromer. The station was renamed Cromer High in 1948, but was closed to passenger traffic in 1954.

Cromer Beach station was opened in 1887 by the Eastern & Midlands Railway, bringing trains from the East Midlands via Melton Constable and Sheringham and greatly strengthening Cromer's popularity with holidaymakers from the East Midlands. The meandering line was run by the Midland & Great Northern Joint Railway (M&GN, or 'Muddle and Get Nowhere') from 1893 to 1936, and by the LNER from 1936 until nationalisation. Direct trains from the Midlands ceased in 1959, though the line from Melton Constable to Sheringham remained open for another five years.

See also BUDDIES.

A line from North Walsham via Mundesley was opened in 1906 to Overstrand (where the station had two coal wharves), and then via LINKS HALT, passing under the top of the Norwich Road and over the Roughton Road and Hall Road to give the Great Eastern its own route to Cromer Beach and Sheringham. It was used by the 'Poppyland Flyer' (average speed 20 mph). The line was closed in 1953. See Constance Rothery, *The Poppyland Flyer: The Story of the Railway Line from Cromer to North Walsham* (Trimingham: Old Station House Press, 1984).

Reading rooms. 1. In 1814, Edmund Peele and Thomas Field opened a subscription reading-room on part of Peele's garden which had fallen onto the beach in a storm. Here visitors could read several daily papers or

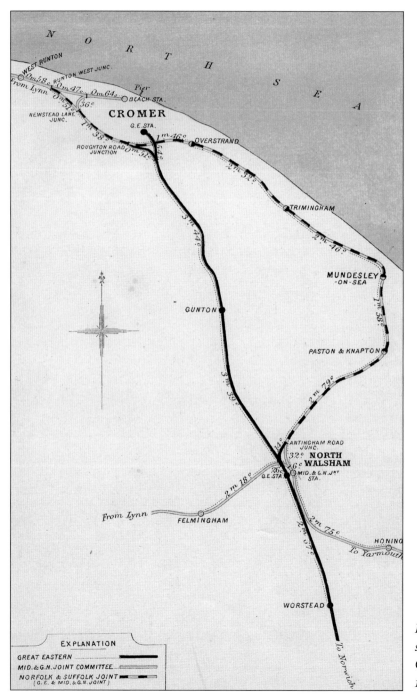

Railways serving Cromer in 1907.

avail themselves of a small library 'for light readers'.[1] In 1827 the local schoolmaster, Simeon Simons, bought the business, extending the building and adding bathing facilities and billiards (*see* BATH HOUSE). When the building was washed away by a storm in 1836, it was rebuilt, but from this date we hear nothing of books, only newspapers.[2] In the morning lounge were London and provincial daily papers, and users were charged sixpence a day, or half a crown a week.[3] It was a convenient place to read the newspapers, which were expensive to buy because of the stamp duty. The establishment continued under Simons' control until his death in 1867, after which the building became briefly a private residence and then a hotel.

2. In 1842 Elizabeth Fry and others founded a reading room for fishermen at the top of the GANGWAY. Mrs Fry wrote: 'it appears a general opinion that *much* good will result from the library, the room and the Benefit Society there is really quite an interest excited about it'.[4] Fowell Buxton offered the land free of charge to build on, and Lady Listowel (the lady of the manor) thought it would add to the value of her property. The Fry family expected to use it occasionally themselves, and asked Buxton to see the Bishop about the matter, hoping to overcome the high church spirit' which was creating divisions amongst potential supporters. The vision was for a social centre,

where it would be possible to buy a cup of coffee as well as read improving books. William Mayes was 'ready to undertake the care of the room with a view of making some profit from the Coffee & the teaching' (of reading?), but without other remuneration.[5]

This seems to have evolved into the FISHERMEN'S AND WORKING MEN'S CLUB OF CROMER which opened a reading room with a small library in the old Methodist chapel, in Chapel Street in 1891 (*see under* LIBRARIES 2).

3. Read's dairy (now demolished; it lay just east of the Parish Hall) had a long upstairs room once used as a dining room; according to Crawford Holden, it was previously known as Cromer Reading Room, and the programme survives of a concert held there in 1865.[6]

4. The Town Hall in 1890 was designed with a reading room on the first floor.[7]

5. A reading room was also provided in the SHIPDEN CLUB.

❡ Lord Battersea provided a reading room in Overstrand for use on winter evenings.[8]

Rechabites. *See* FRIENDLY SOCIETIES.

Rectors of Cromer. *See* VICARS OF CROMER.

❡ **Rectors of Overstrand.** The following table[1] lists the rectors (i.e., ministers of the parish church):

n.d.   John Reymes
1345   Richard de Shipden
1349   Simon Cary of Mundesley
1355   Thomas Goodknape
     (who also held Roughton)
1383   Robert Madeson
1432   William Dolle
     Stephen Clerk
1443   John Wyttelbury
1445   Richard Halyday
     (who also held Itteringham)
1482   William Crowmer, *monk*
1483   James Willyams
1492   Thomas Garforth
1508   Thomas Ward
1526   Robert Stone
1531   Cuthbert Huddysmawth
1546   John Shereborn
n.d.   Thomas Punder
1568   William Harper
1577   William Fourd
1580   Thomas Nabbes
     (also rector of Sidestrand[2])
1599   John Money
1606   Thomas Mundye
     (who had been vicar of Cromer from 1591, and was rector of Thorpe Market in 1600; a Thomas Monday, presumably the same man, was rector of Sidestrand in 1603)
1639   Robert Springall
1641   Charles Warde
1662   Thomas Rule
1670   William Ashmore
     (who became vicar of Sidestrand in 1686 and of Cromer in 1694; he died in 1712)

1714   George Bearfoot
1748   Samuel Johnson
     (who died in office[3])
1779   Edward Moon
     (who in 1792 was also instituted as rector of Thwaite, Suffolk; he resigned the living of Overstrand when he was appointed vicar of Bedingham, Norfolk[4])
1794   George Betts
1822   John Cubitt
     (on the death of the previous incumbent[5])
1841   Paul Johnson
     (also Rector of Sidestrand, and a significant local landowner born in East Runton in 1789)
1871   Forster George Simpson
1892   Lawrence Carter Carr
1947   Harold George McMaking
1958   George Norman Brummitt
1961   Robert Brackenbury Budgett
1974   John Herbert Squibb
1985   Richard Henry Chatham
1995   Simon Habgood
1999   Michael Leslie Langan

❦ **Rectory** (Overstrand).[1] In the time of Thomas Mundye (rector from 1606 to 1639) there was a parsonage house 16½ feet by 8½ feet (5 by 2.6 m) standing on a plot of an acre and a half (or a little less) in what is now known as Paul's Lane. This must have been extended or rebuilt later in the century, for in 1692 it measured 36 feet by 15 feet (11 by 4.6 m). How long this building survived is unclear, but rectors tended to live elsewhere and by 1716, when George Bearfoot was rector, the house on the site (though in good repair) was let to John Thurst; in the 1740s the house was described as a small cottage 'no way fit for any Clergy man or any other Then a very Poor man or a Collectioner to Live in', though the churchwardens remembered that there had once been 'A Conveniently Large Mansion House' on the site. A new house may have been built shortly after this – in 1845 it was a thatched brick-and-flint building with a stable attached.

What is now known as the Old Rectory, a brick-and-tile building 66 feet by 42 (20 by 13 m) with a slate roof and an adjoining stable, was built by the end of the 19th century; it remained in use until a new rectory was built in Harbord Road.

Red House. See HALSEY HOUSE.

Red Lion. When Sherman Cutler was paying rates on the Red Lion in 1767, the property belonged to Mrs Brook(e) of Stalham Hall; she had inherited it from her father, Richard Ellis of Northrepps Hall. Later in the century Robert and Rose Webb became the tenants (one of their sons, John Craske Webb, was adopted by Mrs Brooke's daughter Susannah Ellis Brooke), and the Webb family ran the hotel for over a hundred years.

Local magistrates used to meet at the Red Lion for their Petty Sessions in the second half of the 19th century, as did one of Cromer's FRIENDLY SOCIETIES, the Loyal Baring Lodge of the Manchester Unity Independent Order of Oddfellows.

In 1867 Benjamin Bond Cabbell bought the Red Lion; he sold it in 1883 to John Smith,[1] a Kensington wine merchant, who engaged Edward Boardman as architect[2] and had it rebuilt in 1887 by local builder George Riches, adding an assembly room on the site of the old fishermen's cottages and stables; this was used for auctions and plays, and even for the celebration of mass before the Roman Catholic church was built.[3]

In September 1910, when the owner was Dr Sydney Smith of Beccles, the hotel was advertised as being 'Under entirely new management. Re-decorated and re-furnished.' The new man in charge was Reilly Mead, who was also proprietor of the Grand Hotel at Mundesley (another of Smith's properties). Mead stayed there till at least 1922.

Tom Bolton had the Red Lion from 1954 to 1981, when it was sold to Eric and Mandy Dodson and Douglas and Elizabeth Dodson. It was later sold to builder Reggie Medler.

Red Lion Street. Another name for Brook Street.

Rede's House (Overstrand Road). See SCHOOLS.

Reeve Place. Development of housing

at the corner of Links Avenue and Station Road, built in 2000 on a plot formerly used as allotment gardens.

Refuse disposal. A refuse destructor was built in 1912 in Sandy Lane (on the site later occupied by North Norfolk Mushrooms). The rubbish collected by carts before this had simply been dumped in a farmer's field two or three miles away.

Regal Cinema (Hans Place). *See* CINEMA.

Regattas. Regattas, which developed out of the Whitsun FAIRS and were a precursor of the CARNIVALS, were held annually in the early 19th century. Fishing boats sailed and rowed for prizes.

Regency. *See* DOLPHIN.

Regeneration. Cromer was a qualifying area for European Union funding for the East of England and about £12 million was spent during the period 2001–06 on projects in the town – probably the single biggest co-ordinated development since the end of the 19th century. Whilst the funding was primarily for infrastructure (wider pavements, revised traffic one-way system, building renovations, redesigned pier forecourt etc.), it had to be planned with the aim of improving business in the area, offering skills development, providing employment opportunities and being

sustainable. In 2005 Cromer PPF Ltd was set up as a trust and developed the MERCHANTS' PLACE offices.

Retail trade. *See* MARKETS; SHOPS.

Richmond Court Gardens. Retirement flats built in The Croft in the early 1990s.

Ridge Way. Development of bungalows off Hillside, built by Garden Link Homes of Norwich in the late 1980s.[1]

Roads. *See* LONDON ROAD; ROMANS; *and names of individual streets.*

Rocket House. *See* WATCH HOUSE.

Rocket House Gardens. The land between the Gangway and the Watch House was leased by the council in 1893 when the old lifeboat house at the top was redundant.[1] Tea gardens developed on the slopes were bought in the 1930s by E. C. Ackermann and bequeathed to the town. The sunken gardens and Rocket House Café were installed by the council in 1935–37, though the café had to be rebuilt after being hit by a wartime bomb and again after the 1953 floods.[2] The whole building was demolished and rebuilt *c.* 2004 to the designs of David Bissenet of Purcell Miller Tritton, including a new lifeboat museum on the ground floor with the café above and a lift to convey passengers between clifftop gardens and promenade.

Roman Catholic church (Overstrand Road). Clement Scott wrote to the Roman Catholic Bishop of Northampton in 1886 drawing his attention to the lack of facilities for Roman Catholics to worship when on holiday in north Norfolk. The Bond-Cabbell estate would not sell land to the Roman Catholics, and whilst a site was being sought mass was celebrated during the holiday season in Hastings House (1888), Bracondale (1889) and the Red Lion Assembly Rooms (1889–91). A site was bought from Lord Suffield in 1894 and the present church built upon it in 1895–96 (architect G. Sherrin, builder Chapman of Hanworth). Altar and pews came from the old Willow Lane chapel in Norwich (which had been replaced by the new St John's in 1894).

At first, priests came only for the holiday season and stayed in temporary lodgings – the only Catholic permanently resident in Cromer at the time was a Mrs Evans at Melbourne House. The first full-time minister arrived in 1902, lodging in Station Road; the presbytery was built in 1903–04.[1]

The adjoining church hall was built in 1995–96 (architect Featherstone of Sheringham; builder H. Bullen).

From 2008 the Catholic parishes of Cromer and Sheringham were merged to form the parish of Our Lady and St Joseph.

📖 Fuller details are in Charles Munkman, *The Catholic Revival in North Norfolk: Centenary of Our Lady of Refuge Church in Cromer, 1895–1995* (privately printed).

Roman Catholic priests. The following have served Cromer as full-time priests:

Tea-gardens by the Gangway, part of the Rocket House Gardens.

1902 Thomas Walmsley Carter
*who built St Joseph's in
Sheringham in 1909–10 and
moved there as its priest*

1910 Harold Shelley Squirrell
*who moved on to become rector of
St John the Baptist, Norwich*

1934 Francis G. Armstrong
*from Olney; he had the church
enlarged with a new sanctuary
before moving on to Newmarket*

1941 N. W. E. Gray
moved to Gorleston in 1945

1946 Leonard Tomlinson
moved to Chesham Bois

1949 Frederick Charles Nutt
from Chesham Bois; he died 1971

1972 Joseph Michael Parr
*from Bedford; he later went to
Peterborough*

1977 Francis Hacon
*previously at Fakenham and
Thetford; he retired and died 1989*

1991 Peter Cansdale
*who initiated the building of the
church hall; he retired to* HALSEY
HOUSE *following a stroke*

1996 Peter Brown

Fr Peter Brown retired in 2008, when Fr Denys Lloyd became the first priest of the new combined parish, residing at Sheringham (the presbytery at Cromer being let out).

Romans. Evidence of Roman occupation in this part of Norfolk is scanty, and we are not even certain exactly where the coastline lay. A Roman road ran east and west from Brampton, 11 or 12 miles to the south, where there was a considerable pottery industry; a road also ran from there to the north, but we have no firm evidence that it reached any further than Burgh Hall, near Aylsham.

Some scholars have thought the coastline from Brancaster to Caister-on-sea too long a stretch to have been left unprotected, and have surmised there may have been at least one more Roman fort along this 'Saxon shore', possibly at or near Cromer – in which case one might expect there to have been a road from Brampton right the way to the coast. This whole line of thinking has not, however, been favoured in recent scholarship.

A bronze coin of Claudius II Gothicus (emperor A.D. 268–70) was found just east of Cromer High station in 1958.[1]

Rosebery Road. Plans for Mr Howard's house and shop at the corner of Cliff Road were passed by the council in 1903.[1]

Roughton Road. The original road from Roughton, before the turnpike in 1811 struck across Roughton Heath to join the North Walsham road at Beeches Corner (by Manor Farm, Northrepps).

Royal Cromer Hotel. *See* NEWHAVEN COURT.

Building the Royal Links Hotel.

Royal Links Hotel. In 1892 Lord Suffield, Lord Battersea, Lord Hastings and Lord Carrington joined together with other investors to form the Overstrand Estate Ltd, buying land (behind Carrington Villas) from Harry Smith of Chiswick on which to build a hotel.[1] It was opened in 1895 adjacent to the golf links – both the hotel and the full 18-hole golf course were opened by Lady Hastings on the same day. The hotel could accommodate about a hundred guests,[2] and Lord Suffield, one of the directors, recalled that the building was 'an expensive affair, for there was nothing but a sandhill to build on, and very deep excavations had to be made for the foundations'.[3]

The 'Royal' refers to King Edward VII, who was Patron of the golf club. Distinguished guests staying here included the Duke and Duchess of Connaught and Earl Feversham, and in 1903 an entire floor was taken by the Tungku Bezar and his retinue from the Malay States.[4] Guests also included Sir Squire Bancroft (1841-1926), the actor-manager, who stayed several times and was induced to help local charities.[5]

Built on a commanding height above the town, close to the lighthouse, the hotel offered superior facilities: an early motorist wrote of it that 'the charges, compared with those of the "Angel" at Bury, seemed high. Still, it was more "replete with every modern luxury" than the "Angel"; it possessed bathrooms, for example, which are indispensable to the motorist.'[6]

The hotel was used as barracks during both World Wars,[7] was refurbished after World War 2, but then burned down in 1949.[8] The land was used as a caravan site by a succession of owners before becoming the CROMER COUNTRY CLUB.

Royal Links Pavilion. Built in 1926 as a ballroom for the wealthy guests of the Royal Links Hotel, this building remained untouched by the fire of 1949 but was neglected by the owners of the caravan site until that business was bought by the Blow family in 1964. Under them, the Pavilion became a venue for pop bands including The Who, the Tremeloes, UFO, Queen (Freddie Mer-

cury) and (on Christmas Eve 1977) the Sex Pistols. The Pavilion was burned down in 1978.

📖 Julie Fielder, *What FLO Said: The Story of the West Runton Pavilion and The Royal Links Pavilion, Cromer* (Happisburgh: Edition Books, 2006).

Royal Oak. *See* TUCKER'S HOTEL.

Royal Observer Corps. The Observer Corps ('Royal' from 1941) had a post beside the lighthouse from 1934, moving underground in 1958 and closing in 1968.[1]

Royalty. An early connection with royalty is found in the story of James Stuart, son of Robert king of Scotland. The young prince was on his way to France for his education when he was driven ashore in a gale on 30 March 1423 and was captured by Robert Bacon, a Cromer mariner.

Cromer had many royal visitors between the 1880s and the 1920s. The *Empress of Austria* stayed at Tucker's Hotel (*see* OLD LOOKOUT). The Belgian *Princess Stephanie* and her second husband *Count Lonyay* stayed at Tucker's in 1902 and rented Tudor House in Cliff Avenue in 1905 before moving to The Pleasaunce in Overstrand as guests of Lord and Lady Battersea.[1] *Edward VII* also used to visit Tudor House (hence the royal standard in the glass over the front door), and the same house was where *the Maharajah of Cooch Behar* lived – and committed suicide in 1913.

Princess Victoria (the sister of King George V) stayed at the Royal Links Hotel and was a regular customer of Herbert Mace at BALCONY HOUSE when he had antique furniture displayed outside along the Mount; she also patronised his photographic studio there, being a keen photographer herself.[2]

As a boy, **Prince Philip** stayed at a chalet in the grounds of Newhaven Court and presented the prizes at a gymkhana;[3] he was taught horseriding by Albert Wilkin, who ran a riding school and livery business. The former **King of Greece** and **Princess Ileana of Romania** stayed at Newhaven Court in 1925 and took part in the carnival.[4]

The **Duke of Kent** has visited three times for the Royal National Life-boat Institution.

❡ **Queen Mary** used to visit Lady Battersea at the Pleasaunce; the streets were expected to be cleared of ordinary people before she passed through.

Runton Road. The original road to Runton seems to have led from the church of St Peter, Shipden-juxta-Mare (sited near the end of the present pier) in a westerly direction. Coastal erosion forced the creation (probably between the mid-14th and early 17th centuries) of a new, more southerly, road on the present route beginning with New Street. (Just east of the junction with Westcliff Avenue, on the south side of the road, there was found the bronze

spout of a ewer or similar vessel, depicting an animal head; it dated from the 15th century. Was the pot dropped on the road and broken?[1]

The land on the northern side of the present road used always to be called the marrams; the council first leased it from the Cromer Hall estate in 1895[2] and finally bought it in 1938.[3] The putting course was laid out in 1937–38 (extended in 1947) and the E.B.A. bowling green in 1938, the pavilion being completed in 1939.[4] The car park was formerly referred to as a picnic site, public conveniences being built there in 1960.[5]

Among the houses on this road, numbers 43 to 47 are notable as a late (1934) example of the work of George Skipper.[6]

S

Saffron yard. Saffron, used as a dye and medicinally, was grown in north Norfolk especially in the 14th and 15th centuries; production took place in Cromer in a triangular plot of land just west of the top of the Gangway but had ceased by the 18th century.

St John Ambulance. *See* AMBULANCES.

St Margaret's Lane. Back passage to St Margaret's Terrace, the houses built in the 1880s on the west side of Norwich Road between Upton House and Vicarage Road.

St Margaret's Road. Made up by 1899.[1]

St Margaret's Terrace (Norwich Road). This first row of houses to be built on the Norwich Road was built for the Cromer Hall estate in 1884-85; the architect was Edward May, who had worked on London's fashionable Bedford Park.[1]

St Martin's Church (Mill Road). The original mission hall, serving the new development of Suffield Park, was built in 1897-98 in what was then still part of Overstrand parish; it was named after the old parish church in Overstrand (which at that date was in ruins). Worship had previously been conducted in the station refreshment room! The church built behind the hall was opened in 1967.[1]
¶ St Martin's Church in Overstrand was built on a half-acre of land given by one of the Reymes family in 1339, replacing the first recorded church in Overstrand, which was swallowed by the sea in the reign of Richard II.[2] It was in ruins for many years, and CHRIST CHURCH used instead, but when the population of Overstrand was affluent and growing, St Martin's was rebuilt (architect: Cecil Upcher); it was reopened in 1914.[3]

St Martin's Road. Named after the church opposite.

St Mary's Road. Built in 1894 as part of the Cromer Hall estate development.[1]

St Oran's Place. Courtyard off West Street. The name seems to have been applied to it only in the 20th century; 'St Oran' was originally the name of a house on West Street.

Salisbury Road. Part of the original Suffield Park development plan of 1887.[1] Made up in 1896.[2]

Sandcliff Hotel (Runton Road). Designed by George Skipper and built in 1895 by A. Fox for T. H. Wallis (whose initials are over the entrance).[1] Opened in 1897 by Arthur Wiseman.[2]

Sandringham House. *See* TEA ROOMS.

Savings Bank. Lord Suffield and Thomas Fowell Buxton gave their support to the formation of a Savings Bank in 1824, with an office at George Pank's in Church Street open once a week from 12 to 1 o'clock. The maximum any account could have was £200; funds could be withdrawn at 14 days' notice. Deposits were forwarded to the Bank of England (it was all part of the government's attempt to reduce the National Debt) and account holders were not allowed to have an account with any other savings bank.[1]

This view of the Goldsmiths' school was drawn by Philip Hardwick in 1833.

School Cottages. *See* WEST COTTAGE.

Schools. The ***Goldsmiths' School*** in Cromer was the earliest endowed grammar school in Norfolk,[1] founded by the 1505 will of Sir Bartholomew Rede (*see under* LONDON MAYORS), but it seems to have had no building of its own until 1790. In 1821 the Goldsmiths' Company provided money for the building on the Overstrand Road. Under Simeon Simons the curriculum began to provide an appropriate (rather than classical) education for all local boys (rather than just a few of them). 'In teaching Writing & Arithmetic, Geography & Mapping & even the difficult study of Navigation, Mr Symons seems in an especial manner to excel,' noted the Goldsmiths' Company's Wardens.[2]

The school was closed in 1897 after the Board School started providing universal primary education. The building was sold to R. Hoare[3] and was used for some years as a furniture and cycle warehouse, before being bought in 1926 by Dr Arthur Burton, who turned it into his surgery and built the adjoining house (Rede's House). The school building became a private house after the new surgery was built opposite The Warren.
📖 P. S. Barclay, *A History of Sir Bartholomew Rede, the Goldsmiths' Free Grammar School and the Cromer Exhibition Foundation* (1989).)

Private schools were run by J. W. Greenwood in West Street (boarding, day and drawing) and Mary Leak in Church Street (ladies' boarding and day) by 1830.[4]

In the mid-19th century Miss Magson kept a small school for boys and girls at 10 Chapel Street; from 1860 to 1889 Miss Murrell kept a school at 3 Chapel Street.[5]

The *Girls' Charity School* in East Street[6] (there was a schoolroom at the back of the cottages now known as 21-25 Church Street) was probably the one founded by Mrs Buxton and later supported by Mrs Birkbeck;[7] there was a separate *Infants' School*. By 1872 there was a girls' and infants' school supported by the church.[8]

In 1896, to cater for the increase in Cromer's population, the *Board Schools* (Louden Road/Cross Street) were built; the girls' and infants' department absorbed the earlier girls' school from the outset, but at first boys would go on to the Goldsmiths' School at the age of 7. After the opening of the *Secondary Modern* school on the Norwich Road in 1949, the Cross Street buildings continued to be used for infants and mixed juniors. A new *Infants School* was built on Mill Road in the late 20th century a new *Junior School* on the Norwich Road in 1994, after which the Board School buildings were converted into housing by Reggie Medler.

After the coming of the railways, an astonishing number of small private schools were established in Cromer, mainly offering boarding places. *For details, see the entries on* AVON HOUSE SCHOOL; KING'S COLLEGE; KINGSMILL SCHOOL; LEIGHTON HOUSE SCHOOL; OAKLEIGH; SUFFIELD PARK PREPARATORY SCHOOL; SUSSEX HOUSE SCHOOL; SUTHERLAND HOUSE SCHOOL; WOOD-DENE SCHOOL.

¶ *See also* BELFRY SCHOOL.

¶ **Scole House.** *See* GISSING HOUSE.

¶ **Sea Marge.** Sir Edgar Speyer, a German Jewish financier who helped finance the Metropolitan District Railway and the Promenade concerts, bought the house in 1902 for £6,400 and subsequently spent about £8,000 on rebuilding it,[1] supposedly with 'authentic' Elizabethan oak, brick and tile. The design may be by Sir Arthur Blomfield.

The story goes that Sir Winston Churchill was staying at Pear Tree Cottage in The Londs in 1914 when war broke out; he went to Sea Marge to use Sir Edgar's telephone to ring the Admiralty and mobilise the fleet. Speyer was soon accused of collaborating with the Germans, however, and moved to New York in 1915. (A postwar enquiry cleared him of the charge.) The building later became a hotel.

It was a council home for old people from 1955 to 1990 and afterwards remained empty for several years before being restored to use as a hotel in the 1990s.

¶ **Sea Marge Settlement.** Shown on the 1927 revision of the Ordnance Survey 6-inch map. Here was staff acommodation for Sea Marge, as well as its laundry.

¶ **Sea View** or **Sea View Road.** Former name for that part of HARBORD ROAD, Overstrand, which connects with Paul's Lane.

Sea walls. The first effective sea wall was built by Lowestoft engineer George Edwards in 1838. It ran from the West Cliff to the Gangway. An advertisement described property on the West Cliff as being 'secure from the inroads of the sea, by a magnificent wall of great substance',[1] but in 1845 its western portion failed to prevent the loss of cliff property and had to be replaced by John Wright's 1846 wall. These walls were strengthened and extended by Douglass & Arnott in 1900. All three walls were erected as a direct response to storm damage: the 1837 storm which had washed away the BATH HOUSE, the 1845 storm which had destroyed the earlier jetty, and the 1897 storm which destroyed the 1846 jetty.[2]

Sewage works. The old gas works at the end of Sandy Lane were converted into a new sewage works for Cromer, Sheringham, Overstrand and the Runtons in the 1990s; an extra building for secondary treatment was added in 2000-01.[1]

Sheep's Hill. The name given on maps of 1717 and 1747 to the hill now bounded by Beach Road, Bernard Road and the bottom of Central Road.

Sheep's Pit. Seasonal spring on the south side of Sheep's Hill, on the site of the later railway goods yard. The water would flow down West Street in a channel in front of the houses, which had flagstones to cross the stream. A cobblestone gutter then carried the water down what is now Garden Street, till it reached the cliff edge.[1]

Ship Hotel (Church Street). In 1767, William Ransom was paying rates here. By 1873 it was owned by Nathaniel Field of Runton, who also had interests in shipping – he owned the last collier to unload cargo on Cromer beach; the licensee from 1848 to Field's time was James Witting, a carpenter who was one of the two contractors who built the 1846 jetty. The adjoining premises were connected in 1878, and the bunch of grapes in the stonework over the shop which now occupies part of the ground floor denotes the wines sold when these premises formed the inn's wholesale outlet. The inn was later owned by Morgans brewery, then Watney Mann, who closed it in the early 1980s.

Shipden. The original name of the medieval settlement of Cromer, including 'Shipden juxta Felbrigg' (equivalent to present-day Cromer) and 'Shipden juxta Mare' (now washed away by the sea), each with its own church. The spelling of the name in medieval documents implies that the name means 'sheep valley' rather than having anything to do with ships. (Cf. SHEEP'S HILL.) It is certainly in a valley (even from the top of the 160-foot (49 m) church tower, it is impossible to see much beyond the town because it is down in a dip), but if the sheep contributed significantly to the local economy, it was before the 14th century (*see under* TITHES). (On the other hand, as late as the 1590s Emmanuel Calliard, who had land adjoining Roughton Heath, was in constant dispute with his neighbours over sheep grazing.[1])

Shipden Abbots. Another name for the medieval manor of St Benet's, i.e. the land at Shipden which at the time of the Domesday survey (1086) belonged to the abbey of St Benet's at Holme and supplied the monks there with food. This land was all consumed by the sea centuries ago.[1]

Shipden Avenue. A development of council houses built in 1952.[1]

Shipden Club. A social club formed in 1904 in the IMPERIAL HOTEL. By the beginning of World War 1 it had moved into Hanover House, where it had a reading room, bar and billiard room on the first floor and card rooms on the second floor.[1]

Shipden House. *See* HANOVER HOUSE.

Shooting. *See* HUNTING AND SHOOTING.

Shops. Over the years, some of Cromer's shops have been such well known features of the local community that their permanence must have seemed beyond doubt. In 1665 Cromer shopkeeper **Richard A. Bennet** issued a token (there being a national shortage of small coinage);[1] it showed a horse trotting, and his customers must have regarded him as a permanent part of the local trading scene, though for a long time Cromer's shopkeepers catered only for the daily necessities of local residents: Robert Marten, visiting from London in 1825, noted 'few shops and those quite country fashion – very little inticement to spend money'.[2]

Thomas Field was a grocer and draper at HANOVER HOUSE. He joined with Edmund Peele, who had married his wife's sister, to open a subscription reading room in 1814; this later became the BATH HOUSE. He was succeeded in the drapery business by his son, Thomas W. Field, but in 1868 the business was taken over by Rust's.

The first **Benjamin Rust** was born at Sea Palling in 1753, apprenticed to a Yarmouth grocer, and opened a shop in one of John Kirby's row of ten cottages in Cromer in 1780; he did well enough to be able to buy, in 1798, the shop, house, five cottages, malthouse, yard and gardens. In 1818 he bought property in Trimingham (where his father-in-law had a farm), opening a branch shop there which remained open until 1922; he had a branch in Trunch from 1828 to 1857. The Cromer shop was rebuilt in 1805, and given a new front in 1896,

Rust's main Cromer shop in the early 20th century.

one foot further back from the High Street.[3] By this time John William Rust had taken a different direction, going in for banking on the site later to become Barclays Bank, whilst his brother Benjamin Rust continued to expand the retail business, opening a shop in Sheringham in 1898. The business grew by the 1950s to include branches in Holt, North Walsham, Cley, Watton, Mundesley and Wymondham, and new shops were built: a large one in what had been the Narrows in Church Street, and a small one in Suffield Park, at the corner of Mill Road and Harbord Road. The wine bottling department closed in 1984, and the great enterprise came to an end, Boots the chemist moving into the Church Street shop and the High Street premises becoming a Budgens.

In 1881 **Robert Laurence Randall** arrived in Cromer from Holt, where his father was a watchmaker and gas engi-

neer. R. L. set up in business as a watchmaker, at first working from his home in the newly built Chesterfield Villas, then opening a shop in Bond Street

Robert and Clara Randall and a member of staff outside their Mount Street shop. As well as clocks and watches, the shop sold and repaired bicycles.

and *c.* 1890 moving into Mount Street. As domestic electrical supply spread, he began installing and servicing electrical appliances. Over the years his descendants opened up new branches – at one time there were five shops in Cromer and Sheringham. The surviving electrical business moved in 2009 from Mount Street to 7 Church Street.

A. H. Fox Ltd had a noted furniture shop in Prince of Wales Road (Ambrose Fox lived at Sunnycroft in Meadow Road and is described in the 1901 census as a cabinet maker and upholsterer); by the end of the 20th century the business was reduced to that of funeral directors, though a remnant of their removals and storage business survived as 'Fox of Cromer', despite having moved out of the town.

National chains of supermarkets did not establish themselves in Cromer until Safeway built a store on the former railway goods yard in the 1980s (to become Morrisons later), with the Cooperative moving their store shortly afterwards to the edge of town (Middlebrook Way) and the Homebase store opening on the other side of the Holt Road in 2008.

See also JEWELLERS; PHARMACISTS.
¶ Overstrand in 1861 had only one shop, a grocer's in The Londs; even that was occupied by a fisherman, whose 44-year-old wife described herself merely as a former dressmaker.

Short Street. Old name of Surrey Street.

Signal station. *See* TELEGRAPH.

Skates Hill. The hill immediately north-west of Hall Road where it bends towards Felbrigg Hall, by the railway viaduct. The name Sket is Scandinavian, and was popular in north Norfolk in the late 11th and 12th centuries; before 1066 a man named Skeet held land in Overstrand,[1] though the name is not mentioned in connection with Shipden or Felbrigg. A Roger Skete of Felbrigg is mentioned in a muster of 1577.[2]

Slaughterhouse. Thatched building at the junction of the Metton and Felbrigg roads, just south of the railway bridge over Hall Road; remained a slaughterhouse into the 20th century; later it became a private dwelling house.

Slavery. In 1820 Thomas Fowell Buxton (1786–1845) found the family's London brewery of Truman Hanbury needed little of his attention, so he was able to move to Cromer where he rented CROMER HALL from the Windham family. As a Member of Parliament he led the campaign to abolish slavery, and both Thomas Babington Macaulay and William Wilberforce visited him at Cromer in the autumn of 1822 to discuss this campaign.[1]

When the Windham family decided to have Cromer Hall rebuilt, Buxton moved to Northrepps Hall, which belonged to the Gurney family. His son, also Thomas Fowell, lived at UPTON

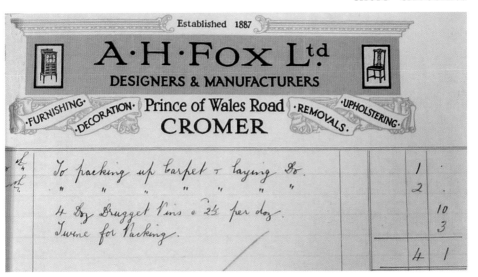

Fox's invoice (very fashionably designed) itemises the pins and string used in carpet-laying.

HOUSE on the Norwich Road; and his grandson, of the same name again, lived at COLNE HOUSE.

The Buxton family continued to work against slavery for many years: Priscilla Johnston, daughter of the first Sir Thomas, was a close supporter and co-worker with him on the campaign and the Dowager Lady Buxton attended a London meeting in connection with the Polynesian slave trade in 1871, just months before her death.[2]

❡ **Slipway** (Overstrand). Work began in the early 19th century on the construction of a 'Morgan's slip' on which a boat could be landed at high tide, with a capstan to haul it up to the top of the cliff for unloading. It was not completed, but the archway in the cliff face can be seen in some old pictures.

Smoke houses. Around the end of the 18th century a smoke house was built for the curing of herrings.[1] By 1836 there were four such buildings: in Church Street, West Street, Brook Street and Pump Street.[2]

Rust's shop had its own smoke house (surviving until the 1960s) for the smoking of gammons etc. at the back of their premises in Garden Street.

❡ A smoke house at 10 High Street, Overstrand, was built in 1880 and last used in 1933.

Smuggling. Ships from the northern provinces of the Netherlands regularly brought goods to Cromer in the 14th century, avoiding duties easily because there was only one 'searcher' (customs officer) for the whole of the East Anglian coastline.[1]

A newspaper report of 1823 mentions gin being seized on the beach. One smuggler was shot by a lieutenant from the preventive service at about this time.[2]

Snooker Club (Brook Street). Licensed club with several snooker tables functioning in Allman's former auction room during the 1990s. *For earlier facilities, see under* BILLIARDS; *for development of the site, see* CLARENCE MEWS.

¶ **South Street.** Turning off Cliff Road, Overstrand, north of Thurst Road.

Southern Bungalow. Built on the Norwich Road as Northern and Southern Bungalows; later amalgamated as the Southern Bungalow Hotel. Used as accommodation for SUTHERLAND HOUSE SCHOOL for a time, and then converted into flats.

Souvenirs.[1] Holiday resorts such as Cromer and Overstrand have long offered objects to entice visitors to spend and then take home a present as a memento of their visit. Local lapidaries made objects of amber and jet (*see* JEWELLERS) and national (and international) entrepreneurs developed their ranges of souvenirs. 'A Present From' or 'A Gift From' plus the name of the village/town/building was an easy way to mass produce items such as confectionery, stationery, clothes, china, books, badges, spoons and food. Noth-

ing was sacred and the trade was well established by the 1850s.

Postcards and letter cards were published by national companies (Valentines, Salmon, Raphael Tuck) and featured paintings by A. R. Quinton and photographs of Cromer, Overstrand, the miller and his daughter, the Garden of Sleep at Sidestrand as well as the famous Frith views. Local businesses, for example the Post Office and jeweller's run by Mrs Fox in Jetty Street and Alfred Collinson Savin promoted their own cards and booklets of views of the beach and buildings using local photographers.

Jarrolds of Cromer were instrumental in selling articles associated with Poppyland and were responsible for a very attractive series of cards featuring poppies, painted by George Norman Parsons, which were also published as a book. Poppyland china proved successful with a pattern produced by Wedgewood exclusively for this firm. Other local shops followed the trend and used the Staffordshire pottery firms; Rounce and Wortley used Barker Brothers, Hewitt & Leadbetter and Willow Pottery from 1913 with a design protected until 1928. Later in the century, Pamela Morton Ceramics produced their own pattern.

Views were also popular and the Scottish firm Smiths of Mauchline produced black lacquered and varnished transfer decorated souvenir ware made of sycamore wood in the second half of

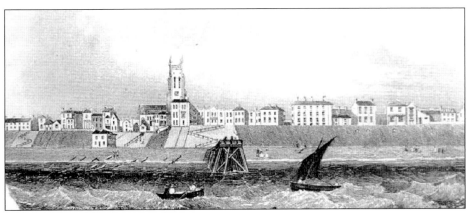

Before the days of picture postcards, Rock & Co produced tiny but accurate and attractive engraved views of resorts, such as this one of Cromer sea-front in 1855.

the 19th century. Microphotographs showing local scenes were also incorporated into small magnifying devices called Stanhopes, made in France.

Crested ware appeared on china sold at Mrs Abel's shop in the High Street in Cromer during the 19th century. The firm W. H. Goss boasted that every town with a coat of arms in the United Kingdom was represented by one of their products and Cromer and Overstrand were no exception to the rule (*see also* ARMORIAL BEARINGS). Spoons, trinket boxes and other metallic items were equally successful. As early as 1845 Ann Cantrill at her bazaar was selling quill pens with 'Cromer Bazaar' woven into the binding.

Local chemist Daniel Davison produced perfume and soap called 'Poppy-land Bouquet', which was featured as an impressive display in his shop window. Between the years 1908 and 1916 Churchman's even produced 'Poppy-land Tobacco'.

Stained and painted glass. Vicar John Gosselin in the 1380s left money for an east window of three lights depicting Mary Magdalene, St Christopher and St Katherine, but there is no old stained glass in Cromer church now – the chancel having been in ruins for 200 years and the side windows partly bricked up. The present east window, typical of its date (1875), is by J. Hardman & Co. of Birmingham. The window at the eastern end of the south aisle is of 1874, by Morris & Co. (William Morris and Edward Burne-Jones), who had done work in Antingham church *c.* 1865 and were now at the peak of their reputation; it is still greatly valued by admirers of Pre-Raphaelite art despite being badly damaged in World War 2.[1]

Architect George Skipper used local

Windows from the Hotel de Paris, depicting the Garden of Sleep and Sheringham beach.

scenes and coats of arms in the windows of the big hotels he designed in the 1880s and 90s: the Hotel de Paris, the Grand Hotel and the Cliftonville.

In the 20th century, Cromer had its own stained glass specialist in Leslie Rees Steers; born in Hartlepool, he moved to Cromer and worked as a bus conductor with Eastern Counties buses before returning to glazing – he worked on glass in Cromer and Roughton churches as well as in Norwich Cathedral and Kings College Cambridge.[2]

Station House. *See* BUDDIES.

Station Road. Made up in 1896.[1] Early plans for estate sales show this being called Overstrand Road and what we know as Beach Road being called Station Road.

Steam laundry. *See* LAUNDRIES.

Stevens Road. Strictly speaking, the road is in Northrepps. In 1941 the land was being used for poultry rearing (over 1,000 birds).[1] After being bombed, pre-fabricated bungalows were built on it.

Stocks. In 1607 a woman of Southrepps, having borne an illegitimate child, was sentenced to be put in the stocks in Cromer for three hours on the next market day as well as in Southrepps on the Sunday.[1] The punishment seems to have been the standard one meted out by the magistrates of the day, though why Cromer was stipulated is a mystery, unless it was to advertise her sin to the largest number of people. (Southrepps had no market.) The stocks are likely to have been in the vicinity of the church and market-place.

Stonehill Way. Stone Hill is so named on Bellard's 1747 map.[1]

Plans to erect concrete industrial units here were approved by the council in 1976.[2]

Storey's Hill. Name (on the 1838 Ordnance Survey map) of the hill on which Cromer railway station was later built.

Street names and numbering. Nameplates for the streets of Cromer were ordered by the Local Board's Highways Committee in 1889.[1]

In 1969 house numbering was imposed for the first time on Holt Road, Roughton Road, St Martin's Close, Ar-

One of Cromer's earliest street signs.

bor Road, Carrington Road, East Grove, Northrepps Road, Cliff Drive, Colne Place and Arbor Hill, and rationalised in Park Road, Howards Hill, Canada Road and Bernard Road. When the letters went out from the council obliging residents in these streets to display house numbers, one resident was reported as saying, 'I think it is rather high-handed and – dare one say it? – it seems to smack of Communism.'[2]

Suffield Court. *See* SUFFIELD PARK HOTEL.

Suffield Park. In 1815 the manor of Cromer Gunners, including the land now known as Suffield Park, was bought by the 3rd Lord Suffield, who had a marine villa built at the centre of Cromer sea-front (now the HOTEL DE PARIS). In the 1820s there was an idea of developing Cromer 'in a manner to fit it for a watering place of large and fashionable resort'; the London architect

---

CROMER CHARACTERS
THE 3RD LORD SUFFIELD

Edward Harbord (1781–1835) became the 3rd Lord Suffield when his brother died in 1821. As a young man his dress was 'recherché and fantastic', but the effeminate impression this gave was wholly misleading: he could run a mile easily in five minutes, sometimes racing for money against professional athletes, and he wrestled and boxed. He founded the Norfolk cricket club, and his exertions on the beach helping the lifeboat in Cromer led him to propose a county-wide lifeboat service.

In the House of Lords he was the leading spokesman for the abolition of the slave trade and a prime mover in prison reform – both issues dear to the hearts of other Cromer notables (Thomas Fowell Buxton of Cromer Hall in the case of slavery, and Elizabeth Fry in the case of prison reform).[1]

who sketched out rough plans for villas in the valley was Robert William Jearrad, whose later work was to include laying out the Lansdowne estate in Cheltenham, with its large houses and villas perhaps reflecting what Cromer might have looked like had Lord Suffield taken up his offer of working for him free of charge.[1] (*See also* NORTH LODGE.) But the Cromer project came to nothing, and it was left to the 5th Lord Suffield to develop the district. He was instrumental in bringing the railway to Cromer and, with the second station about to be opened, he began selling building plots in 1887.

The area was part of the parish of Overstrand; the administrative boundary was changed from 31 December 1895 to include it in Cromer,[2] but ecclesiastically it remained part of Overstrand parish for another 50 years.

☐ *See* Rochelle Mortimer Massingham, *Up the Park! A History of Suffield Park, Cromer, Norfolk* (Cromer Museum, 1999).

Suffield Park Hotel. Built opposite the railway station (Cromer High) after the 1887 auction sale of building plots on Lord Suffield's estate, and owned from 1901/02 by the City of London Brewery.[1] The hotel part could accommodate 50 guests, but closed in 1929 and was shut off from the pub, remaining derelict until demolition in 1962. Jack Carpenter was licensee from 1925 to at least 1962. The pub closed in 2000 and the building was converted into flats called Suffield Court.

Suffield Park Preparatory School. In the late 19th and early 20th centuries this school occupied the building later called Linkside, in Park Road; its sanatorium was on the other side of the road, facing Carrington Road. The school had two masters.[1] One of its pupils (from 1904 to 1908) was E. J. Moeran, from Bacton, who was to become well known as a composer.

Summer house (Warren Woods). A white structure used for worship by the Quaker Gurney family in the 19th century on days when they were unable to drive to the Meeting House in Swafield. It had a table with a drawer for a large Bible they used. The building survived until World War 2.[1]

Summerhouse Close. Developed for housing in the 1990s. The name is the old field name of the land.[1]

Surrey House (Surrey Street). Built in 1880 on the site of a coal-yard belonging to Jeremiah Cross. The ground floor was used as the Cromer & District Labour Club and subsequently by the Crescent Club (later renamed Blazer's).

Surrey Street. Road created *c.* 1820 and taking its present name from Surrey House.

Sussex House School. In 1907 this

small private school was offering 'experienced Home Care for young and delicate boys'.[1]

Sutherland Court. *See* HERNE CLOSE.

Sutherland Court Gardens (Overstrand Road). Housing development created in the 1990s on part of the grounds of the former SUTHERLAND HOUSE SCHOOL, after which it was named.

Sutherland House School. Originally established in Ipswich, the school moved to Cromer in the 1940s, occupying Southern Bungalow and a house in Cliff Avenue; in 1946 they took over The WARREN, and in 1959 HERNE CLOSE. BRACONDALE was also used for a time. The school amalgamated with Runton Hill School in 1990 and moved onto the Runton Hill site in West Runton (which became a Kingswood Centre when the combined Runton & Sutherland School in turn closed a few years later).

Swacking Cuckoo. Name of a piece of woodland next to the railway line at the top of the Holt Road. 'Swacking' appears in dialect dictionaries with the meaning of 'large', 'whopping', 'whacking'. *See also* CUCKOO LANE.

Swann's Yard. Small yard behind the Ship public house in Church Street. Mrs Swan kept a butcher's shop here.

T

Taxation, Medieval. Taxation lists of 1334 and 1449 can be studied to show the relative prosperity of Shipden/ Cromer and of other nearby places. Shipden's assessment is very much less than that of the Blakeney ports, and was not reduced despite the loss of land to the sea – the churchyard was already being eroded (*see under* CHURCHES), so the most significant losses of land may well have occurred before 1334:

	1334 assessment			1449 assessment		
	£	s	d	£	s	d
Shipden [=Cromer]	2	18	0	2	18	0
Runton	3	6	2	2	16	2
Sheringham	3	14	0	3	14	0
Sidestrand	4	0	0	3	0	0
Holt	5	4	0	4	17	4
Salthouse	7	0	0	5	1	4
Cley	10	0	0	10	0	0
Wiveton	13	0	0	6	0	0
Snitterley [=Blakeney]	12	0	0	7	0	0

Taxis. Cromer taxis and taxi drivers were first required to be licensed in 1890, when the Local Board set the fares for journeys between the Gangway and Cromer High station at one shilling, and for longer journeys at one shilling and sixpence.[1] The first order for licence plates and badges (two dozen of each)[2] was clearly too cautious, for despite drivers' initial reluctance to comply with the law, it was only a year before the Board was issuing 49 drivers' licences;[3] in 1893 the number had risen to 68 despite a decision to exclude those living in Runton.[4] There were soon stands for 40 cabs, mostly on the Runton Road and Prince of Wales Road close to the big new hotels.[5]

The first we hear of any attempt to oust the horse-drawn cabs is in 1903, when 'an application by Mr. J. T. Sharp for permission to ply for hire with a motor car was read but not acceded to' by the council; the minute does not say whether it was Mr Sharp or his motor car that they were worried about.[6]

The council seems later to have abandoned licensing as too much work, and it was not reintroduced until the 1980s. Of the longer established firms, Blue Star Taxis operated from the late 1940s for over 50 years, after which one of its owners started Ace Cabs Cromer. Crisp's operated from 1948 for nearly 60 years (using, from the 1960s to 2000, premises formerly used by Flaxman's – a Mr Flaxman was driving a Cromer taxi shortly after World War I), being succeeded by L.G. Taxis.

Tea rooms. The high duty levied on tea was slashed in 1784, bringing to an end the widespread practice of smuggling it and making it much more affordable. Mary Hardy's diary entries reflect this: on 7 May 1781 she and her husband 'went to Cromer & dined at Mr Alsops' (this was the King's Arms, later known as the CROWN AND ANCHOR) – no mention of tea – but on 12 May 1791 her family party of four ladies and two gentlemen 'dined & drank tea at the Kings Arms'.[1] By 1817 the WELLINGTON had a

Horse-drawn cabs wait on the rank at the foot of the Norwich Road.

The Wellington, with its tea-room balcony, is seen in a painting of the early 1890s. Right of centre is the Belle Vue Hotel and on the extreme right is Kingston House.

first-floor tea-room with a balcony giving a fine sea view.[2]

Other than the public houses, Cromer's first tea room is said to have been Bay House, in Garden Street; by World War 1 a Miss Little was running a large tea room on the ground floor of Kingston House (at the corner of Garden Street and the High Street, opposite the Wellington), where the basement had two kitchens and a larder.[3]

For much of the 20th century the most prominent tea rooms in Cromer were to be found opposite the church in the Tudor Café. Originally a simple two-storey house with attic rooms, home to the Clarke family and known as

Sandringham House, it was bought by Mrs Loynes, a Belgian who had married locally and ran the café at the Rocket House Gardens. She added a third storey to Sandringham House, faced the upper storeys with mock Tudor beams and extended it over the garden at the back. Its success lay partly in its being the only restaurant in Cromer large enough to accommodate coach parties of visitors, and there was consternation when it was learned that Mrs Loynes, at the age of 74, was retiring and had sold the premises.

See also Blue Danube; Victorian Tea Rooms.

¶ Mrs Emily Harrison had a dairy in Overstrand before World War 1; by the time of the 1916 directory it was a 'dairy & tea room'.

Telegraph. When England feared invasion by Napoleon, chains of telegraph stations were established using flags or semaphore shutters to connect coastal observers with each other, with the fleet and with the Admiralty in London. By 1806 Cromer had a telegraph station on the cliff top near the lighthouse, the high position being necessary if its flags were to be seen through telescopes from the stations at Beeston or Trimingham (part of a line from Holkham to Yarmouth). Stations had two resident signallers.[1] 'Upon the appearance of any ship of war off the coast,' wrote a contemporary, 'signals are hoisted from the different stations,

The telegraph station is just visible next to the lighthouse (1809 or just after).

the answer to which tells the *number* of the ship, from which the commanders at the signal-posts, by referring to their books, immediately learn her name and force.' The Cromer station appears to have fallen out of use by the early 1830s.[2]

The electric telegraph was invented in the 1830s, and in 1858 (just a few years after the first submarine cable was laid from England to France) the Submarine Telegraph Co. commissioned Glass, Elliot & Co. to lay their longest cable, running from Cromer to Weybourne and then across the sea to Hanover; there was a land line from Cromer to London by way of Norwich and Newmarket. The following year another cable was laid from Cromer to Heligoland and Tonning in Denmark. A building behind Tucker's Hotel was used as a telegraph office, which in December 1860 was equipped with eleven of the latest pneumatic relay instruments.[3] 'There were several clerks, of different nationalities, to translate the messages received, but owing to small ships an-

choring the cable was often damaged, and the service was discontinued'.[4] In fact the Danish cable had been cut when it fell into Prussian hands during the war between Denmark and Prussia in 1864. The Hanover cable, damaged early in 1864, was never repaired and the Cromer telegraph station was closed either late in 1864 or in 1865.[5]

The domestic telegraph companies were bought out by the government in 1870, after which the Post Office rapidly expanded the service to rural areas. In the 1880s and 1890s the Post Office's telegraph office in Cromer was open between 8 a.m. and 8 p.m. (and on Sunday from 8 a.m. to 10 a.m.), but this did not give businesses or emergency services direct access to telecommunications equipment. Lloyds established a signal station in Cromer in 1882 as part of a network all round the coast 'to give notice of vessels in distress and requiring assistance, the state of the wind & the weather' etc.[6]

In 1892 Sir Edward Birkbeck proposed in the House of Commons that all coastguard and lifeboat stations should be linked by telegraph.[7] ¶ In 1888 the Cromer Local Board gave the Post Office permission to erect telegraph poles to extend the telegraph to Overstrand.[8]

Telephones. Cromer and Wroxham were the first Norfolk towns to have telephones, outside of Norwich and Yarmouth. The GPO converted their second telegraph line from Norwich into a telephone trunk line, to which the National Telephone Co. connected a local magneto exchange with eight subscribers;[1] permission was given by the council in 1895 to erect a telephone line between Cromer and North Walsham, running up Bond Street, Cross Street and Love Lane, across the brickfield and up to the railway station at the top of the Norwich Road.[2] (The NTC took a five-year lease on 5 Church Street in September 1907.[3])

Within a year or two, telephones were installed for five of Cromer's hotels (all built in the 1890s), both railway stations, doctors, chemist, vet, estate agent, solicitors, a dozen tradesmen who supplied the hotels – all of these evidently regarding the telephone as a useful business tool rather than a mere status symbol – and for Lord Suffield and the golf club.[4]

When the GPO took over the system at the beginning of 1912, Cromer telephone exchange had one (female) operator, who was paid eleven shillings a week.[5]

The new exchange building on Louden Road, with Dutch gables, was erected in 1936, and remained in use until 1985, though the switchgear had by that time already been housed in a utilitarian building next door.

❡ Overstrand had a telephone exchange opposite the junction of the Coast Road and Mundesley Road.[6]

Tennis. The game of lawn tennis was not invented until 1874, when one of the participants in the first match ever played is said to have been Clement Scott. Rye refers to tennis being played both 'on and off the sands'. The local tennis club was formed in 1908.

Cliff House in 1914 had two tennis lawns and tennis was being played by local private girls' schools.[1]

The Locker-Lampson family were very keen on tennis, and built covered courts at Newhaven Court – the company

A tennis match on the lawn of Cromer Hall in the 1880s.

formed for the purpose in 1924 included among its shareholders not only local citizens but Sir Robert McAlpine (which presumably means his firm built the courts) and Slazengers.[2] Many great players, including Suzanne Lenglen,[3] stayed and played here before it was burnt down in the early 1960s.

The tennis club on the opposite side of the Norwich Road, renowned for its grass courts, added squash courts to its facilities in 1979–80.[4]

Terrace. Older name for The CRESCENT.

Terrace Road. Name given in the 1861 census to Surrey Street.

Theatre. In the 19th century touring companies of 'barn-stormers' would come for a three-day visit, performing several plays in a barn near what is now the bottom of Mount Street, or at one of the pubs.

The Town Hall functioned as a theatre from 1890 until 1963 – Lillie Langtry appeared here for a week in 1906. Later buildings occasionally used for plays include the Women's Institute hall in Garden Street and the hall of the Cromer High School, but the sale of the Town Hall in 1963 left the Pavilion Theatre on Cromer pier as the town's main theatre. 📖 For further details see Christopher Pipe, *The Story of Cromer Pier* (Poppy

Pupils from WOOD-DENE SCHOOL *in Cliff Avenue play on the beach, 1986/87. The school later provided a number of pupils for theatre, film and television work.*

land Publishing, 1998). *See also* ACTORS.

¶ **Thurst Road.** Thomas Thurst was licensee of the White Horse in Overstrand from 1790; the pub was put up for sale after Mrs Thurst's death in 1828. The name is sometimes, most appropriately, spelled Thirst. A plot of building land here was sold in 1897 for £25, and £450 spent erecting two houses.[1] Further development of land that had once belonged to the pub took place in the early years of the 21st century under the name of White Horse Gardens.

Tithes. Tithes were the church tax of one tenth of farm produce. In the 1380s, the tithe payable in Cromer worked out as follows:[1]

	£	s	d	
corn	15	0	0	33%
lambs/wool	1	6	8	3%
fowls/sucking pigs	1	6	8	3%
heather/hay		6	8	< 1%
wood	13	6	8	29%
herrings	13	6	8	29%
dairies/dovecote		6	8	< 1%
hemp/brushwood		2	0	< ¼%
eggs		1	6	< ¼%
mill		13	4	1½%

Thus it is clear that Cromer's wealth did not come from wool, but from trade in corn, wood and herrings.

Tourism. It was in the 1780s and 1790s that the large families of QUAKERS discovered the delights of Cromer and started a fashion for taking long holidays here. A North Walsham solicitor selling a Cromer property in 1801 boasted that 'Cromer is situated in the most romantic part of the county of Norfolk, and is much resorted to by genteel families during the summer season, having an extremely pleasant beach, with several bathing machines.'[1] As more and more houses were taken over by their friends and relatives for the season, inns such as TUCKER'S HOTEL sprang up or were modernised and ordinary families rearranged their lives to accommodate visitors. BUILDERS embarked upon speculative projects and landowners saw fresh possibilities in any vacant plot that overlooked the sea, such as NORTH LODGE PARK. Progress was not uniform, however, as the adjacent panel testifies. Only later, with the advent of the railways, did tourism boom.

Tourist Information Centres. 1. An early attempt to help visitors to Cromer find accommodation was conducted by Francis Pank, who by the beginning of the 19th century kept at his houses a Register of Lodgings 'where, for the trifling sum of one shilling, every relative information may be had, as to size, number of beds, price, when vacant, &c.'[1]

2. The first Council-run Tourist Information Centre was the little

Complaints about poor holiday seasons are nothing new. On 21 August 1850 the Bury and Norwich Post *printed this contribution:*

Cromer, August 19.
The number of visitors to this delightful watering place has not been so great this summer as in former seasons, and we regret to say that many of the inns and lodging houses have been unoccupied. Attempts have been made to get up some races on the beach, and if they take place there will doubtless be a great influx of company.

The writer goes on to extol the many attractions of Cromer and its locality, and was presumably part of a campaign to promote the resort. Ten years later, Thomas Boulter at Tucker's Hotel found business 'a total failure', and it was 'very little better' in 1861, when he told Benjamin Bond Cabbell (the owner) that he could not continue. Compare this with the following letter from Mrs E. Rogers (who rented a house in West Street) to her landlord Benjamin Bond Cabbell or his agent. It is dated 9th January 1861; the original has no punctuation whatever. A covering note from Mr Cabbell indicates that Mrs Rogers owed five quarters' rent.

I take the Libety of writing to Ask A grate favour As I have Had A very Bad sumer in leten the House wich make us feel very unhapy As whe cannot pay the Rent this year. I though whe should Be Able to pay A part But I Am very much Afrid that whe cannot. I Am sorry to say that I have not got mor then five pounds After paying Buts A tacks And set [*rates and tax etc.*]. Sir, the Resen is I had to By meny things for the House when I took it And this year I was oblige to pay for them. As it Have Been a Bad Sumer for my peple As wel As my slef, But if you will elow me to stay till michaelmas And see if I makes A better Sesen, if not I shall Be oblige to Leave the House thow I shall Be sory After spenden so much in painting A papern And putting up stores to make it fit for leten

Sir I shall Bee Anches [*anxious*] to hear

(Transcribed from NRO: MC 97/7, 538 x 1. The 1861 census shows that Eliza Rogers, 33, was a dressmaker with a baby girl and had, on census night, just one lodger, a local youth. Her husband Ellis Rogers, then aged 30, was a carpenter.)

thatched building at the top of the Gangway.

3. When Eastern Counties buses no longer required their booking office at the bus station, the Tourist Information Centre was moved there.

4. A new information centre was opened on the Meadow car park in 2008, designed to offer information on North Norfolk to local people as well as tourists. Architects Stead Mutton of Sheringham included solar power and underground heat pumps in the design, which also included new public toilets to replace those at the junction of Louden Road and Bond Street.[2]

Town criers. Savin lists the following 'bellmen': Tom Kennedy, John Mack (1841–89), James Mack and R. Warner. Dick Laurence was town crier in the 1930s and was reappointed in 1952[1] and was succeeded by Alfie Howard (*see under* CARNIVALS) and later by the appropriately named Jason Bell. A record of 1897 states that the town crier had to provide his own bell (one such bell found its way to Cromer Museum), though the Council had the bell after World War 2 when they had nobody to ring it.

Town Hall. Built in 1890 (architect George Skipper)[1] as a theatre and meeting place. Its attached garage housed the fire engine; the latter was subsequently moved into a building on the other side of Canada Road, and the vacated garage used as a scenery and prop store and in 1905 converted into dressing rooms.[2]

The Cromer Town Hall Company, formed in 1889, was dissolved in 1964.[3] The building was used as a warehouse by Rust's, then in the 1990s as a Co-op shop before the building of their new store in Middlebrook Way, and then became a plumbers' merchants, the offices being used variously by architects, accountants, solicitors and others.

See also ARMORIAL BEARINGS; THEATRE.

Trams. Before the advent of the railway, there was a proposal to run a tram service from Norwich to Cromer. It would probably have made for shorter journey times than coaches could achieve, because the horses would have found it easier to pull a vehicle along metal rails than over the indifferent road surface.

Trent House (Overstrand Road). Built (as Trent Cottage) *c.* 1890; it had more than an acre of ground including meadow, kitchen garden, stables etc. Henry Broadhurst MP lived here.[1]

Tucker Street. Named 'Hotel Street' in the map accompanying the sale of the Cromer Hall estate in 1852, on account of the importance of TUCKER'S HOTEL. The street was widened on the north side in connection with the building of the Metropole Hotel in 1893,[1] and by some six feet on the south side at the expense of the churchyard in 1896.[2] The road was made up in 1894.[3]

CROMER CHARACTERS
GEORGE COOKE TUCKER

Tucker came to Cromer as a tide-waiter (customs officer) and stayed to become one of the place's most influential figures. Taking over the only hotel (the Hotel de Paris had not yet been founded), he invested £100 in the extension of the turnpike road from Norwich and Aylsham,[1] clearly foreseeing that Cromer's new-found popularity as a seaside resort would be enhanced if people could reach the place more easily. His inn's location was the best – it was opposite the church, it was the terminus for coaches to and from Norwich, and 'directly under the Cliff, on which it is situated, the Bathing Machines are every morning drawn out upon the sands'.[2] One diarist in 1821 wrote of 'Tucker's Inn, which is the principal Inn in Cromer, and the Master of it is nearly King of Cromer.'[3] Under his reign the inn was used for lifeboat dinners, meetings of the Poor Law board, magistrates' Petty Sessions etc. Another diarist praised the 'obliging Landlord . . . & Landlady & their most civil and attentive Daughters . . . the cleanliness of the House . . . the ready attention of the servants'.[4] Tucker died in 1842, aged 90 (his iron gravestone is in the churchyard just opposite the site of his inn).

Tucker's Hotel. A two-storey building is shown on this site in a map of 1717.[1] It was originally called the Royal Oak (under which name it is included in the rates list for 1767). In 1788 it was taken over by John Wilson, formerly a waiter at the Feathers, Holt; he renamed it the New Inn, and seems to have been the first person to turn it into an inn meeting the requirements of a nascent holiday resort.

In the early 19th century the hotel was taken over, and rebuilt, by George Cooke Tucker, who thus gave his name not only to the hotel but to the street it stood in.

The business was taken over by Thomas Boulter, who is also listed as a brewer, auctioneer and estate agent. In 1860 he found the business 'a total failure' and it was 'very little better' the next year, so he told owner Benjamin Bond Cabbell in October 1861 that he could not continue; in 1862 came James Chapman, who sold it in the early 1870s to the Jarvis family, who kept it for decades, along with the Hotel de Paris.

Tucker's was used as a billet for troops during World War 2. It suffered war damage and was demolished in January 1958. A small hotel continued trading under the name of 'Tucker's Family Hotel' in the house next to Brunswick House (overlooking the Gangway) until the 1990s.

See also OLD LOOKOUT.

Tucker's Tap (Jetty Street, adjoining Barclays Bank). The tap room associated with Tucker's Hotel; later called Tucker's Cottage. It was connected to the network of underground TUNNELS which linked Tucker's with its annexe on the Promenade, and with the Hotel de Paris and other properties. It remained part of the same property as the Hotel de Paris even as late as the 1964 sale.

Tudor House (Cliff Avenue). Designed by A. F. Scott for a Mr Livock of Oulton, this house was built in 1901. In its early years there were 26 servants here, and guests included Princess Stephanie (daughter of Leopold, King of the Belgians) and her husband Count Lonyay.[1] The building became a hotel in the 1920s, remaining a Christian holiday home until 2007. It was then converted into flats

under the name of Tudor Villas.

Tudor Café (Church Street). *See* TEA ROOMS.

Tudor Villas. *See* TUDOR HOUSE.

Tunnels.[1] Underground tunnels have certainly existed in Cromer, though their extent, purpose and interconnection have often been exaggerated. The best attested led from the Bath House via Lower Tucker's Hotel to Tucker's Hotel itself and the cellars of the Hotel de Paris and Belle Vue Hotel. These may have been linked to the King's Head and to the tunnel which until the second half of the 20th century could be entered behind Lane's wallpaper shop (the High Street/Jetty Street) and followed under Imperial House where it divided, one branch going eastward under Barclays Bank and along Tucker Street until it reached the basement of the Metropole Hotel, while the other branch led to the cellar of Hanover House and thence towards the church.

Most reports describe the tunnels as lined with brick, though that from Hanover House towards the church may have been of stone; both types had niches, perhaps for candles to provide light.

Were these tunnels once used by smugglers? On the Norfolk/Suffolk border, Gorleston vicarage was built with large cellars which are supposed to have been used for the storage of smuggled goods, and until the late

19th century they were connected by a tunnel to a landing stage.[2] Cromer's tunnels appear to have linked the cellars of the town's leading merchants (Field's and Rust's in the High Street and Ditchell's barn in Tucker Street) with the boathouse which stood on the shore where the Bath House was later built. This could suggest a desire to move goods covertly from landing place to trading warehouses, but hard evidence is lacking.

Another very tentative interpretation could be based on reports that the tunnel under Tucker Street emerged on the cliff face in front of the Red Lion, which is close to the Napoleonic fortifications. Could tunnels have led there from stores of ammunition kept in the church tower? Savin tells us that the battery volunteers' arms were kept in the church, and when the gallery in the tower was taken down over 400 cartridges were found behind the woodwork, thought to have been placed there during the Napoleonic war.[3] Moreover, Benjamin Rust from his shop just opposite (also connected to the tunnels) sold flints for guns. The idea of such a tunnel may therefore not be as fanciful as it appears.

Turnpike road. The Norwich to Aylsham and Cromer Highway Act was passed in 1811, permitting the extension of the Norwich–Aylsham turnpike to Cromer. For the most part it followed existing roads, but improvements to the road surface were financed by tolls (the nearest toll house to Cromer was at Crossdale Street). Capital was invested by local landowners and by anyone who saw a need to improve communications. Tolls continued to be collected until the railway reached Cromer in 1877.

📖 A booklet by Valerie Belton, *The Norwich to Cromer Turnpike* (the author, 1998), is based on a study of the surviving archives; unfortunately, there is a gap in the archives covering the years when the road was extended to Cromer.

U

Ufford's Hall. One of the medieval manors of Cromer, lying to the west of Cromer Gunners; CROMER HALL was the manor house. Before 1066 the lord of the manor was Osbern; the Normans ejected him and gave it to Roger Bigod (or Bigot), the tenant in 1086 being Thurston.[1] The Ufford family owned it in the 14th century, the Arnold family in the 15th; Robert Underwood bought it in 1581 and passed it to his son James (they are both buried in the church) whose widow married a Wyndham. It remained in that family until its sale to Benjamin Bond Cabbell in 1852.[2]

Upton House (Norwich Road). On the site of The Crossway House, which with its orchard, yard and garden had before 1802 been part of Susannah Ellis Brooke's property occupied by 'Widow Webb &c.'[1] (A house is shown here on Bellard's map of 1717, the owner's name there being Robert Frary.)

The Crossway House was pulled down and rebuilt a few yards further back from the road in 1884; it was called Upton House after the Essex property of the Buxton family who lived here.

The house became a hotel in 1936, then from 1963 to 2008 a home for the elderly, then converted into offices.

V

Vicarage. In 1272 the Rector of St Peter's church, Shipden, had a house with twelve acres of land, which must have been lost to the sea during the course of the following century.

The next recorded clergy house was built in the 1380s, somewhere between the present Bath House and Red Lion steps; the land on which it stood extended to three-quarters of an acre in 1627, but had entirely succumbed to the sea by 1709.[1] In 1784 the vicar was living in rented accommodation, there being no parsonage house;[2] in the first half of the 19th century the vicar lived in West Street.

Scattered portions of GLEBE rented to the Cromer Hall estate were exchanged in 1843 for a single piece of land on which a new vicarage was built in 1854; the architect was Thomas Jeckell;[3] this gave its name to Vicarage Road. In the 1890s the house was reckoned to need 14 servants![4] It was sold on the change of incumbent in 1946/7 and a larger house in Cromwell Road became the vicarage; by the 1970s, however, this was thought to be too large and a new house was built behind it to give the vicar more manageable accommodation.

Vicarage Road. On the site of GLEBE LANE, this road connects the former VICARAGE with the Norwich Road. The houses were built from the 1890s on, including designs by Norfolk architects A. F. Scott, John Newman and George Skipper.

📖 See A. D. Boyce, *Harmonious Houses in Exquisite Surroundings* (Cromer Preservation Society Guides, 2008), pp. 12–15.

Vicars and Rectors of Cromer. The following were rectors:

1337   John de Lodbrok
       who initiated the church rebuilding programme
1349   Robert Broun de Wyngreworth
       who was also rector of Forncett; he died in 1353
1353   William de Mirfield
       who was rector of Gimingham in 1342
n.d.   John Winter
       probably of the Winter family of Barningham Winter

1364 Richard Gosseline de Eriswell

1375 John de Stalham
a canon of Hickling Priory

1381 Robert Ellalle
who seems to have retired when the
Carthusians took over from Hickling
Priory as patrons of the living

The following were Vicars:

1384 John Gosselyn of Eriswell
who in his will (proved 1389)
left, amongst other bequests to the
church, 10 lb. of silver for a new
east window; if he is the same as
the John Goscelyn who in 1354 had
a Sedgeford merchant imprisoned
in Norwich castle for a debt of £40,[1]
then he was a merchant of some
consequence

1389 John Hermere
whose will was proved in 1403

1403 Richard Bishop
previously (1378) vicar of Paston

1429 Richard Milham
who is buried in the chancel

1437 Simon Norman
who in 1439/40 acquired some
property in Bawdeswell (together
with the chaplain there, and other
people);[2] *he died in 1450*

1450 Geoffrey Champneys
also known as Galfr. Gaminsewyn,
who later resigned and became vicar
of St Stephen's Norwich; a radical
cleric with Lollard sympathies, he
bequeathed a Lollard book to his
successor at Cromer

1462 Robert Hayle
or Hayles or Hellys or Heylis,
who seems to have come from a
Roughton family; he died in 1479
and was buried in the chancel

1497 William Tugge *or* Tukke
who was also parson of Gunton; he
died in 1521 and was buried in the
chancel

1521 William Smith

1549 or earlier
Robert Roston *or* Ruston
possibly the same as the Robert
Ryston, canon, whose brass was in
the church at Beeston Regis and
hence may have been a canon of
Beeston Priory

1554/5 John Harlow
who had been a canon at Walsing-
ham, and vicar of Binham in 1551;
he was dead by 1574

1584 or earlier
Stephen Roberts
who was sued in that year for ne-
glecting to repair the vicarage house

1584 William Burton

1587 Simon Harward

1591 Thomas Munday
(various spellings, of which he him-
self generally preferred Mundye) a
preaching vicar, and schoolteacher
– he had been licensed to teach
grammar at Aylsham in 1584;[3] *he*
was also rector of Thorpe Market
in 1600, and of Sidestrand (where
he was buried) 1600–39 (marrying
Mary Secker there in 1634); he was
appointed rector of Overstrand in

1606

1601   John Money *or* Mony
      who was also vicar of Overstrand

1605   Richard Watson
      probably the same as the Watson
      who was vicar of Calthorpe a few
      years earlier

1626   Richard Talbot

There follows a period of some confusion in the records – the 1640s and 1650s were the period of the Civil War and Commonwealth when ecclesiastical appointments were made in new ways. At some point William Talbot seems to have become Vicar but was an absentee minister, living in another parish. A Thomas Talbot is recorded as having created a vacancy by his death in 1663, which is difficult to square with the next few perplexing records:

1659   Robert Smyth
      appointed on the previous incum-
      bent's death

1661   Henry Brignell
      was appointed, but there is no record
      of him ever taking office

1662/3 Robert Fawcett
      who was also vicar of Roughton

1670   William Ashmore

1676   Michael Frere

1694   William Ashmore
      who was also vicar of Overstrand
      (1670) and rector of Sidestrand
      (1686); when he died in 1712 he was
      separated from his wife but was able
      to leave property in Cromer to John

Kirby as well as the residue of his estate to a son in London[6]

1716   Timothy Bullimore
      owner of Stalham Hall; his wife
      Elizabeth was a daughter of William Ellis of Northrepps; Bullimore
      became a master at Norwich Grammar School, went on to minister in
      Oulton and Stalham, and died in
      1750

1723   Wormly Martin

1729   Framlingham Price

1743/4 Wormley Martin (senior)
      of Southrepps; also rector of Beeston
      Regis from 1756

1763   Wormley Martin (junior)
      son of the previous incumbent

1768   Richard Sibbs[7]
      ordained deacon 1766, priest 1769;
      he was also curate of Sheringham
      (1768–1804) and incumbent of Sustead (1769–84) and (from 1778) of
      West Beckham[8] *and became rector*
      of Thurgarton in 1781;[9] *he married*
      a daughter of Cromer merchant
      Anthony Ditchell and is buried in
      Cromer church

1804   John Short Hewett
      baptised in Bengal in 1779; Cromer
      was his first living

1807   George Glover
      Archdeacon of Sudbury and for 58
      years rector of Southrepps; Larry
      Banville wrote in his diary for 9
      September 1807 the he 'heard a good
      sermon preached by Mr Glover all
      about charity, but he have none of it.
      I suppose he would not give a penny

to a poor man if it would save his life.' Glover, who was closely involved politically with Lord Suffield, died in 1862[10]

1831   William Sharpe

William Sharpe in old age

Vicar of Gimingham. An evangelical, he would not accept the living of Cromer until he had found a suitable curate, because he did not want to leave Gimingham and be succeeded there by a non-evangelical. 'Mr. Sharpe . . . was four and a half feet tall with a head disproportionately large; his wife topped a comfortable six feet. Sharpe had but one eye and that already beginning to lose its sight. He preached standing on a stool, with his notes held high to his eye.'[11] Sharpe evidently had

a sharp sense of humour, for he referred to the argumentative Sir John Boileau as 'Sir John Boil-over'. After his retirement, Sharpe continued to live in Louden Road

Frederick Fitch

The following was first Vicar and later Rector:

1852   Frederick Fitch
in whose time the church was restored; he died in 1897

The following was Rector:

1896   James F. Sheldon
who had been rector of St Leonard's, Exeter since 1887;[12] later moved to Birmingham; he returned to lead the beach mission in 1906, 1908 and 1911[13]

The following were Vicars:

1905   Willliam F. T. Hamilton
*who had been a vicar in Woking; he
retired in 1916*

1916   Edmund Mapletoff Davys
*previously at Babbacombe, Devon;[14]
in 1938 he became Rector of Horton
in the diocese of Gloucester[15]*

1939   A. Gilbert Barclay
*a son of Ellen Buxton; he was previ-
ously Rector of Great Holland; in
1946 he became Rector of Langley in
Kent[16]*

1947   Daniel T. Dick
*who had been Vicar of Gorleston
and then at Beverley Minster; from
Cromer he retired to Wroxham[17]*

1960   Charles W. J. Searle-Barnes
*who then went on to become Vicar
of Tonbridge[18]*

1971   Derek Osborne
*who moved to Emmanuel Church,
Northwood, but returned to live in
Cromer in his retirement*

1984   David Hayden
*who became Archdeacon of Norfolk
in 2002*

2002   David Court
*formerly Vicar of Mile Cross in
Norwich*

Victoria Restaurant. *See* LECTURE HALL.

Victoria Terrace. Name used **1.** in the
1851 census for the dwellings on the
Promenade; **2.** for certain houses in
Vicarage Road in the 1890s.

Victorian Tea Rooms (Meadow Road).
Converted in the early years of the 21st
century from the coach house belonging to GORDON HOUSE.

Virginia Court Hotel (Cliff Avenue).
Built 1899-1900 (architect George Sher-
ring of London; builder Richard Chapman of Hanworth) as a gentlemen's club
house: the 1901 census shows a resident
steward, cook (wife of the steward) and
footman. The club was started by local
doctors and gentry, and offered a dining
room, smoking room and reading room.
It was running at a loss by 1924, and the
original company liquidated; the club itself bought the house and contents but
was wound up in 1932.[1]

W

War. *See* FORTIFICATIONS; MILITIA; WORLD
WAR 1; WORLD WAR 2.

War memorial. W. D. Caröe's design,
incorporating statuettes of a soldier, a
sailor, an airman and a nurse, was approved at a series of public meetings in
1919, against fierce opposition from the
Vicar, who thought the crucifix a pop-
ish symbol. It was unveiled in 1921.[1]

An additional memorial tablet was
placed in the church in 2010 recording
the deaths of those who had served in
later conflicts, including Afghanistan.

Warnes Close. Land owned by H. Bullen & Sons (managing director: Norton Warnes), once used for the pasturing of ponies and donkeys. In the 1950s it was turned into a cricket ground, with the later addition of two small blocks of flats and a new surgery for the town's doctors, opened in 1969.

Warren, The. House on the Overstrand Road, originally called The Cottage; if there was actually a warren here, it would have been of some economic importance: accounts for the neighbouring Felbrigg estate show payments for many hundreds of rabbits a year in the 1670s and 1680s, with a carefully managed stock of between one and two thousand rabbits on that warren – but the Felbrigg warrener 'grew rich, married, and woud noe longer endure the hardship of a warrener's life'.[1] That the sandy hills of Cromer and Overstrand have long been attractive for rabbits

is evident in the name of Conisburgh Hill (spelled 'Cunny Borowe hill' in a document of 1626) – coney being an old word for rabbit.[2]

As late as the 1851 census there was a warrener in Cromer, James Smith, then aged 50, but as he lived in 'West Road' it seems likely that he was employed on the Cromer Hall estate rather than on the eastern side of Cromer.

The Cottage was bought by Robert Barclay c. 1820 when he married a daughter of Joseph Gurney of the house next door (The GROVE). He added to it, as did his son Joseph Gurney Barclay; the next Robert Barclay built HERNE CLOSE, and The Warren was therafter used as a holiday home for various other family members – Gilbert Barclay remembered it as 'a very rambling house with five staircases, ideal for children on rainy days to play hide and seek',[3] and the 1901 census shows seven servants living in.

The Warren about 1890.

The house was used by SUTHERLAND HOUSE SCHOOL from 1946 and demolished in 1975 to make way for the WARREN COURT flats.

The house also gave its name to the road constructed on the land formerly belonging to the house after its sale in 1935.

Warren Court. Flats built in the 1970s to house tenants of the Greater London Council;[1] the site was previously occupied by the house known as The WARREN.

Warren Woods. *See* LIME KILN; SUMMER HOUSE.

Watch House, The. Built ?1830[1] to replace WEBB'S HOUSE, and used as a coastguard station in the 19th century; rockets were launched from its grounds (so it was also known as the Old Rocket House) and there was a bowling green in front, belonging to the Red Lion – the Ellis/Brooke/Webb family once had considerable shipping interests and owned property on each side of the Gangway and on the seaward side of what became North Lodge Park, but it was rapidly being lost to the sea through erosion.

The Watch House remained in use by the COASTGUARDS until 1895.

Water supply. A parcel of land near the rectory house in 1383 was called Well Yard because it had a spring.[1] Until late in the 19th century, Cromer people obtained their water from shallow wells, from pumps and from the two becks flowing down to the sea, and the quality (if not the quantity) seems always to have been esteemed. As early as 1633, the Norwich gentleman Anthony Mingay, concerned for his health, wrote: 'I doe determine, God favouringe, this sumer to make use of the waters; and to that purpose have gott the Doctor Martine to ride to Cromer to make perfect triall of a water thereabout; and if that prove not, then, God willing, I am for Tunbridg.'[2] This seems to imply some sort of spa, but whether it was in Cromer itself or elsewhere in the vicinity is unclear.

The original town pump was in front of Fountain House at the junction of West Street and Church Street, and gave its name to Pump Street (later called Chapel Street). In mid-Victorian times it was opened for an hour in the morning and an hour in the afternoon, and water was charged at a penny a pail.[3] As late as 1888, though beyond repair, it was in sufficiently regular use to warrant being replaced with a new one.[4]

A second pump was known as Happy Jack.[5] This is presumably the one which was in Louden Road, against the wall of the Meadow at the corner of West Street.

A pump mentioned in 1813 near the bottom of the Norwich Road was for the use of the cottages on the Upton

House site;[6] this was known as Brown's Yard (John Brown was a maltster in Cromer in 1825) and his successor on the site, J. W. Baker, was able to sell water to the public from his wells when other supplies ran dry in the summer. Nearby was a property occupied by Mrs Chadwick, who had to fetch water from a well until permission was given in 1869 to lay a pipe and pump.[7] When Cromer Museum was given a pump by a Trimingham farmer, they sited it over a well which would have served the occupants of East Cottages.[8]

S. Jarvis sank the 'town well' in 1868. A water company was set up in 1875 and sank an 81-foot (24.7 m) well and a 400-foot (122 m) borehole at the pumping station in Roughton Road. The reservoir at the top of Arbor Hill appears on the Ordnance Survey map of 1887.

These developments still did not meet the needs of all the summer visitors – in August 1888 supply was stopped at certain hours of the day[9] and on 1 September a local paper reported that 'the company's mains have been completely stopped since last Sunday, and one or two trucks of water are instead delivered to householders by the Waterworks Company free of charge, but as in so many cases this is not nearly sufficient, householders have to pay men for water fetched from the parish pump and other sources'.[10] The Royal Links Hotel (built 1892) had its own deep well and pump house.

New works were added to the pump-ing station in Roughton Road[11] in 1892, and this seems to have rendered the town pump redundant since it was converted to a drinking fountain the following year.[12] A water tower was erected for the Great Eastern Railway at the top of the Norwich Road, in 1896/97, holding 50,000 gallons; it was demolished in 1974, after the cessation of all railway traffic at the neighbour-ing High station.[13]

The Urban District Council took over the waterworks by compulsory purchase in 1901.[14]

In 1902 arrangements were made for obtaining water from a borehole at Metton in order to see Cromer through the summer months; this was not needed after the middle of October, but a new well at Metton was ordered, the tender of Thomas Tilley & Sons of London being accepted for carrying out the work, which began in 1903.[15] In the same year it was agreed to build a larger reservoir on the very high ground at Aylmerton, water being pumped there from Metton.[16]

A new filtration plant was opened at the Metton pumping station in 1914 to remove iron deposits.

Water Works Lane. Another name for Roughton Road, at a time when the waterworks were there.

Waterloo Street. Name given in the 1840 tithe map to what became known as Garden Street.

Weavers. Although Cromer was outside the main areas of weaving in Norfolk, it seems that some weaving was carried out here in the first half of the 16th century: the wills of Thomas and John Barker, proved in 1549 and 1555 respectively, describe them as linen weavers, and that of Simon Daynes (1557) describes him as a worsted weaver.

Webb's house. Old house on the east cliff, belonging to Alexander Webb. It was apparently built of timbers salvaged from wrecks, and was famously crooked. In the 1820s it was occupied by the coastguard, who in 1828 asked permission from the owner to demolish it and rebuild further inland, since it was only six feet from the cliff edge and was 'Daily in expectation of being washed Down & forsed into the sea'.[1]

See also WATCH HOUSE.

Wellington (Garden Street). Originally built probably between 1790 and 1795 as a smaller house and renamed in honour of the Duke of Wellington's victory at Waterloo in 1815 (Garden Street was still called Waterloo Street by the tithe surveyors in 1840). On the street corner were fishermen's cottages, in one of which Henry Blogg is said to have been born; these were demolished and the pub extended to include nine bedrooms as well as its brewhouse, bar and tap. The costs of extension seem to have been too great for licensee John Whitting to bear, for the *Norwich*

Mercury of 22 March 1817 advertised the bankruptcy sale of the Wellington.[1]

In 1822 a play was put on at the Wellington: a playbill in Cromer Museum gives prices for 'Pit' and 'Gallery'. By this time the inn was in the hands of Thomas Brown (it is listed in Pigot's directory as the 'Lord Wellington', though this was not its original name), and by 1826 Robert Sunman, a carpenter and wheelwright who in 1838 would build Sheringham's first lifeboat and who went on to become licensee of Sheringham's Windham Arms. (There was also a Robert Sunman who was a cordwainer in Gresham, and moved to Sheringham *c.* Michaelmas 1807.) In 1830 'that well accustomed Tavern called the Wellington Inn at Cromer, with good Yards and Stables, now in the occupation of Mr. Brown or his under tenant, who is under an agreement to quit at Michaelmas next', was advertised to be let by its owner, William Temple of Southrepps. Thomas Brown is listed in the 1830 directory as brewer on Norwich Road with livery stables and a lodging house in Garden Street.

The pub's licensee in the 1830s and 1840s was Tabitha Ransom, who is also listed as licensee of the Norfolk Hotel – it is not clear whether this was the Wellington or another establishment. The pub was later owned by Philip Primrose of the Trunch Brewery. William Walpole Amis, the licensee, became its owner in 1882.

The original building was burnt down and rebuilt in the 1890s; it was bought by Steward & Patteson in 1932; when offered at auction in 1975 it failed to reach its reserve.

A new pub sign in 1998 bizarrely depicted a Wellington bomber; fortunately it was short-lived!

See also TEA-ROOMS.

Wellington Street. Old name for Garden Street.[1]

Wells. *See* WATER SUPPLY.

West Cliff Hotel. *See* DOLPHIN.

West Cottage (Louden Road). Formerly known as School Cottages. The plot is shown on the tithe map of the 1840s as extending to a cluster of buildings on Church Street; at this date the piece is owned by the Vicar, Rev. William Sharpe, and is described as 'house, outbuildings, school & yard'. The building consisted of two cottages until, in 1866, it was converted into Cromer's first cottage hospital, under Mrs Stokes as matron. Crawford Holden noted that the old mortuary could still be seen at the back of the building. After the new hospital was built just along the road, William Harrison kept a school here.

West Parade Hotel (Runton Road). Built in the 1890s next to the Grand Hotel. Later became flats and the Anglia Court Hotel.

West Street. One of the older roads of Cromer, lined on one side by humble cottages and the WHITE HORSE pub. It was the way into Cromer from Gresham and other villages, whose farmers would have brought their corn here either to the MALTINGS or for export via the GANGWAY. It later formed the approach to the town for visitors arriving by train from the Midlands.

Westcliff Avenue. Developed in phases (starting in the 1930s) on the site of allotment gardens. Nos 14–20 evens, 9–13 odds were built for the council in 1951[1] and retailers were invited to tender for the two shops at the southern end in 1953 – shops later combined into one and then converted into a flat in the 1990s, by which time local residents were well served by the Safeway supermarket only a short walk away.

Weylands. Part of the King's private manor, held from 1240 by the family 'de Weyland', then from the 15th century by the Paston family; it was bought in the 18th century by George Anson, and in the 19th century by the Repton family, then by William Henry Scott, and in 1862 by Benjamin Bond Cabbell MP (who was already lord of Ufford's Hall manor).[1]

The house called Weylands was built in 1871 for Francis Hoare, and demolished in 1974.

Weylands Court (Overstrand Road). Flats built on the WEYLANDS site.

Whaling. A will of 1483 refers to a cottage in Cromer called 'Bloberhouse', which suggests a connection with whaling.[1] In the 18th century Kings Lynn saw heavy investment in whaling (an Act of 1771 exempted whalers from paying duty on their catches and protected whalers from being pressed for the Navy),[2] and c. 1791 a ship trading from Cromer is described as a 'Greenland-man', i.e. a whaler.[3]

Wheelwrights. As late as the 1930s there was a wheelwright – a Mr Rogers – in the Holt Road.[1]

White Horse. The rates list of 1767 includes reference to land 'formerly belonging to the W[t] Horse', so the pub must be significantly older than that. In 1879/92 it was owned by James Watts of Erpingham; then Benjamin Cook of Aylsham from 1898; then Morgans Brewery of Norwich; then the Norwich Brewery.

Bostock's Menagerie set up their show for a day in the adjoining yard in 1890, and the Goldsmiths' Company paid for all the boys at their school to go.

A room at the pub was used from 1939 as a rest-room for off-duty firemen.[1]

It is said to have a ghost.

❡ The White Horse in Overstrand is mentioned in licensing lists from 1789. It was the property of the Weybourne brewery by the 1840s (their licensee, Robert Summers, also acted as a fish

merchant), then Steward & Patteson from 1897.[2] The present building is largely the work of Norwich builders J. S. Smith.[3] In July 1913, weekly sales were estimated at about five barrels of draught beer, nearly three dozen pints of bottled beer and about 3½ gallons of spirits.[4] The Codling family were licensees from the 1880s to just before World War 2. The building was altered internally in 2006–7 following its purchase by Darren and Sarah Walsgrove.[5] *See also* THURST ROAD.

White House. 1. Building on the corner of Jetty Street and Tucker Street, owned by the Rust family and used by them for banking purposes from 1864. (In the 17th and 18th centuries there had been another large house on the site, belonging to Cromer vicar, William Ashmore and bequeathed by him to John Kirby.[1]) The present house was conveyed to Barclays Bank in 1888 and altered in 1898 and 1921 by Edward Boardman & Son.[2] *See also* BANKS.

2. House at the end of Hartington Road, once a hotel. Plans for building nine new starter homes in the grounds were approved in 2000.[3]

3. Original name of a house in Cromwell Road, built 1909–10,[4] which later became the vicarage.

4. House on the Holt Road, built in Overstrand (near the Overstrand Hotel) but removed brick by brick to Cromer when its original site was threatened with erosion.

White House Estate. Estate of prefabricated bungalows built in the grounds of the WHITE HOUSE in Hartington Road but approached from Jubilee Lane. The road came under Northrepps (part of Erpingham Rural District) until 1952, when Cromer's boundary was altered to include this development and exclude a portion of land south of the Cromer–Overstrand railway line.[1]

White Lion. A house near the Gangway which was lost in one of the cliff falls; since it was called the White Lion, one supposes it was an inn.

Wills. Rye (*Cromer Past and Present*, pp. lxv–lxxx) gives an almost complete list of the surviving wills (proved at Norwich) of Cromer inhabitants from 1484 to 1796. Later wills are indexed in published volumes held in reference libraries and the Norfolk Record Office. The original wills, or copies of them, are available on microfilm in the Norfolk Record Office and the Norfolk Studies Library in Norwich.

Withy bed. *See* OSIER BED.

Women's Institute hall. *See* MEETING HALLS AND ROOMS.

Wood-Dene School. A house in Cliff Avenue called Wood-Dene housed a small private school in the mid-20th century. It reverted to private accommodation, but in January 1986 Mrs Diana Taylor (ignorant of the previous school's existence) started a new Wood-Dene School here with five pupils; after two years the pupil roll had grown to 76, and the school was moved to Aylmerton Hall, where it continued until 2009. *(Picture: page 188.)*

Workhouses. *See* POOR LAW.

Working Men's Club. *See* READING ROOMS.

World War 1. Cromer was the scene of much army training – the lighthouse hills and the field opposite the golf clubhouse were used by the army to

World War 1 soldiers encamped with their horses on the Meadow. Note the bell tents.

Ladies of some social status volunteered to work as nurses in the military hospitals.

practise trench-digging, and the Mission Hall (St Martin's church) in Suffield Park was taken over as a canteen for the soldiers.[1] Soldiers in the Middlesex Yeomanry left Reading for what they thought would be active service, but found themselves passing through Cromer en route for Mundesley![2] With the need for men to serve in the army, the golf course was reduced to nine holes so that green-keeping staff could be laid off, and 13 acres of the main course were put under the plough.[3]

So many of the soldiers encamped in the district were Roman Catholics that the little church on the Overstrand Road was not big enough, even with some of the congregation spilling over into the garden outside, and mass had to be said in the Marlborough Hotel and even in the Town Hall, where there was a congregation of over 700.[4]

Privately financed war hospitals were established in COLNE HOUSE and the RED HOUSE in Cromer; in Overstrand, facilities made available at Overstrand Hall and the Pleasaunce, including what later became the village hall.[5]

Lady Suffield and other local ladies opened a War Hospital Supply Depot in 1915, sending dressings etc. to hospitals at home and abroad.[6]

Sewing party in the Red House hospital.

With the loss of business from holiday visitors during the war the town suffered considerable financial hardship, and even appealed to the government to billet troops in the empty hotels.[7] They were unsuccessful at first, though soldiers were later billeted in, for example, the Grand Hotel.[8]

See also WAR MEMORIAL.

World War 2. East coast towns were declared an evacuation area in 1940; on 2 June nearly 800 children left Cromer Beach station for the Midlands.[1]

The top of the church tower was used as an observation post for fire watchers. The golf course was used for initial training, with practice trenches, mortar emplacements and weapons pits and a pillbox erected in 1941–42; similar activities were conducted on Smallhopes Hill in Overstrand.[2] Some 40 acres of the golf course were requisitioned for cultivation,[3] and the army

occupied Fearns Field and dug air raid trench shelters in North Lodge Park.[4]

Eastern Counties started using gas-fuelled buses in Cromer in 1942.[5]

See also BOMB DAMAGE; FORTIFICATIONS.

Writers. A splendid satire on certain Cromer visitors appeared in a magazine of 1806: 'There is a gentleman here, Mr. L., who generally passes three or four months at Cromer, during which time he writes a novel for the circulating libraries, consisting of five or six volumes, and they tell me they are very pretty reading. Here is another, likewise, who is a poet and dramatic writers; he has (for he told me so himself) written eleven plays within these three years, nine of which are now in the hands of the Drury-lane manager; he has not, however, yet received an answer, but expects one every day, and has left word at his lodgings in town, that every two-penny post letter should be instantly forwarded to him.'[1]

Sir **Arthur Conan Doyle** stayed at the Royal Links Hotel and heard the story of Black Shuck, which inspired his tale of *The Hound of the Baskervilles*. Although that story is set on Dartmoor, the description of Baskerville Hall is notably similar to the appearance of Cromer Hall.

E. F. Benson (1867–1940) used to stay with Lord and Lady Battersea at The Pleasaunce and derived inspiration for some of his ghost stories from the district.[2]

Henry Gee, resident in Suffield Park in the early 21st century, followed his palaeontology studies by working as an editor on the science journal *Nature*, and in his spare time writing science fiction and a book on the science behind J. R. R. Tolkien's fantasy.[3]

Anthony Hope (real name Sir Anthony Hope Hawkins, 1863-1933), barrister and novelist (author of *The Prisoner of Zenda*), stayed frequently in Overstrand.[4]

A. C. Swinburne (1837-1909) stayed at the Bath Hotel (*see* BATH HOUSE) with his friend Theodore Watts-Dunton in 1883, whilst waiting for Louie Jermy's cottage at Overstrand to become available. They came to Overstrand for further autumn holidays in 1884 and later, their last visit being in 1904. It was in this region that he wrote part of *A Midsummer Holiday*, which includes several poems about Cromer and the cliff path. **Theodore Watts-Dunton** (1832-1914) wrote his novel *Aylwin* while staying in this district. A letter he wrote to his fiancée, Clara Reich, implies that she had been at Cromer in 1905, for he tells her how anxious he was when he heard of the fatal accident when the Cromer Express was derailed at Witham – until he realised it was not the train she was travelling on. The two of them had been in Cromer and Overstrand together before their marriage, so maybe it was in this year and he had had to return to London before she did. She was certainly visiting Cromer in 1906 and in 1910.

George R. Sims and **Henry Pettitt** were among other regular guests at the Jermy cottage; while staying at their 'cottage by the sea in Cromer' they wrote for the West End stage.[5]

Florence Barclay, who had a holiday home in Overstrand during World War 1, was the author of a number of popular novels including *The Rosary* (1909). A devout evangelical, she believed fiction should portray only characters worthy of emulation.

Florence Barclay at her writing desk.

See also NEWHAVEN COURT; POPPYLAND; *and the information on Alice Sargant under* GUIDEBOOKS.

X

Y

X-rays. Although Cromer hospital did not acquire an X-ray department until 1914, there was a local case which involved possibly the earliest use of X-rays in England. (*See panel.*)

¶ Yeomans. *See* HILL FARM.

York Mews. Small group of houses built in Corner Street in the early years of the 21st century for Peter Storey, whose butcher's shop in Garden Street backed onto this land. The name was already in use when there was a crab boiler house here before 1981.

AN INTERESTING CASE

In 1895, Laurence Reynolds of Overstrand was shot in the head by a boy with a revolver. Dr Dent operated at Cromer hospital to drain the wound and remove fragments of bone, but the bullet remained in the skull. After remaining unconscious for three weeks, the patient opened his eyes

'Do you know me, Larry?' *inquired the doctor.*

'That I do and all.'

On being asked how he felt, he replied: 'Rarely thirsty and I could do with half a pint of Bullard.'

A few weeks later he was taken to an eye specialist in Norwich, who was so interested in the case that he had X-ray equipment sent over from Germany and used it to locate the bullet. This was in the year that Roentgen produced his first X-ray photographic plates. Dr Dent noted that Larry Reynolds recovered, apart from damage to the vision in his right eye, and was still alive, aged 76, in 1932. Dent notes that he and Dr Fenner had 'with the patient's ready acquiescence . . . purchased Larry's head as we desired to make a section of the track followed by the bullet,' but it looked as though the patient might well outlive the doctors.[1]

York Road. Built in 1893.[1] Made up in 1896.[2]

York Terrace. Row of houses in York Road.

Young Men's Christian Association. In 1908 a branch of the YMCA was established in Cromer and took rooms over Jarrold's shop in Church Street. Here they provided holiday accommodation, a billiard room, reading and writing rooms and a photographic darkroom. There were lectures and debates, outings and a cricket club.[1] Later in the year GORDON HOUSE in West Street was bought as a holiday home. The organisation carried on charitable work amongst the troops in World War I, having a branch in Cross Street

Gordon House as a YMCA holiday home.

and a canteen in a hut on the Meadow, staffed by volunteers from the district; officers regarded this as a more desirable social centre than the pubs, and it had the advantage of giving the men some female companionship.[2] The branch was dissolved in 1928.[3]

Z

Zoo. 1. Cromer's first zoo was opened in 1962 by Coco the Clown on a four-acre site on Howards Hill, which was bought from the Cromer UDC by Coco's daughter Mrs Olga Kerr and her husband Alex, well known as a lion tamer. Lions, tigers, pumas, a bear (Yogi), an elephant (Marjorie) and many birds were kept, as well as a monkey who was famous for smoking cigarettes offered by the visitors.

Mrs Kerr announced her intention of finding a buyer in 1981[1] – an application to the council for having a circus here was refused[2] – but the zoo had to be closed on Christmas Day 1983.

2. 'Amazona' zoo (specialising in animals from South America) was opened in 2008 as a summer tourist attraction on 15 acres of land leased from the Cromer Hall estate, between Hall Road and Roughton Road. It was planned by Ken Sims who had owned the wildlife gardens at Thrigby Hall for more than 30 years.[3]

Houses on the west cliff (Melbourne House at the far end).

Loading ballast bags, which had to be shifted across the boat when tacking against the wind.

The no. 2 rowing lifeboat Alexandra *could not reach the wrecked* Sepoy *in 1933; it was replaced by the* Harriot Dixon *motor lifeboat. Beach launching required good waders!*

SOURCE REFERENCES

Abbreviations for record repositories are as follows:

NHER   Norfolk Historic Environment
Record
(Database maintained by
Norfolk Museums & Archaeology
Service)

NLP   Cromer Town Council
(North Lodge Park, Cromer)

NNDC   North Norfolk District Council

NRO   Norfolk Record Office
(in Norwich)

TNA: PRO   The National Archives
Public Record Office
(at Kew)

Actors

1 *Observer* 25th September 1796, p. 3; Philip H. Highfill, Jr, and others, *A Biographical Directory of Actors, Actress, Musicians, Dancers, Managers and Other Stage Personnel in London, 1660–1800* (Carbondale and Edwardsville: Southern Il-linois University Press, 1993), pp. 178–81. The parish register for West Beckham contains an entry for the baptism of Elizabeth Leake, daughter of Alexander and Margaret Leake, on 18th September 1776, but she would then have been three or four years old if the same register is correct in recording her age as 73 at the time of her burial on 3 May 1846.

2 Dent, *Reminiscences of a Cromer Doctor* edited by Derek Barker, p. 28.

3 Dent, p. 27.

Advowson

1 Walter Rye, *Some Rough Materials for a History of North Erpingham*, vol. 3, pp. 622–3.

2 For a full account of the landowning Reymes family, *see* Alwyn Leslie Raimes, 'Reymes of Overstrand' in *Norfolk Archaeology* xxx (1952), pp. 15–64.

3 NRO: DN/REG 24:31.

4 *The Times* 18 December 1848, p. 2.

Albion

1 Pigot's directory of 1839 lists him as a brewer and beer retailer, but gives no address. The 1843 tithe apportionment shows him at a house and yard in this location, and names Pank as owner.

2 Tithe apportionment (1843) showing Mary Brookes at a beer house, cottage, building and yard owned by John Breese.

3 Petty Sessions proceedings. Savin/Crawford Holden give Mary Brookes at The Albion from 1826, but give no source.

Alfred Road

1 A. D. Boyce, *Pretty Villas & Capacious Hotels* (Cromer Preservation Society, 2006), pp. 3–4.

Almshouses

1 NRO: NNAS Frere MSS, mentioning 'the almshouse at C.' immediately after mentioning the vicar Robert Hales; cf. glebe terrier 1723 (NRO: DN/TER 52/3/4).

2 Savin, p. 88.

Ambulances

1 Neil R. Storey, *Cromer St John Ambulance and Auxiliary War Hospitals during the First World War: Historical Notes* (unpublished).

2 Dent, *Reminiscences of a Cromer Doctor* (edited by Derek Barker), pp. 79–80. Cf. 'Reliving ambulance history' in the *Eastern Daily Press* 31 March 2000, p. 31; *Cromer, Sheringham and District Weekly Press* 27 February 1915, p. 6, col. 7.

Arbor Hill

1 Glebe terrier in NRO (MC 989/1, 801 x 7).

2 Cromer Gunners court book, 1755.

Armorial bearings

1 Rye, *Some Rough Materials,* p. 3.

2 Sales particulars of the Grand Hotel, 1925, in the Norfolk Heritage Centre.

3 Bernard Burke, *The General Armory of England* (Harrison, 1864), p. 246.

4 Rye, *Some Rough Materials,* pp. 5–6.

Artists

1 Sydney D. Kitson, *The Life of John Sell Cotman* (London: Faber, 1937), p. 129.

2 Kitson, pp. 111, 127, 356, 360; letter to Dawson

Turner, 17 October 1841 (NRO: MC 2487/56 977x3).

3 The picture was bought for Norwich Castle Museum in 1976: *The Journal* 5 March 1976.

4 *Ellen Buxton's Journal 1860–1864* (London: Bles 1967).

5 The *Eastern Daily Press* of 3 December 1901 says that 'the well-known artist, Mr Edward Pocock' died at the Norfolk and Norwich Hosptial at the age of 58, but another Edward Pocock, described as 'An Artist Painter of St Stephens', died in Heigham workhouse on 3 October 1905 at the age of 59.

Assembly room

1 *Norwich Mercury* 30 August 1828; cf. also 9 August.

Auction rooms

1 Poster in NLP, advertising auction in the Lecture Hall of building land in Station Road, 12 October 1937.

2 NNDC: PLA/19781574.

Avon House School

1 Savin, p. 134; Local Board committee minute book (NLP: CR61), pp. 12–13.

2 Photograph *c.* 1903 reproduced in Philip Bligh, *A History of Cromer Beach Mission 1883–2007* (Lulu, 2008), p. 108.

3 Valuation Office fieldbook (TNA: PRO IR 58/62395), hereditament no. 243.

Bacon, Robert

1 Jonathan Hooton, *The Glaven Ports: a Maritime History of Blakeney, Cley and Wiveton in North Norfolk* (Blakeney: Blakeney History Group, 1996), pp. 30–37, 524–6, 71.

Bailey Road

1 Planning permission was granted in 1981: NNDC: PLA/19810989.

Band of Hope

1 Crawford Holden notes and prospectus in Cromer Museum.

2 NRO: MC 97/114, 541 x 1.

Bands

1 Letter from Thomas Boulter to Benjamin

Bond Cabbell, 8th August 1853. NRO: MC 97/1.

2 Article by Lt.-Col. Newnham-Davis in the *Pall Mall Gazette*, reprinted in the *Norwich Mercury* 3rd August 1904, p. 6.

3 Letter to the author from Richard D. Andrews, secretary of the Northampton Light Orchestra, 13th October 1998.

Bandstands

1 A. Boyce, *An Esplanady Sort of Place* (Cromer Preservation Society, 2004), p. 12.

2 Cromer UDC *Contract Ledger*.

Banks

1 Cf. John M. Barney, 'Building a Fortune: Philip Case, Attorney, 1712–1792' in *Norfolk Archaeology* 43:3 (2000), p. 450: this was an extremely wealthy lawyer in one of the chief ports of the country, yet 'Philip never operated a bank current account – in the most active years of his career there was no bank in Lynn – but "banked" with the general merchanting firms of his sons-in-law, at first with Everard Browne and later with W. & T. Bagge, obtaining from them bills on Child's Bank in London in order to make his own payments and depositing with them bills received which in general they deposited with Child's. But he also had loan accounts with both firms . . . and bought from them building materials, household coal and wine.'

2 Harold Preston, *Early East Anglian Banks and Bankers* (Thetford: the author, 1994), entry no. 70.

3 For background information on the history of the Gurneys and Barclays banks, see Harold Preston, *Early East Anglian Banks*, entry no. 1, and P. W. Matthews, *History of Barclays Bank Limited* (London: Blades, East & Blades, 1926), pp. 103ff.

4 Harold Preston, *Early East Anglian Banks*, entry no. 38; A. D. Boyce, *The Old Lloyds Bank: Bank House, Church Street, Cromer* (Cromer: Cromer Preservation Society, 2001), p. 2.

5 Planning application approved April/May 1975 (NNDC: PLA/19750309, 19750545; described as 'new' in October 1976.

Baptist Church

1 NRO: SO 197/4 C. See also *Cromer Preservation Society Newsletter* 31 (2008), p.3.

Barkers Herne

1 Bellard's 1747 map in Cromer Museum; also NRO: AYL 90 (map not later than 1749).

Bath House

1 White's directory. The building is depicted in a drawing by S. Wilkin dated 1814, now in Dawson Turner's extra-illustrated set of Blomefield in the British Library (Add. MS 23,028), fol. 122, and copy in Cromer Museum.

2 Unpublished history of the Bath House (together with notes on the proprietor, Simeon Simons) by Christopher Pipe, deposited in Cromer Museum. For details of the internal arrangement of the building, see the *Cromer Preservation Society Newsletter* no. 5 (2005), pp. 3–4.

Bathing, and bathing machines

1 *Norwich Mercury* 5 June 1779, p. 2.

2 J. Green to Hamond, 20 August 1796, in NRO: HMN 4/210/6/1.

3 Quoted by George Tatem in a letter to Hamond, 20 September 1804 (NRO: HMN 4/389/9).

4 *Norwich Mercury* 14 May 1830, p. 3, col. 2 (sale notice for the New Inn).

5 John Thornton's diary in 1821 (Northants Record Office: Th. 3183) says eight; Henry Marten's *Journal of an Excursion to Cromer* a few years later says seven.

6 John Timpson, *Timpson's Adaptables* (Norwich: Jarrold, 1997).

Beach huts

1 *Cromer and North Walsham Post* 1912.

Beach Road

1 *Jarrolds' Directory of Cromer and Neighbourhood* (London: Jarrold, 1889). Cf. Skipper's plan in the RIBA drawings collection in the Victoria & Albert Museum, PB 486, showing the road as 'New Station Road'.

2 A. D. Boyce, *Pretty Villas & Capacious Hotels* (Cromer Preservation Society, 2006), p. 16.

Beckhythe

1 Karl Inge Sandred, *The Place-Names of Norfolk, Part Three: The Hundreds of North and South Erpingham and Holt* (Nottingham: English Place-Name Society, 2002), p. 26.

Beckhythe Manor

1 Valuation Office fieldbook: TNA: PRO IR 58/62406, hereditament no. 1368 (dated April 1915).

Beef Meadow

1 NRO: AYL 90.

Belle Vue

1 Reminiscences of Mr Self, noted by Crawford Holden (Cromer Museum: CCH 6/57/1), last page.

Bells

1 For background information see Ronald Hutton, *The Rise and Fall of Merry England: the Ritual Year 1400–1700* (Oxford: Oxford University Press, 1994), pp. 45, 52, 97, 221, 222.
2 NRO: 23240 Z 92, and 12994.
3 Alan Davison, *Deserted Villages of Norfolk* (North Walsham: Poppyland, 1996), p. 59.
4 Rye, *Cromer Past and Present*, p. 103. The name of Thomas Artis is documented in the Yarmouth area at this period.
5 Gilbert Barclay, *Random Reminiscences* (1946 typescript in Cromer Museum, CCH 1/2/1), p. 12.
6 UDC Fire Brigade Committee Minute Book (NLP), pp. 62, 63.
7 *Eastern Daily Press* 15 May 1976, p. 15.
8 L'Estrange, *The Church Bells of Norfolk* (Norwich, 1874). Lady Buxton's funeral was held at Overstrand church in March 1872 (*Ipswich Journal* 30 March 1872, p. 7).

Belmont Hotel

1 Advertisement reproduced in A. D. Boyce, *Pretty Villas & Capacious Hotels* (Cromer: Cromer Preservation Society, 2006), p. 9.

Bernard Road

1 Local Board minute book 2 (NLP: CR3), pp. 432–3, where the proposed width of 20 feet is objected to.

2 UDC minute book 7 (NLP: CR8), pp. 163, 340–42.

Billiards

1 Plan by Simeon Simons in connection with the proposed sea defence works of 1845 (NRO: MC 999/9, 801 x 9).
2 Correspondence of Simeon Simons, 1841, in Goldsmiths' Company archives in London.
3 Sales particulars, 1925, in the Norfolk Heritage Centre.

Bishop's Manor

1 Christopher Pipe, *The Story of Cromer Pier* (North Walsham: Poppyland Publishing, 1998), p. 12.
2 Rye, *Cromer Past and Present*, pp. 35–6.

Blacksmiths

1 Alehouse recognizance in NRO (C/Sch 1/7/11).
2 Pigot's directory 1830; White's directory 1836.
3 Pigot's directory 1830; in White's directory of 1836 he has been succeeded by Elizabeth Curtis.
4 See Pococke watercolour in Cromer Museum (1163.pcx).
5 The Ordnance Survey map of the 1880s shows just the one among the cottages near the White Horse. Pigot's directory in 1839 lists Sewell Burton in West Street and William Watts in the White Horse yard; White's directory (1836) lists only Sewell Burton in West Street, succeeded (1864 edition) by William Burton. This may be the blacksmiths shop recorded in the 1901 census in Cabbell Road, on the site later occupied by the extension to Allen's garage.
6 White's directory 1864.
7 1901 census.
8 Cromer UDC PSW final apportionment 8 December 1902 (NLP), for Back Corner Street; the house is described as house, blacksmith's shop & land.
9 Kitty Lee, *The History of Cromer Lifeboats and Crews: H. F. Bailey 777, 1939–1945* (1991), p. xiv. Cf. UDC *Register of Factories and Workshops*, entry no. 6.
10 UDC *Register of Factories and Workshops*, entry

no. 66; the premises were inspected in 1931.
11 Ordnance Survey 1:2,500 map (1906; survey revised in 1905).

Blazer's
1 TNA: PRO BT 31/26174/170079.

Blue Danube Café
1 UDC Parks & Open Space Committee Minute Book (NLP: CR31), p. 219.

Boating lake
1 Cromer UDC *Contract Ledger*.

Bomb damage
1 *Wartime Norfolk: the Diary of Rachel Dhonau, 1941–1942* edited by Robert Malcolmson and Peter Searby (Norwich: Norfolk Record Society, 2004), pp. 175 (footnote), 208.
2 PD 523/153.
3 C. E. Knight, *The Auxiliary Hospitals of the British Red Cross Society & St. John Ambulance in Norfolk 1914–1919* (Norwich: Order of St. John of Jerusalem and the British Red Cross Society Norfolk County Joint Committee, 1989).

Bond Street
1 Local Board minute book 3 (NLP: CR4), pp. 11, 15.
2 UDC minute book 7 (NLP: CR8), pp. 2–3.

Bowls clubs
1 Alfred Salter's magic lantern lecture notes.

Bracondale
1 Cf. Gilbert Barclay, *Random Reminiscences* (1946 typescript in Cromer Museum, CCH 1/2/1), p. 13.
2 Charles A. Munkman, *The Catholic Revival in North Norfolk: Centenary of Our Lady of Refuge Church in Cromer, 1895–1995* (privately printed), p. 16.

Breaker's Lane
1 NRO: AYL 90 (map not later than 1749).
2 Map of lands belonging to Nathaniel Smith, in NRO (with photocopy, FX 264/1).

Brewing
1 TNA: PRO SC 8/128/6390 and SC 8/198/9895.

Brickfields
1 According to the Valuation Office fieldbook, no. 6 was occupied from October 1898 (TNA: PRO IR58/62402, hereditament no. 937), but cf. 1891 census return.
2 TNA: PRO IR58/62399, hereditament no. 654.
3 NRO: NRS 1707.
4 Letter to the Goldsmiths' Company, 1821, in Goldsmiths' Hall, London.

Brickfields Cottages
1 *Jarrolds' Directory of Cromer and Neighbourhood* (London: Jarrold, 1889).

Brook Street
1 Cromer Local Board minute book 2 (NLP: CR3), p. 60.
2 UDC minute book 4 (NLP: CR5), p. 62.

Brownshill
1 NNDC: PLA/190021.

Brunswick Street
1 Plan of 1884 in NRO (NCC Road Orders box 6, bundle no. 2); also first edition of the Ordnance Survey 25" map.

Bulls Row
1 Valuation Office fieldbook, dated 1914 (TNA: PRO IR58/62402, hereditament no. 968).
2 See sketch maps in the NRO: COL/2/75/1–6.

Burnt Hills
1 NRO: AYL 90.

Bus services
1 Sale prospectus for the 1891 sale of building plots on the Cromer Hall estate (NRO: WD 123, 385 x 5).
2 Susanna Wade Martins and Tom Williamson, *The Countryside of East Anglia: Changing Landscapes, 1870–1950* (Woodbridge: Boydell, 2008), citing J. Hibbs, *The History of British Bus Services* (Newton Abbot: David & Charles, 1989).
3 Constance Rothery, *The Poppyland Flyer* (Trimingham: Old Station House Press, 1984), p. 33; Maurice Doggett, *Eastern Counties: the First 50 Years* (Norwich: Eastern Counties Omnibus Company, 1981), pp. 1, 2, 31, 40–41.
4 *North Norfolk News* 14 February 2008, p. 5.

Butts
1   Robert Baxter's will (proved 1650) in NRO: MS 21584, 369 x 1.
2   Indenture dated 14 January 1824 offered for sale by Sylvan Manuscripts in 2008.

Cabbell Road
1   UDC minute book 7 (NLP: CR8), pp. 85, 126–7, 147.

Cabbell Road: Benjamin Bond Cabbell
1   *The Times* 13 August 1852, p. 5, col. f, and 11 December 1874, p. 10, col. f.
2   Hamon Le Strange, *History of Freemasonry in Norfolk, 1724 to 1895* (Norwich: Goose, 1896), pp. 83, 129–30, 232.
3   Rye, *Cromer Past and Present*, pp. 31–2.

Cadogan Road
1   UDC minute book 7 (NLP: CR8), pp. 85, 126–7, 147; but in minute book 8 (CR9) it seems still to be referred to as an intended new road in 1902.
2   H. W. C. Davis, 'Cadogan, George Henry, fifth Earl Cadogan (1840–1915)', rev. H. C. G. Matthew, *Oxford Dictionary of National Biography*, Oxford University Press, 2004; online edition, Jan 2008 <http://www.oxforddnb.com/view/article/32235 – accessed 4 Nov 2009>.
3   Gerald Gliddon, *The Aristocracy and the Great War* (Norwich: Gliddon Books, 2002), pp. 259–60.

Cambridge Street
1   UDC minute book 7 (NLP: CR8), pp. 2–3.
2   Mace advertisement in *Jarrolds' Directory of Cromer and Neighbourhood* (London: Jarrold, 1889).

Cannon
1   Plan by Simeon Simons in connection with the proposed sea defences of 1845 (NRO: MC 999/9, 801 x 9).

Carlyle Road
1   Deeds of 40 Cromwell Road described in Philip Bligh, *A History of Cromer Beach Mission 1883–2007* (Lulu, 2008), p. 254.

Carnivals
1   Edmund Bartell, *Observations on Cromer as a Watering Place* 2nd ed. (London: for J. Taylor 1806), p. 21.
2   1912 carnival programme in Cromer Museum (CCH box 7/65/11); for details of carnivals in the 1920s and 1930s see Christopher Pipe, *The Story of Cromer Pier* (North Walsham: Poppyland Publishing, 1998), pp. 64–5, and the related file of cuttings and programmes in Cromer Museum. There is also in Cromer Museum a photograph of a 'carnival float' dating from the 1880s.

Carrington Road
1   UDC minute book 5 (NLP: CR6), pp. 94, 104–5.
2   *Cromer and North Walsham Post.*

Carrington Villas
1   National Telephone Company directory 1899/1900, listing Lord Suffield at 'Carrington villa'.

Carrwood House
1   William Leary & John Vickers, *A Methodist Guide to Lincolnshire and East Anglia* (Bognor Regis: World Methodist Historical Society, 1984), p. 38.
2   Ordnance Survey 6" map, 1st ed., Norfolk sheet XI NE, 1888 (surveyed 1885).

Cavendish Road
1   Deeds of 40 Cromwell Road described by Philip Bligh, *A History of Cromer Beach Mission 1883–2007* (Lulu, 2008), p. 254.

Cemeteries
1   UDC minute book 7 (NLP: CR8), p. 320; plans for the new cemetery, chapel and caretaker's lodge were approved in 1901 (minute book 8 (NLP: CR9), pp. 229–31). Information on Durrant from a descendant (and cf. Cromer Museum CCH 6/58/1).
2   UDC minute book 9 (NLP: CR10), pp. 13, 36.

Central Road
1   UDC minute book 8 (NLP: CR9), p. 461; cf. pp 149 etc. for mention of planning approvals granted subject to road being made up.

Chapel Street

UDC minute book 4 (NLP: CR5), pp. 346-7.

Chaplains

Rye, *Cromer Past and Present,* pp. 137-9.

Charities

Will of James Payn: Rye, *Cromer Past and Present,* p. 85.

Norfolk Quarter Sessions Order Book 1650–1657 (Norfolk Record Society, 1955) (NRS vol. XXVI), p. 95.

Local Board committee minute book (NLP: CR61), p. 88. Papers of the Howes bequest in NRO: PD 523/142.

Overstrand glebe terriers in NRO: DN/TER 115/6. Cf. *Reports of the Commissioners . . . concerning Charities and Education of the Poor,* 1815-35, Norfolk volume, p. 215.

Chesterfield Hall

North Norfolk News 8 June 2000, p. 8.

Chesterfield Villas

Dent, *Reminiscences of a Cromer Doctor* edited by Derek Barker, pp. 52-3.

Christ Church, Overstrand

Pevsner/Wilson, p. 632.

Valuation Office fieldbook (TNA: PRO IR 58/62409), hereditament no. 1700.

Church Rock

Eastern Daily Press 5 & 12 July 1979.

Church Street

Local Board minute book 2 (NLP: CR3), p. 410.

Local Board minute book 3 (NLP: CR4), p. 317.

Churches

Richard Fawcett, 'Medieval Masons' in *An Historical Atlas of Norfolk* edited by Peter Wade-Martins, 2nd ed. (Norwich: Norfolk Museums Service, 1994), pp. 58-9. Dr Fawcett omitted Cromer from his article on the Wiveton mason in the *Antiquaries Journal* because the porch is so heavily restored, and because it is so difficult to be sure of its date; but he

points to similarities between its mouldings and those in the north porches of Blakeney and Walpole St Peter churches.

2 Will of Richard Chylde (1459), translated by Walter Rye (NRO: Rye 134, p. vii).

3 Cf. Reinhard Strohm, *The Rise of European Music 1380–1500* (Cambridge University Press, 1993), pp. 74-6, 108, 208.

4 Plans in NRO: PD 523/50.

5 Architect's report, drawings etc. in NRO: PD 523/51.

6 Ibid.

7 Restoration papers 1862-70 in NRO: PD 523/53.

8 Alfred Heath, *Cromer Church Organs Past and Present* (Holt: Rounce & Wortley, 1912).

Churchyard

1 Tithe apportionment (1 acre, 28 perches).

2 Local Board committee minute book (NLP: CR61), p. 70, referring to land bought from Mr Fitch adjoining Church Street, to be made into a path; cf. p. 236 for final approval of churchyard plans in 1896.

3 Rye, *Cromer Past & Present,* p. 94.

4 Plans of churchyard alterations 1896 in NRO: PD 523/67.

5 Plan and register by A. F. Scott, showing old and new locations of each stone, in NRO: PD 523/67.

6 NRO: PD 523/69.

7 A photograph of the 1850s shows the western wall of the churchyard constructed of unknapped flints and surmounted only by shaped brick coping: Cromer Museum image CRO1258.

Cinemas

1 Skipper plans in Cromer Museum(CRRMU: 1998.9.31).

2 Peart, *The Picture House in East Anglia,* pp. 14, 24, 86. The company documents are in TNA: PRO BT 31/22039/133773.

3 See *North Folk* (October 1987), pp. 48-50.

Clare Road

1 *Cromer & North Walsham Post* 17 January 1891, p. 5.

2 UDC minute book 9 (NLP: CR10), p. 210.

Cf. Rochelle Mortimer Massingham, *Up the Park! A History of Suffield Park, Cromer, Norfolk* (Cromer Museum, 1999), p. 15 of the original (A4) edition.

3   Karl Inge Sandred (*The Place-names of Norfolk. Part Three*, Nottingham: English Place-name Society, 2002) refers to a supposed hamlet of Clare in the medieval settlement of Shipden, but the notes he was working from seem to have completely misconstrued a Domesday reference to a place called Clare in Tunstead hundred.

Clarence Mews

1   A. F. Scott's drawings were offered for sale on eBay in September 2008.

Clement Scott Mews

1   Jamie Edghill and Keith Entwistle, *Cromer Fire Brigade 1881–2006* (Cromer: Poppyland Publishing, 2006), p. 82. Planning permission was granted for eight residential flats on the site in 1978 (North Norfolk District Council PLA/19781101).

Cliff Drive

1   Lord Templewood, *The Unbroken Thread* (London: Collins, 1949), pp. 286-7.

Cliff House

1   Map of lands belonging to Nathaniel Smith, in NRO (with photocopy FX 264/1).

2   *Morning Chronicle* 17 June 1801.

3   Lord Templewood, *The Unbroken Thread* (London: Collins, 1949), p. 60.

4   For comment on the additions to the house, cf. Templewood, *The Unbroken Thread*, p. 291.

Cliff Lane Cottage

1   Cromer Museum, CRRMU.1981.80.116:INT.

Cliff Road

1   UDC minute book 5 (NLP: CR6), pp. 94, 104-5.

Cliffside House

1   Van Moppes retired in 1917 and died in 1943. For the company history, see <http://www.vanmoppes.ch/?id=1/2/1/1>.

Cliftonville Hotel

1   Boardman's 1888 plans and elevations for the property at the corner of West Street and Prince of Wales Road (outfitter's, grocery & draper's) built by John Downing & Son are in the NRO (BR 35/2/44/10).

2   Letters in A. F. Scott's letter-book 1894-5 refer to him building a 'house' in Runton Road; Churchyard is first listed at Runton Road in the register of lodging house keepers 18 May 1896 (NRO: PS 24/23/1). According to Cromer Museum, the application to the UDC for the dining room was dated 25 August 1898; Pevsner gives the date as 1897.

Clocks

1   Letter of 14 June 1863 in NRO (PD 523/53); transcription by Crawford Holden in Cromer Museum (CCH box 7/63/62); letter from Holden in the *Eastern Daily Press* 4 April 1975.

2   *Eastern Daily Press* March 1975.

Coaches

1   White's directory 1836.

2   Ibid.

3   NRO: MC 26/1, pp. 117, 89-90.

4   Rye, *Cromer Past and Present*, p. 146. He presumably means Roughton, not 'Runton'.

5   Newspaper report of 17 September 1909 in Crawford Holden's papers in Cromer Museum.

6   Printed poster offereed for sale on eBay in August 2010.

7   *The Guide to Orange Coach Tours from Cromer* (36-page booklet in collection of the author).

Coastguard cottages

1   Cf. Edmund Bartell's general comment some 30 years earlier that 'the houses, in general, are indifferent, and the rents very high' (*Cromer Considered as a Watering Place* 2nd ed. (London for J. Taylor, 1806), p. 9).

2   TNA: PRO ADM 7/11, folios 108/129 and 168/188.

3   Valuation Office fieldbook (TNA: PRO IR 58/62409, hereditaments 1694 and 1695.

Coastguard station

1   Ordnance Survey 1:2500 map (1906; survey revised 1905).

Colne Cottage

1 George W. E. Russell, *Lady Victoria Buxton* (London: Longmans, Green, 1919).

2 *Eastern Daily Press* 17 December 1999, p. 13. Sale particulars in NRO (C/C 17/210).

Colne House

1 Ground plan by G. Pank dated 1820 in Cromer Museum (CRRMU.1992.17.11). Mrs Partridge had died 15 December 1819 aged 70 (her memorial inscription is reproduced in Rye, *Cromer Past and Present*, p. vi). See also sale particulars 1831 (CRRMU.1992.17.1).

2 Abstract of title in Hansell's papers in NRO (document 222).

3 For Henry Samuel Partridge's ancestry, see John Burke, *A Genealogical and Heraldic History of the Commoners of Great Britain* (London, 1836), vol. III, pp. 332–4. Partridge acquired the estates of Great and Little Hockham in 1811 and resided at Hockham Hall near Thetford. He became a magistrate and Deputy Lieutenant of Norfolk. Papers relating to the grant to him of the freedom of Norwich in 1813 are in the NRO: MC 55/34, 506 x 3.

4 Gilbert Barclay, *Random Reminiscences* (1946 typescript in Cromer Museum (CCH 1/2/1), p. 11.

5 C. E. Knight, *The Auxiliary Hospitals of the British Red Cross Society and St. John Ambulance in Norfolk 1914–1919* (Norwich: Order of St. John of Jerusalem and the British Red Cross Society Norfolk County Joint Committee, 1989).

6 *North Folk* 4 (November 1987), pp. 54–5. The statement on p. 54 that 'Colne House was built in 1710 for Lord Buxton' seems quite without foundation.

Colne Lodge

1 Photograph with history written on the back: CRRMU.1981.80.576.

Compit Hills

1 NRO: AYL 90.

Congregational Church

1 NCC Road Order book 12, pp. 203–14, in NRO. Notices calling the requisite Vestry meeting had been fixed on the church door, on the doors of the two Wesleyan churches, and

'on a Building annexed to the Coffee Tavern known as a Lecture Hall and used on Sundays by Congregationalists'.

2 Stephen Wright, 'Amyraut, Paul (b. 1600/01)', *Oxford Dictionary of National Biography*, Oxford University Press, Sept 2004; online edition, Oct 2005 <http://www.oxforddnb.com/view/article/457> – accessed 4 Nov 2009.

Connaught Road

1 UDC minute book 9 (NLP: CR10), p. 210. Cf. Rochelle Mortimer Massingham, *Up the Park! A History of Suffield Park, Cromer, Norfolk* (Cromer Museum, 1999), p. 15 of the original (A4) edition.

Conservative Club

1 The 13th annual meeting was reported in the *Norfolk Chronicle* of 17 May 1918 (p. 5, col. 3).

Corner Street

1 Local Board committee minute book (NLP: CR61), pp. 184–5; UDC minute book 7 (NLP: CR8), pp. 340–2; book 8 (NLP: CR9), p. 74.

Cottage

1 *Eastern Daily Press* 7 September 2005, p. 16.

Council

1 Local Board minute book 1, p. 3.

2 *North Norfolk News* 10 November 1978.

Council: Lord Suffield

1 Charles Harbord, 5th Baron Suffield, *My Memories 1830–1913* (London: Herbert Jenkins, 1913), p. 315.

Council offices

1 Fountain House was let on a monthly tenancy in 1901, and the council's tenancy of the offices at the Town Hall extended until 31 March 1902: UDC minute book 7 (NLP: CR8), pp. 386, 412.

Craigside

1 Valuation Office fieldbook (TNA: PRO IR 58/62405, hereditament no. 1292). The site was bought for £505 and the building cost about £2,500 to erect. First listed in the register of lodging house keepers 24 March 1902 (NRO:

PS 24/23/1).

Crawford Road
1   UDC minute book 9 (NLP: CR10), pp. 210, 375.

Crescent, The
1   *Norwich Mercury* 21p. 3, col. 6. Henry Marten's Journal refers to the row as being partly let and partly still vacant in 1825.
2   Plans and elevations in Boardman archive in NRO (BR/35/2/25/7), showing the unimproved terrace. The balconies were added in 1897 (A. D. Boyce, *Cobbles to Cupolas* (Cromer Preservation Society, 2004), p. 7).

Cricket
1   *Cromer: A Descriptive Poem* (London: for J. Ridgway, 1806), p. 46.
2   Letter from Thomas Keith to Benjamin Bond Cabbell, 31 January 1860 (NRO: MC 97/7, 538 x 1). The letter merely refers to the cricket ground, without saying where it was or was planned to be.
3   Crawford Holden's notes in Cromer Museum, box 7.
4   NRO: MC 97/116, 541 x 1.
5   Savin, p. 138.
6   Neil R. Storey, *Cromer St John Ambulance and Auxiliary War Hospitals during the First World War: Historical Notes* (unpublished).
7   *North Norfolk News* 11 June 2009, p. 2.
8   Constance, Lady Battersea, *Reminiscences* (London: Macmillan, 1922), pp. 329-30.

Croft, The
1   Sketchmap in NRO (Rye MS 134).
2   Grenville Astill in *The Countryside of Medieval England* (Oxford: Basil Blackwell, 1988), pp. 47-50.

Cromer
1   Rye, *Cromer Past and Present,* p. 18.
2   Eilert Ekwall, *Concise Dictionary of English Placenames*. Ekwall does not consider the possibility of 'mere' (as a placename element) meaning 'boundary'.

Cromer Convention
1   Philip Bligh, *A History of Cromer Beach Mission*

1883-2007 (Lulu, 2008), pp. 149-54.

Cromer Hall
1   Thomas Fowell Buxton, *Memoirs* (Everyman edition), p. 53.
2   NRO: WKC 7/97, 404 x 5, and plans held at Felbrigg Hall.
3   *Observer,* 30 November 1829, p. 2; *Norfolk Chronicle* 28 November 1829, p. 2, col. 6.
4   NRO: MC 97.
5   Rye, *Cromer Past and Present,* pp. 31-2.
6   Dent, *Reminiscences of a Cromer Doctor* edited by Derek Barker and privately printed by him), p. 23.

Cromer Ladies' Bible Association
1   *Report MDCCCXXXVIII* (Norwich: Fletcher, 1839). Cf. *Memorials of Hannah, Lady Buxton,* p. 104.

Cromer Mutual Improvement Society
1   Dent, *Reminiscences of a Cromer Doctor* edited by Derek Barker, p. 16; *Cromer & North Walsham Post* 17 January 1891, p. 5.

Cromwell Road
1   *Cromer & North Walsham Post* 11 April 1891, p. 5, col. 4.

Cross Street
1   UDC minute book 7 (NLP: CR8), pp. 2-3.

Crown
1   NRO: Rye 33, vol. 4, fol. 2523.

Crown and Anchor
1   *Mary Hardy's Diary* (Norwich Record Society, 1968), pp. 41, 75, 79, 80, 83, 128.

Cuckoo Lane
1   NRO: AYL 90.
2   G. F. Leake, *East & West Runton: Two Villages, One Parish* 2nd ed. (Cromer: Poppyland Publishing, 2006), p. 36.
3   *Oxford English Dictionary* 2nd ed (1989), under 'how, howe' n^2.

Dairy Farm
1   Map of 1865 in possession of C. J. Wright of Cromer (and photocopy in Cromer Museum).

2 Ordnance Survey 1-inch map, Old Series (1838).

Dancing

1 John Thornton's diary (Northamptonshire Record Office: Th 3184).

Danish Pavilion

1 Valuation Office fieldbook (TN: PRO IR 58/62406), hereditament no. 1343. The original three-acre plot was bought on 27 June 1900 for £1,563; a further acre was bought on 9 November 1901 for £800.

Danum House

1 TNA: PRO IR58/62406, hereditament no. 1380; *Cracroft's Peerage* (on-line).
2 Dent, *Reminiscences of a Cromer Doctor* edited by Derek Barker, pp. 82-4. The Norwich local studies library's copy of Charles W. Barclay's history of the Barclay family contains a letter written from The Corner House, Overstrand, thanking him for his interest and sending him a copy of the book in 1926. (Rev. Charles Barclay was the husband of Florence Barclay.) Beverley as a medical student is mentioned a number of times in Shephard T. Taylor's *Diary of a Norwich Hospital Medical Student, 1858-1860* (Norwch: Jarrold, 1930), with a photograph of him taken at this time (opposite p. 140); also frequently in the same author's *Diary of a Medical Student during the Mid-Victorian Period, 1860-1864* (Norwich: Jarrold, 1927), with a later photograph of Beverley facing p. 2.

Dentists

1 Dent, *Reminiscences of a Cromer Doctor* edited by Derek Barker and privately printed by him, p. 16.
2 UDC *Register of Factories & Workshops*, entry no. 68.

Ditchell's house and barn

1 See drawing in Cromer Museum (2014.pcx).

Doctors

1 Although his will, dated 25 December 1794, describes him as 'of Cromer', it is clear from the wording that he only expected to be here during the season. He is rated for a house in the rating list of 1772-73, but not in the 1772 list.
2 P. J. & R. V. Wallis, *Eighteenth Century Medics (Subscriptions, Licences, Apprenticeships)* (Newcastle upon Tyne: Project for Historical Bibliography, 1985).
3 See his will, Norwich Consistory Court, 1796; also cf. Hannah Buxton's reference to staying at his lodgings in 1793 (*Memorials of Hannah Lady Buxton*, p. 5).
4 *Cromer Preservation Society Newsletter* 18 (2004), p. 1.
5 A. Boyce, *Cobbles to Cupolas* (Cromer Preservation Society), p. 11.
6 *Eastern Daily Press* 28 October 1978, p. 20.
7 *North Norfolk News* 22 March 1974, p.1, and 19 January 1979.
8 A. Boyce, *An Esplanady Sort of Place* (Cromer Preservation Society, 2004), p. 3.

Doctors: William Henry Ransom

1 *Dictionary of National Biography*.

Doctor's Steps

1 UDC minute book 4 (NLP: CR5), pp. 164, 178-80.
2 John S. Mannings, *Cromer: A Descriptive Poem* (London: Ridgway, 1806), p. 7.
3 NRO: NCC Road Order Book 12, pp. 203-14, 225-6, and box 26, bundle no. 2, relating to diversion of the path in 1883-84.

Dolphin post

1 *Oxford English Dictionary* 2nd ed., sense 6b (b).
2 Rye, *Cromer Past and Present*, pp. 39-43. The documents on which Rye based his summary are now in the NRO (COL/2/75/1-2).

Donkeys

1 Simeon Simons' report on attendance record, 1833; letter dated 4 July 1837; report of 1849 leavers – all in R.III.174 at Goldsmiths' Hall.
2 John Thornton's diary (Northants. Record Office, Th. 3183).
3 Map of *c.* 1868 in the NRO: Rye MS 134.
4 William Frederick Starling, *Memories of Aylsham* (Aylsham Local History Society, 2000), pp. 80-81.
5 Information from the late Mrs G. ('Nonnie') Wright of Aylmerton, who with her husband

used to run the pony rides until the council put a stop even to these.

6 Eric Puddy, *A Short History of the Order of the Hospital of St John of Jerusalem in Norfolk* (Dereham: Starling, 1961), p. 108.

7 Victoria Leggett, 'Donkeys banned from Cromer beach' in the *Eastern Daily Press*, May 2010.

Driftway

1 Tithe map 1840.

Durrant's Farm

1 TNA: PRO MAF 32/714/492 (National Farm Survey).

East Cottages

1 *Journal* 16 December 1977.

Ebenezer Cottage

1 Information from C. J. Wright, who renovated the cottage.

Edinburgh House

1 Register of Lodging House Keepers (NRO: PS 24/23/2), listing Florence Rebecca Dennis on 9 April 1906.

2 *North Norfolk News* 3 August 2000, p. 1; Jamie Edghill and Keith Entwistle, *Cromer Fire Brigade 1881–2006* (Cromer: Poppyland Publishing, 2006), pp. 91–2.

Electric lighting

1 John Thornton's diary (Northants. Record Office: Th 3183).

2 UDC minute book 6 (NLP: CR7), p. 314.

3 UDC minute book 7 (NLP: CR8), p. 396.

4 UDC minute book 8 (NLP: CR9), p. 360.

5 UDC minute book 9 (NLP: CR10), pp. 183, 237.

6 UDC minute book 9 (NLP: CR10), p. 299.

Ellenhill

1 The North Norfolk District Council approved the original residential development of bungalows in 1978 (PLA/19781161); the houses at the bottom of the road were added early in the 21st century.

Erosion

1 Walter Rye, *Eastern Counties Collectanea* (1873) vol. i, pp. 37–9; SPD Eliz. 38/8; Hearth Tax assessment 1664.

Factories

1 UDC minute book 9 (NLP: CR10), p. 187; *Register of Factories & Workshops*, entry no. 28.

2 UDC *Register of Factories & Workshops*, entry no. 34.

3 UDC *Register of Factories & Workshops*, entry no. 69.

4 NNDC: PLA 19751544, 19760520, 19790838.

5 *Eastern Daily Press* 4 April 1952 and 20 November 1952.

6 *North Norfolk News* 2 November 2000, p. 8.

Fairs

1 *Owen's New Book of Fairs* new ed. (1802).

Faldonside

1 Dent, *Reminiscences of a Cromer Doctor* edited by Derek Barker, p. 75.

Falls

1 Philip Hardwick's 1839 plan (in Goldsmiths Hall) of houses which it was thought to build nearby show a 'proposed bridge' over the beck slightly seaward of the existing one.

Fearns Field

1 White's directory, 1890. See also Rochelle Mortimer Massingham, *Up the Park! A History of Suffield Park, Cromer, Norfolk* (Cromer Museum, 1999), pp. 8 & 19 of the original (A4) edition.

2 Valuation Office fieldbooks (TNA: PRO IR 58/62405, hereditaments 1211 etc.; also IR 58/62408, *passim*). The lease was for 99 years.

3 Valuation Office fieldbook (TNA: PRO IR 58/62408, hereditament 1553).

4 NRO: MC 501/216, 754 x 4.

Fern House

1 Crawford Holden notes in Cromer Museum.

Festival of Music, Drama and Dance

1 *Cromer Town Guide and Trade Directory 2000/1*, pp. 17–19.

Field system

1 Diary of Sir Philip Skippon, of Foulsham, quoted in *Norfolk Archaeology* vol. xxii, p. 159.

2 Map of 1717 in NRO, showing strips in a field called the South Field. Cf. also court book of the manor of Cromer Gunners, 1739, in which pieces of land surrendered by John Cook are described as lying 'in the Westfield'.

Fire brigade

1 *William Windham's Green Book 1673–1688* edited by Elizabeth Griffiths (Norfolk Record Society, 2002) (NRS vol. LXVI), p. 65.

2 Papers of the manor of Cromer Lancasters (NRO: MS 20978).

3 *Norfolk Archaeology* vol. xv, p. 222.

4 Jamie Edghill and Keith Entwistle, *Cromer Fire Brigade 1881–2006* (Cromer: Poppyland Publishing, 2006), pp. 6-8. The date given by Savin for the foundation of the fire brigade is 1880; E. R. Priest, writing in 1899, gave it as 1881.

5 Local Board minute book 1 (NLP: CR2), pp. 8, 73.

6 Ibid., pp. 292-3, 340, 355; UDC Fire Brigade Committee minute book no. 1 (NLP), pp. 89-92.

7 Local Board minute book 2, pp. 33-4.

8 Local Board minute books 2 (NLP: CR3), p. 436, and 3 (NLP: CR4), p. 61.

9 UDC minute book 6 (NLP: CR7), pp. 262, 283.

10 UDC minute book 5 (NLP: CR6), p. 209.

11 UDC Fire Brigade Committee minute book no. 1 (NLP), p. 15, 35, 37, 39, 42.

12 Ibid., pp. 127, 135-41.

13 UDC minute book 9 (NLP: CR10), pp. 351-2, 384; Fire Brigade Committee minute book no. 1 (NLP), pp. 5, 6, 10, 14, 19, 22. The public inquiry into the proposed new building was in January 1904.

14 UDC Fire Brigade Committee minute book no. 1 (NLP), pp. 296-6, 300.

15 Ibid., pp. 105, 110.

Fishing

1 TNA: PRO SC 8/102/5100.

2 Cellarer's roll, 1415-1416, published by Norfolk Record Society (vol. xvii), pp. 81, 83, 85.

3 Carol Rawcliffe, *Medicine for the Soul* (Stroud:

Sutton, 1999), p. 177.

4 Diary of Sir Philip Skippon of Foulsham, 1667, quoted in *Norfolk Archaeology* vol. xxii, p. 159. It is something of a puzzle to know how the fish got there – the main route to Cambridge would have been up the up the Ouse from Lynn, so why land the fish at Cromer? (Cf. N. J. Williams, *The Maritime Trade of the East Anglian Ports, 1550–1590* (Oxford: Clarendon, 1988), p. 55.)

5 John Thornton's diary (Northants. Record Office: Th 3183).

6 *Eastern Daily Press* 12 September 1977.

Fletcher Hospital

1 See Boardman archive (NRO: BR 35/2/49/1-4).

Football

1 Indenture of 12 September 1741 relating to lands later Colne House, among Hansell's papers in NRO, document 222.

2 Savin, p. 130.

3 Dent, *Reminiscences of a Cromer Doctor* edited by Derek Barker, pp. 68-9.

4 *Norfolk Century* (Eastern Counties Newspaper Group, 1999), p. 106.

5 *Cromer, Sheringham & District Weekly Press* 9 October 1915, p. 1, col. 1.

6 Constance, Lady Battersea, *Reminiscences* (London: Macmillan, 1922), pp. 329-30.

Fortifications

1 Davis' edition of the Paston letters, vol. 1, p. 237, and vol. 2, p. 533.

2 B. Cozens-Hardy in *Norfolk Archaeology* xxvi, pp. 311-12.

3 Ordnance Surveyors' Drawing, 1816 (British Library).

4 Report of Maj. Alex Bryce to Lt Gen. Sir James Craigg, 12 December 1803 (TNA: PRO WO 30/100), p. 155.

5 Peter Kent, *Fortifications in East Anglia*; R. W. Ketton-Cremer, *Norfolk Portraits*, p. 166. Source materials at TNA: PRO (HO 50/80 and WO 30/100).

6 Plan accompanying Cromer Hall estate sales particulars, 1852.

7 *An Historical Atlas of Norfolk* 2nd ed. edited by

Peter Wade-Martins (Norwich: Norfolk Museums Service, 1994), p. 174.

8 Detailed history of the development of the battery, its staffing, equipment etc. may be found in the fort record book in The National Archives (TNA: PRO WO 192/67).

9 Norfolk Landscape Archaeology (Gressenhall), Sites & Monuments Record, no. 32566 <http://www.heritage.norfolk.gov.uk/SingleR esult.aspx?uid=MNF32566>.

10 UDC Parks & Open Spaces Committee minute book (NLP: CR31), p. 226.

11 Christopher Bird, *Silent Sentinels* (Guist Bottom: Larks Press, 1999), pp. 16–17, 20. Norfolk Landscape Archaeology (Gressenhall), Sites & Monuments Record, nos 32525 and 32569 <http://www.heritage.norfolk.gov.uk/Sing leResult.aspx?uid=MNF32525> and <http: //www.heritage.norfolk.gov.uk/SingleResu lt.aspx?uid=MNF32569>. See also Cromer Museum, record of oral information received, which claims that the coastal battery's guns were 4½-inch.

Foulness

1 See Knight's chart of the coast of Norfolk, 1801, in the Hydrographic Office at Taunton (I.29, shelf Qe), which suggests that the beach and shallow water at Overstrand extended a couple of miles out from the present cliffs; in fact Overstrand is not marked at all, only Foulness extending from the lighthouse as far as Sidestrand church.

Fountain House

1 UDC minute book 4 (NLP: CR5), p. 188.

2 White's directory, 1864; Savin.

3 UDC minute book 6 (NLP: CR7), pp. 426–7, 442–3; minute book 7 (CR8), pp. 189, 217.

4 TNA: PRO IR 58/62400, hereditament no. 793. The purchase price was £2,000.

5 *Cromer Preservation Society Newsletter* 3 (2001), pp. 2–3.

Friendly societies

1 E. W. Brabrook, *Provident Societies and Industrial Welfare* (London, 1898), p. 73.

Fulcher Avenue

1 'Sentimental Journey Closes Mundesley-

Cromer Line' in *Eastern Daily Press* 7 April 1953. See also *EDP* 27 May 1952.

Furze Hill

1 Ordnance Survey 25" map, surveyed in 1885.

Gangway

1 *Jarrolds' Directory of Cromer and Neigbourhood* (London: Jarrold, 1889).

2 UDC minute book 8 (NLP: CR9), pp. 155–6.

3 Ibid., p. 401.

4 Michael Brackenbury, *Cromer Lifeboat Station 1919–1997* (unpublished report in Norfolk Landscape Archaeology files at Gressenhall), pp. 24–5.

5 TNA: PRO ADM 7/11, folios 108/129 and 168/188. The tithe apportionment describes the property as 'granary, cottage, fish house, coal shed and yard', which makes one wonder if the surveyors had noticed it had been converted into cottages, but does seem to confirm that it was used as a granary, as Savin says, and not just as a warehouse, as some later writers have suggested.

Garden Street

1 NNDC: PLA/197601418.

Gardens

1 *Robson's Commercial Directory of London & the Nine Counties* vol. II, 20th ed. (London: William Robson, 1839), p. 20.

2 TNA: PRO IR58/62399, hereditament no. 609.

3 1901 census; the books were offered for sale on eBay in August 2010 by a Hampshire bookseller.

4 NHER 6477, 30482.

5 TNA: PRO MAF 32/714/492 and (for Overstrand) MAF 32/732/504.

6 *Norfolk Allotments: The Plot so Far* (Norfolk Recorders, 2007).

Gas works

1 Thomas Keith to Benjamin Bond Cabbell, 10 May 1859. NRO: MC 97/6, 538 x 1.

2 Company annual report 1877 (NRO: C/Scf 3/1/1).

3 Shown on Ordnance Survey 6" map, 1st ed. (1886), surveyed 1885.

Giglers Croft

1 1717 map of lands belonging to Nathaniel Field, in NRO (with photocopy FX 264/1); spelled 'Jiglers' in Bellard's 1747 map in Cromer Museum.
2 Glebe terriers 1627 and 1709 (NRO: DN/TER 52/3/1-2).

Gissing House

1 Terence Richards, *A Visitors Guide to Overstrand Past and Present* (Overstrand Parish Council, 2001; amended edition 2005).

Glendon House

1 Valuation Office fieldbook (TNA: PRO IR 58/62406), hereditament no. 1322.

Golf

1 Charles Harbord, 5th Baron Suffield, *My Memories 1805–1913* (London: Herbert Jenkins, 1913), p. 83. Cf. *Norfolk Weekly Standard* 6 October 1888, p. 2, quoting the *Star*.
2 Compton Mackenzie, *Octave One (1883–91)*, cited in Julian Earwaker and Kathleen Becker, *Literary Norfolk: An Illustrated Companion* (1998; Aurum Press, 2003), p. 131.
3 *Norwich Mercury* 17 July 1895, p. 2, col. 5.
4 Crawford Holden notes in Cromer Museum (CCH 5/46/10, apparently based on Sir Malcolm's autobiography).
5 Elevation by A. H. Fox in NRO (Gunton 115/466).

Gospel Hall

1 Information from Jack Earl, whose brother was one of the Trustees of the Brethren congregation.

Grand Hotel

1 Bond-Cabbell was granted a liquor licence for the hotel as early as 1889: North Erpingham Register of Licences C (NRO: PS 24/7/1).
2 TNA: PRO BT 31/15338/39542.
3 Dent, *Reminiscences of a Cromer Doctor* edited by Derek Barker, p. 24.
4 Sales particulars in Norfolk Heritage Centre.
5 Jamie Edghill and Keith Entwistle, *Cromer Fire Brigade 1881–2006* (Cromer: Poppyland Publishing, 2006).

Grange, The

1 Valuation Office fieldbook (TNA: PRO IR 58/62406, hereditament no. 1334). The date of sale was 21 July; Player is described as of Nottingham.
2 Dent, *Reminiscences of a Cromer Doctor* edited by Derek Barker, pp. 82–3.

Grange Avenue

1 NRO: BR 277/3.

Grange Court

1 Dent, *Reminiscences of a Cromer Doctor* edited by Derek Barker, pp. 30, 75–7.
2 Charles A. Munkman, *The Catholic Revival in North Norfolk: Centenary of Our Lady of Refuge Church in Cromer, 1895–1995* (privately printed), p. 34.

Grangegorman

1 Valuation Office fieldbook (TNA: PRO IR 58/62406, hereditament no. 1350). The sale in 1904 had cost £1,200 and subsequent expenditure on the house £1,500.
2 For details of Edward Lyttleton's life, see the *Oxford Dictionary of National Biography*.

Grove, The

1 Verily Anderson, *Friends and Relations* (London: Hodder, 1980), p. 203.
2 Plans and elevation in Boardman archive (NRO: BR 35/2).
3 Gilbert Barclay, *Random Reminiscences* (1946 typescript in Cromer Museum, CCH 1/2/1), pp. 8–9.

Grove Farm

1 Valuation Office fieldbook (TNA: PRO IR 58/62404), hereditament nos 1190, 1197.

Guidebooks

1 C. L. S. Linnell & A. B. Douglas, *Gresham's School History and Register 1555–1954* (Holt: Gresham's School, 1955), admissions year under the year 1777.
2 This identification is based on an inscription on a copy of the *Guide* bought by R. C. Fiske from the library of the Cromer solicitor P. E. Hansell. See the British Library catalogue for details of her other works.

3 UDC minute book 8 (NLP: CR9), p. 410.

Guilds

1 N. J. G. Pounds, *A History of the English Parish* (Cambridge University Press, 2000), pp. 273–6.
2 Wills of Richard Chylde (1453) and Robert Stronge (1498) summarised by Rye in NRO: Rye 134. Cf. Rye, *Cromer Past and Present*, for more.

Gunner's Manor

1 Rye, *Cromer Past and Present*, pp. 39–40. Cf. Stowe Charter 205 in the British Library – a grant of 1467 from Simon Gunnore to Hugh Reymes, 'clericus', of all the lands in Shipden which had come to him from his mother Cecily, and which had formerly belonged to Alan the son of Galfrid.

Gypsies Close

1 NRO: AYL 90.

Hall Road

1 Plan in possession of C. J. Wright (and photocopy in Cromer Museum); cf. correspondence in NRO: MC 97/15-16, 538 x 3.

Halsey House

1 *Building News* 20 October 1908. The land was originally purchased from the Trustees of the Bond-Cabbell estate on 20 January 1900 for £4,300 and £13,500 was subsequently spent in building on it; purchase of a further seven-eighths of an acre took place in January 1904 for £1,750, with £450 being spent on it subsequently: TNA: PRO IR58/62398, hereditament no. 577.
2 *Cromer, Sheringham & District Weekly Press* 27 February 1915, p. 6, col. 7.
3 C. E. Knight, *The Auxiliary Hospitals of the British Red Cross Society & St. John Ambulance in Norfolk 1914–1919* (Norwich: Order of St John of Jerusalem and the British Red Cross Society Norfolk County Joint Committee, 1989). The sale to Torwood Estates was for shares, not cash: NRO: MC 2547/1-2, 980 x 5.

Hampshire Gardens

1 *Hansard* Commons debates 26 April 1990, vol. 171, col. 293w.

Hanover House

1 *Cromer Preservation Society Newsletter* 9 (2002), pp. 2–3.

Happy Valley

1 Norfolk Landscape Archaeology site no. 6452.

Harbord House

1 Shown as 'Carrington Villas' on 1st (1886) edition of the Ordnance Survey 6" map, surveyed in 1885. Lord Suffield is listed in the 1899/1900 telephone directory as at 'Carrington Villa'. Called 'Harbord House' in 1914 in the Valuation Office fieldbook (TNA: PRO IR 58/62405, hereditament no. 1208), which notes that it 'was originally two houses' and gives Lord Suffield as the occupier. See box 115 of the Gunton papers at the NRO for site plan and floor plan by Edward Boardman, 1878.
2 Plan of ground floor in NRO: Gunton collection B115/494.
3 Charles Harbord, 5th Baron Suffield, *My Memories 1830–1913* (London: Herbert Jenkins, 1913), p. 314.
4 North Erpingham Register of Licences C (NRO: PS 24/7/1). A provisional licence was issued to Hon. Harbord Harbord on 29 September 1890, but not renewed. A licence was issued to Harry Smith for the Royal Cromer Golf Links Hotel as early as 1891.

Harbord Road

1 Auction plan of building plots 1887, reproduced by Rochelle Mortimer Massingham in *Up the Park! A History of Suffield Park, Cromer, Norfolk* (Cromer Museum, 1999).
2 UDC minute book 5 (NLP: CR6), pp. 94, 104-5.
3 NRO: Gunton collection B115/471.
4 Gerald Gliddon, *The Aristocracy and the Great War* (Norwich: Gliddon Books, 2002), p. 260.

Hartington Road

1 Auction plan of building plots 1887, reproduced by Rochelle Mortimer Massingham in *Up the Park! A History of Suffield Park, Cromer, Norfolk* (Cromer Museum, 1999).
2 UDC minute book 7 (NLP: CR8), pp. 340-42, 445-6. Estimate accepted in 1901: minute book 8 (NLP: CR9), pp. 69-72.

Hastings House

1 Register of John Morton, vol. 3, no. 147.

Herne Close

1 Map of lands belonging to Nathaniel Smith, in NRO (with photocopy FX 264/1).

Herne Court

1 A. D. Boyce, *Aspects of Design in Cromer* (Cromer: North Norfolk District Council, 2007), p. 15.

Historians

1 *Who was Who* vol. 3; *The Times* 26 February 1929.
2 *Cromer Past and Present*, p. 129.
3 *Some Rough Materials for a History of North Erpingham*, vol. i, p. 324.

Holly Cottage

1 *Cromer Preservation Society Newsletter* 18 (2004), p. 1.
2 White's directory.
3 Reminiscences of Mr Self (whose horses they were), recorded by Crawford Holden (Cromer Museum: CCH 6/57/1, last page).

Homecolne House

1 Information supplied by the warden in 2000.

Hospital

1 *Cromer, Sheringham & District Weekly Press* 18 November 1916, p. 1, col. 3; Dent, *Reminiscences of a Cromer Doctor* edited by Derek Barker, p. 77; UDC minute book 9 (NLP: CR10), p. 243.
2 Plans 1928–39 are in the Boardman archive in the NRO: BR 35/2/49/5-7.
3 *North Norfolk News* 25 February 1976; *Eastern Daily Press* 26 September 1978, p. 14.
4 *North Norfolk News* 19 February 1982, p. 20.
5 *North Norfolk News* 30 July 2000, p. 1; 7 September 2000, pp. 1, 3.
6 Gerald Gliddon, *The Aristocracy and the Great War* (Norwich: Gliddon Books, 2002), p. 260.

Hotel de Paris

1 There was a Matthias Goggs, builder, in Ash Close, Swaffham, who in 1858 won the contract for demolishing the old Mansion House in Swaffham and building in its place a Corn Exchange. He had just built the Corn Exchange in Dereham (opened in 1857).
2 Edward & Wilfrid L. Burgess, *Men who have Made Norwich* (Norwich: E. Burgess, 1904), pp. 222–30.
3 Dent, *Reminiscences of a Cromer Doctor* edited by Derek Barker, p. 58.

Hotel de Paris: 3rd Lord Suffield

1 'Harbord, Edward, third Baron Suffield (1781–1835)', rev. H. C. G. Matthew, *Oxford Dictionary of National Biography*, Oxford University Press, 2004 <http://www.oxforddnb.com/view/article/12232> – accessed 15th April 2010.

Howards Hill

1 Map of lands belonging to Nathaniel Smith, in NRO (with photocopy FX 264/1).

Hunting and shooting

1 Ground floor plan by Donthorn in RIBA drawings collection at London's Victoria & Albert Museum: SB 70/18 (1) – this was a version that was not in the end executed, but the final plans (SD 120/5 (3)) show an unlabelled room which could well have been intended to serve the same purpose.
2 Vic Brown, *The Foxhunters of Norfolk, 1534 to the present day* (Hindringham: JJG Publishing, 2006), pp. 56, 59, 64–8, 82, 84, 88–9.

Ice house

1 Letter from Philip Barnes to Benjamin Bond Cabbell, 2 July 1853 (NRO: MC 97/1).

Iceland

1 William of Worcester says that Iceland was discovered accidentally by Robert Bacon of Cromer, but see Jonathan Hooton, *The Glaven Ports*, pp. 64-66, 71.

Imperial Hotel

1 Ephemera in Cromer Museum.
2 NRO: SO 197/4 C.
3 For details of a fire at the flats in 1987, see Jamie Edghill and Keith Entwistle, *Cromer Fire Brigade 1881–2006* (Cromer: Poppyland Publishing, 2006), pp. 87–8.

Inkpot

1 RIBA photograph album A317/21–22; A. D. Boyce, *Pretty Villas & Capacious Hotels* (Cromer Preservation Society, 2006), p. 16.

Isolation hospital

1 Local Board committee minute book (NLP), 1890s *passim*.
2 UDC minute book 5 (NLP: CR6), pp. 321, 442–3 etc. The site was purchased from Edmund Skipper for £300 in 1898 (minute book 6 (NLP: CR7), pp. 282–3), the plans were prepared by A. F. Scott (minute book 9 (NLP: CR10), pp. 209, 211) and the builder was J. W. Collins of Downham Market, whose bill was £2,750 (minute book 7 (NLP: CR8), p. 232). The work was completed in 1901 (minute book 8 (NLP: CR9), p. 103).

Ivy Farm

1 Valuation Office fieldbook (TNA: PRO IR 58/62407), hereditament no. 1409.

Jetty Street

1 Map of lands belonging to Nathaniel Smith, in NRO (with photocopy FX 264/1).
2 UDC minute book 4 (NLP: CR5), p. 2.

Jewellers

1 *North Norfolk News* 24 January 2008.
2 A. C. Savin, *A Short Guide to the Geology of Cromer and Neighbourhood* (Norwich: Fletcher, 1887), estimates that about five pounds weight of amber was found annually all along the Norfolk coast, and about twenty pounds of jet.

Jubilee Lane

1 UDC minute book 8 (NLP: CR9), pp. 91–3.

Kennel Burn

1 Gilbert Barclay, *Random Reminiscences* (1946 typescript in Cromer Museum: CCH 1/2/1), p. 4.

King's College

1 Kelly's directory 1904, 1912, supplemented by information from Vaughan's descendants.

King's Head

1 NRO: FOS 611.

Kingsmill School

1 UDC Parks & Open Spaces Committee minute book (NLP: CR31), p. 199.

Lancaster's Manor

1 Rye, *Cromer Past and Present*, pp. 37–8.

Laundries

1 UDC *Register of Factories & Workshops*, entry no. 17. The East Cliff Model Laundry was running in 1909, when Mrs Churchyard of St Aubyns was a customer according to an invoice offered on eBay in 2010.
2 UDC Fire Brigade Committee minute book 1 (NLP), pp. 239–40. Details of the company's 1898 registration are in Cromer Museum.

Lecture Hall

1 Poster in NLP, dated Thursday 19 October.
2 *Cromer & North Walsham Post* 13 June 1891, p. 5, cols 4–5; lease dated 31 January 1895 (in the possession of Peter Stibbons); Jean R. Grose, *Those Were Their Days* (Ingatestone: R. S. Grose, 1999), p. 76.

Libraries

1 Edmund Bartell, *Cromer Considered as a Watering Place* 2nd ed. (London: for J. Taylor, 1806), p. 23.
2 *Norwich Mercury* 20 October 1804, p. 2, col. 3.
3 Catherine Ward, *The Cottage on the Cliff* (1823), pp. 164, 203.
4 NRO: MC 26/1, p. 115.
4 James Stone's diary (NRO).
5 NRO: PD 523/51.
6 Valuation Office fieldbook (TNA: PRO IR 58/62395), hereditament no. 212.
7 NRO: MC 97/118, 541 x 1.
8 E.g., advertisement in the *Eastern Daily Press* 9 June 1936.
9 Bronwen Phillips, *A History of Cromer Primary School in Relation to the Changes in English Elementary Education* (unpublished college dissertation, ?1972; copy in Norfolk Studies Library).
10 NRO: SO 197/4 C.
11 Constance, Lady Battersea, *Reminiscences*

(London: Macmillan, 1922), p. 330.

Lifeboat houses

1 Henry Marten, *Journal* (MS in NRO: MC 26/1, 504x), 14 September 1825.
2 NRO: MC 97/116, 541 x 1; plans for the replacement lifeboat house are in MC 97/109, 540 x 9.
3 Christopher Pipe, *The Story of Cromer Pier* (North Walsham: Poppyland Publishing, 1998), pp. 58–9. For a detailed description of this lifeboat house compiled at the time of its removal, see Michael Brackenbury, *Cromer Lifeboat Station 1919–1977* (unpublished report in Norfolk Landscape Archaeology files at Gressenhall).

Lifeboat service

1 *Norwich Mercury* 20 October 1804, and thereafter every week till 20 December.

Lifeboat service: Henry Blogg

1 See photo in Neil R. Storey, *The Twentieth Century: Norfolk* (Stroud: Sutton, 1999), p. 112.
2 *Eastern Daily Press* 19 February 1976.

Lifeboats

1 John Thornton's diary (Northants. Record Office: Th 3183).
2 UDC minute book 9 (NLP: CR10), p. 30.

Lighthouses

1 N. J. Williams, *The Maritime Trade of the East Anglian Ports, 1550–1590* (Oxford: Clarendon Press, 1988), p. 229, citing W. J. Hardy, *Lighthouses: Their History and Romance* (1895), pp. 25, 62–3.
2 Neville Long, *Lights of East Anglia* (Lavenham: Terence Dalton, 1983), pp. 11–16. The Gunton collection in the NRO includes a paper of 1679 (inserted loosely in a rental for Cromer Gunners 1644–63) with the entry 'Sir John Clayton kt for the lighthouse'. For another account of the history of the lighthouse, see the Trinity House website <http://www.co.uk/html/tlh15.htm>/.
3 *A Guide to Cromer, by a Visitor* (Cromer: Leak, 1841), p. 5.
4 Long, pp. 16–22; Edmund Bartell, *Cromer Considered as a Watering Place* 2nd ed. (London: for

J. Taylor, 1806), pp. 33–4.
5 Capt. Manby's survey of the east coast, quoted in Crawford Holden's notes in Cromer Museum (box 5).
6 Rye, *Cromer Past and Present*, p. 68.
7 John Chandler, *The New Seaman's Guide and Coaster's Companion* 22nd ed. (1840).
8 *A Guide to Cromer, by a Visitor*, p. 6.
9 *North Norfolk News* 1981.
10 Long, p. 162; *Eastern Daily Press* 6 April 1977.
11 UDC Parks & Open Spaces Committee minute book (NLP: CR31), p. 76.

Lime kilns

1 Glebe terrier (NRO: MC 989/1, 801 x 7).
2 See also map in NRO (AYL 90), naming 'Limekiln Close' in this vicinity.

Links Avenue

1 UDC Register of New Dwellings.

Literary mentions

1 T. S. Norgate, *Essays, Tales and Poems* (Norwich, 1795), pp. 211–13.
2 Rye, *Cromer Past and Present*, p. 145.
3 Julian Earwaker and Kathleen Becker, *Literary Norfolk: An Illustrated Companion* (1998; Aurum Press, 2003), pp. 35, 128. Edwin Brock's story appeared in *An Another Thing* (1998).
4 Vol. 56 (21 March – 29 August 1885), p. 511.
5 'On a Friend's Escape from Drowning off the Norfolk Coast' (1954).

Local government

1 Lucy Maren, 'The shiring of East Anglia: an alternative hypothesis', *Historical Research* 81: 211 (2006), pp. 1-27.

Loke, The

1 So called in the plan accompanying the particulars of sale of the Cromer Hall estate, 1852.
2 Local Board minute book 3 (NLP: CR4), p. 269.
3 UDC minute book 5 (NLP: CR6), p. 177.

London Mayors

1 *Dictionary of National Biography*.
2 TNA: PRO SC 8/25/1201.

London Mayors: Bartholomew Rede

1 Valerie Hope, *My Lord Mayor: Eight Hundred Years of London's Mayoralty* (London: Weidenfeld & Nicolson in association with the Corporation of London, 1989), p. 184.

London Road

1 N. J. Willliams, *The Maritime Trade of the East Anglian Ports, 1550–1590* (Oxford: Clarendon Press, 1988), pp. 51–4.

Londs, The

1 Map in NRO: WD 100.
2 Valuation Office fieldbook (TNA: PRO IR 58/62407), hereditament nos 1413ff.

Long House, The

1 See undated (late 18th-century) map of Cliff Piece among Gunton collection estate papers at NRO.
2 Tithe apportionment.

Lord Nelson Coffee Tavern

1 Printed prospectus in the NRO: MC 97/117, 541xi.
2 See newspaper account, among Crawford Holden's notes in Cromer Museum, of the 'newly built' hall on 7 October 1881.

Love Lane

1 Map in NRO: AYL 90.

Lynewood Road

1 UDC Register of New Dwellings.

Macdonald Road

1 A. D. Boyce, *Pretty Villas & Capacious Hotels* (Cromer Preservation Society, 2006), pp. 3–4.
2 UDC minute book 5 (NLP: CR6), p. 8.
3 UDC minute book 7 (NLP: CR8), pp. 163, 340–42.
4 UDC Register of New Dwellings.

Maltings

1 Cellarer's Roll, 1415-16, published by Norfolk Record Society (vol. xvii), pp. 59, 61.
2 *William Windham's Green Book 1673–1688* edited by Elizabeth Griffiths (Norfolk Record Society, 2002) (NRS vol. lxvi), p. 232.
3 Cromer Lancasters manorial papers in NRO:

MS 20978. Since it had previously been owned by two generations of the Kirby family, and before them by Lownd and before him by Frayer, it is almost certain that this malthouse dated back to the 17th century.

4 Norwich Consistory Court wills 1830, no. 51 (will written in 1820).
5 Susanna Wade Martins, *Changing Agriculture in Georgian and Victorian Norfolk* (Cromer: Poppyland Publishing, 2002).

Manors

1 *A History of the English Parish* (Cambridge University Press, 2000), p. 277.
2 Kelly's directory, 1900; cf. Valuation Office fieldbook (TNA: IR 62393, hereditament no. 99) where the house, on a 21-year tenancy from 1891, is simply 44 Cabbell Road.

Marine View

1 UDC minute book 9 (NLP: CR10), p. 150. Cf. pictures in Cromer Museum: drawing by S. Wilkin (1814) copied from drawing in Dawson Turner's extra-illustrated set of Blomefield in the British Library – showing beach huts but no house here; Johnson lithograph (1831; ref. 4030.pcx) and early photos (1850s; refs. 2253.pcx and 5681.pcx) – showing original form of house; photo showing three storeys and bays (1864-67; ref. 1833.pcx).

Markets

1 Rye, *Cromer Past and Present,* pp. 18, 44–6.
2 Carlisle, *Topographical Dictionary* (1808); also the *Universal British Directory* of c. 1792. Savin (p. 2) says the market ceased 'about the beginning of 1800'.
3 UDC minute book 4 (NLP: CR5), pp. 351, 374.
4 News and correspondence in the *North Norfolk News* during June 2000.

Marrams

1 Neville Long, *Lights of East Anglia* (Lavenham: Terence Dalton, 1983), pp. 49–50.
2 *Oxford English Dictionary* <http://dictionary.oed.com> entry for 'marram, *n.*' draft revision Dec. 2000.

Marrams Avenue

1 UDC Register of New Dwellings.

Meadow car park
1   NNDC: PLA/19830706.

Meadow Cottage
1   Valuation Office fieldbook (TNA: PRO IR 58/62406), hereditament no. 1351.

Meadow Road
1   *Jarrolds' Directory of Cromer and Neighbourhood* (London: Jarrold, 1889).

Melbourne House
1   Simeon Simons, letter to J. Lett, 25 May 1821, in Goldsmiths' Hall Library.
2   Tithe apportionment. In the 1861 census, Celia Hogg (aged 80) is described as a 'retired innkeeper's wife'.
3   NRO: Rye Ms 134, datable to 1868 by its inclusion of the lifeboat house and its omission of the completed Edinburgh House. Melbourne House does not appear on the plan drawn up for Bond Cabbell when the creation of Prince of Wales Road was first proposed in 1865. Names of the builders in Savin, p. 127.
4   Notes by A. C. Savin and C. Crawford Holden in Cromer Museum.

Melbourne slope
1   A. Boyce, *An Esplanady Sort of Place* (Cromer Preservation Society, 2004), p. 19.

Meteorological station
1   UDC minute book 8 (NLP: CR9), pp. 256, 362. Shown on the Ordnance Survey 6-inch map of 1930 (survey revised 1927).

Methodist chapels
1   The plans are in the Boardman archive (NRO: BR 35/2/35/4).
2   NRO: SO 197/4 C.
3   Ibid.
4   P. S. Barclay, *A History of the Trustees of 'The Cromer Working Men's and Fishermen's Reading Rooms' and the Property at No. 11 Chapel St. Cromer* (1988), in NRO.
5   Willliam Leary and John Vickers, *A Methodist Guide to Lincolnshire and East Anglia* (Bognor Regis: World Methodist Historical Society, 1984), p. 38.

Metropole Hotel
1   UDC Contract Ledger.

Mickelburgh House
1   UDC minute book 8 (NLP: CR9), p. 7, giving permission for the addition of a bay window.

Middlebrook Way
1   *Hansard* Commons debates 14 June 1979, vol. 968, col. 275w.

Midwives
1   Interview in the parish magazine, in CCH box 7 in Cromer Museum. Her records are in the NRO.

Militia
1   NRO: MS 5364, 5 B 6.
2   Inspection return in NRO: MS 66.
3   Charles Harbord, 5th Baron Suffield, *My Memories 1830–1913* (London: Herbert Jenkins, 1913), p. 97.

Mill Road
1   Road map of 1697, included in Dawson Turner's extra-illustrated set of Blomefield, vol. xxix (British Library Add. MS 23,052, fol. 113).
2   Map in NRO among papers concerning proposed site for new vicarage (PD 523/72).
3   UDC minute book 8 (NLP: CR9), pp. 69–72.

Mills
1   Marriage licence by the Bishop of Norwich, listed in Rye, *Cromer Past and Present*, p. lxxxi.
2   NRO: PD 523/145 (and photocopy FX 264/1).
3   See NRO: WKC 1/425, 393 x 6.
4   Larry Banville, *The Banville Diaries: Journals of a Norfolk Gamekeeper, 1822–44* (London: Collins, 1986).
5   Pigot's directory, 1830. Several members of the Sharpen family are mentioned in the 19th-century parish registers of Gresham.
6   The tithe apportionment shows 'Mill Hill' at this location as arable land, tenanted by Joseph Curtis; it does not mention the mill itself. The file for NHER 15430 says it ceased working in 1830, but does not adduce any evidence.
7   NHER 6802. The Ordnance Survey 6-inch map (1930; survey revised 1927) calls it 'old

mill'.

Motor garages

1 *The Crab Line* issue 134 (24 November – 7 December 2007), pp. 1, 6; private information from the Allen family; *Cromer Preservation Society Newsletter* 31 (2008), p. 3.

Mount Street

1 Local Board minute book 3 (NLP: CR4), pp. 11, 15.
2 UDC minute book 5 (NLP: CR6), pp. 46, 47. The name 'The Mount' appears at least as early as 1840.
3 UDC minute book 7 (NLP: CR8), pp. 2–3.

Music

1 Savin, p. 119.
2 Lt.-Col. Newnham-Davis in the *Pall Mall Gazette* 3 August 1904.
3 Sales particulars, 1925, in the Norfolk Heritage Centre.
4 Frank Meeres, *Norfolk in the Second World War* (Chichester: Phillimore, 2006), p. 25.

New Street

1 *Norfolk Chronicle* advertisement 21 September 1839.

Newhaven Court

1 *Eastern Daily Press* 22 March 1979.
2 Savin, p. 80.

Nonconformity

1 *The Compton Census of 1676: A Critical Edition* edited by Anne Whiteman with assistance of Mary Clapinson (London: Oxford University Press for the British Academy, p. 215.

North Cottage

1 P. S. Barclay, *History of Sir Bartholomew Rede* (1989).

North Lodge and **North Lodge Park**

1 Plans, views and elevations in Goldsmiths Hall, London, with photocopies in Cromer Museum.
2 Joan B. Huffman, 'Buxton, Lady Victoria (1839–1916)', *Oxford Dictionary of National Biography*, Oxford University Press, 2004 <http://www.oxforddnb.com/view/article/55114> – accessed 21 April 2009.
3 UDC Parks & Open Spaces Committee minute book (NLP: CR31), pp. 40, 51.

North Row

1 Valuation Office fieldbook (TNA: PRO IR 58/62402), hereditament no. 910.

Old Coach Road

1 UDC minute book 8 (NLP: CR9), pp. 304–5.

Oliver Court

1 Planning application approved in 1982 (NNDC: PLA/19820555).

Olympia

1 NNDC: PLA/19751234.

One-way streets

1 Local Board committee minute book (NLP: CR61), pp. 10–11.
2 *Eastern Daily Press* 15 June 1956.

Organs

1 Alfred Heath, *Cromer Church Organs Past and Present* (Holt: Rounce & Wortley, 1912).
2 Rye, *Cromer Past and Present*, p. 99.
3 The earliest reference found by Pounds to any organ in an English parish church was in 1433: N. J. G. Pounds, *The History of the English Parish* (Cambridge University Press, 2000), pp. 437–9.
4 *Journal* 30 December 1977, p. 5.

Osier bed

1 Pigot's directories 1830, 1839; Kelly's directory 1929.

Overstrand

1 Karl Inge Sandred, *The Place-Names of Norfolk, Part Three: The Hundreds of North and South Erpingham and Holt* (Nottingham: English Place-Name Society, 2002), p. 26.

Overstrand Court Hotel

1 Valuation Office fieldbook in TNA: PRO IR 58/62406, hereditament no. 1326, and cf. 1368 for Beckhythe Manor – information dated April 1915.

Overstrand Hall
1 Cromer Lancasters court book, 1782.
2 *The Times* 27 December 1892, p. 12, col. c.
3 C. E. Knight, *The Auxiliary Hospitals of the British Red Cross Society & St. John Ambulance in Norfolk 1914–1919* (Norwich: Order of St. John of Jerusalem and the British Red Cross Society Norfolk County Joint Committee, 1989).

Overstrand Hotel
1 Boardman plans in NRO: BR 35/2/71/6.
2 Edward & Wilfrid L. Burgess, *Men Who Have Made Norwich* (Norwich: E. Burgess, 1904), pp. 222–30.
3 Company documents in TNA: PRO BT 31/ 8659/63161.
4 Valuation Office fieldbook (TNA: PRO IR 58/62406), hereditament no. 1331.
5 Information from the library of the *Eastern Daily Press*. Unsafe parts of the building were demolished by an order of 8th November 1949 (to be completed by 5th December) and the rest of the buildings was condemned to demolition by an order of 18th June 1951, to be implemented within one month.

Overstrand Lodge
1 Terence Richards, *A Visitors Guide to Overstrand Past and Present* (Overstrand Parish Council, 2001; amended edition 2005).

Parish hall
1 Bishop's licence for use for overflow services, 1903, in NRO: PD 523/47.

Park Road
1 UDC minute book 5 (NLP: CR6), pp. 94, 104–5.

Paston family
1 Davis' edition of the Paston letters, vol. 1, pp. 45, 176.

Paul's Lane
1 Kelly's directories, 1900 & 1922.
2 Kelly's directry 1922.
3 Valuation Office fieldbook (TNA: PRO IR 58/62407), hereditament no. 1417.

Photographers
1 Much information on photographers is found in Savin, sometimes derived from the printed directories, but the details (especially of who had the studio in Garden Street) seem confused.
2 The Valuation Office fieldbook of about 1913-15 (TNA: PRO IR58/62397, hereditament no. 421) shows Mary Mack's occupancy as 'practically a Tenancy at Will at the nominal rent of a few shillings a week' but does not mention any studio.
3 UDC *Register of Factories & Workshops*, entry no. 51.
4 Embossed stamp on mount of photograph of King's College school in St Mary's Road (in collection of Dave Travagline).
5 Recorded interview with Peter Stibbons, 1975.

The Pleasaunce: Cyril Flower
1 Summary of Cyril Flower's life from booklets by A. R. V. Daubeny, at <http://www.feltwellnorfolk.freeserve.co.uk/written/feltwell_parish.htm>.

Police station
1 Valuation Office fieldbook (TNA: PRO IR 58/62409), hereditament no. 1696.
2 *Cromer Preservation Society Newsletter* 8 (2002), p. 1.

Poor Law
1 *Robson's Commercial Directory of London & the Nine Counties*, vol. II. 20th ed. (London: William Robson, 1839), p. 2.
2 A. Campbell Erroll, *History of the Parishes of Sheringham and Beeston Regis,* p. 85; Peter Wade Martins (ed.), *An Historical Atlas of Norfolk* 2nd ed. (Norwich: Norfolk Museums Service, 1994), pp. 142–5.
3 Tithe apportionment map (1840), plot no. 119. Cf. plan of proposed sea wall etc. (1845) in NRO (MC 999/801 x 9).

Population
1 Domesday Book.
2 State Papers Domestic.
3 Armstrong, *History and Antiquities of the County of Norfolk* (Norwich: for M. Booth, 1781), vol. iii, p. 40. Blomefield (followed by Rye) gave

the figure as 520; one or the other is clearly a misprint, and the earlier and later figures for Cromer would seem to favour 250 rather than 520 as being the correct figure.

4 *The Compton Census of 1676: A Critical Edition* edited by Anne Whiteman with the assistance of Mary Clapinson (London: Oxford University Press for the British Academy, 1986), pp. cxix, 195n, 215. The incumbent was asked for the number of communicants (i.e., men and women over the age of 16), but the figure of 68 for Cromer is certainly an error. Dr Whiteman, noting that according to Blomefield there were 520 communicants in 1603 (but see note 3 above), suggests that the correct figure might have been 680, but this makes no sense when compared with the Hearth Tax assessment of 1664 which listed 66 houses. Moreover, the rate of baptisms and burials recorded in the parish register for the 1690s is consistent with a population of approximately 300. It seems that when the Compton census was being held, the vicar of Cromer did not read the question on the paper carefully enough, and reported the number of households rather than the number of communicants. Dr Whiteman argues (p. lxvii) for a multiplier of 4.25 for converting households into total population at this period.

5 Visitation returns transcribed by Crawford Holden (Cromer Museum: CCH box 7/63/53).

6 Office of National Statistics. Census output for 1961–2001 is Crown copyright and is reproduced with the permission of the controller of HMSO. For details of how the censuses have been compiled and the difficulties of comparing one year with another, see <http://www.visionofbritain.org.uk/census/index.jsp>.

7 *The Compton Census of 1676*, p. 215.

Port

1 Rye, *Cromer Past and Present*, p. 48.

2 William of Worcester says that Iceland was discovered accidentally by Robert Bacon of Cromer, but see Jonathan Hooton, *The Glaven Ports*, pp. 64–66, 71.

3 *The Papers of Nathaniel Bacon of Stiffkey. Volume IV: 1596–1602* (Norwich: Norfolk Record Soci-

ety, 2000), pp. 94–5.

4 Customs jurisdiction would likewise have varied over the years, sometimes coming under Yarmouth and sometimes under Lynn: see E. M. Carus-Wilson & Olive Colman, *England's Export Trade 1275–1547* (Oxford: Clarendon, 1963), pp. 182, 185 (wool) and 190–1, 192–3 (cloth).

5 TNA: PRO E 178/6367. Strictly speaking, Blakeney did not become a head port in its own right until 1786; before that, it was a creek under the head port of Yarmouth – see N. J. Williams, *The Maritime Trade of the East Anglian Ports, 1550–1590* (Oxford: Clarendon, 1988), p. 5.

6 TNA: PRO E 178/6927; <http://www.norfolkinsight.org.uk/census> – accessed 2 November 2010.

Post Offices

1 *Universal British Directory* (c. 1792).

2 Pigot's directory 1830.

3 *Cromer, Sheringham & District Weekly Press* 24 July 1915, p. 1, col. 2, describing A. F. Scott's house as 'the old Post Office'. Cf. map in older editions of Ward Lock's Red Guide to Cromer.

Pound

1 Ordnance Survey 25-inch map, old series (1838). Tithe map, plot 169.

Prince of Wales Road

1 Photograph 20829 in RIBA photograph collection.

Printers

1 The printer was called Silence; copies of the handbill are in the Goldsmiths Hall archive (R.III.170).

2 UDC *Register of Factories & Workshops*, entry no. 42; Kelly's directory 1929.

Prior Bank

1 Dent, *Reminiscences of a Cromer Doctor* edited by Derek Barker, p. 75.

2 NRO: Hansells papers. E. M. Hansell was a director of the Cromer Club House Co. Ltd.

Prior Bank Orchard

1 Outline planning permission gained in 1986

(NNDC: PLA/19861766).

Promenade

1 UDC minute book 5 (NLP: CR6), p. 444.
2 *North Norfolk News* 12 February 1982, p. 3.

Public houses

1 *The Papers of Nathaniel Bacon of Stiffkey. Volume IV, 1596–1602* (Norwich: Norfolk Record Society, 2000), pp. 230-31.

Quakers

1 Julian Earwicker and Kathleen Becker, *Literary Norfolk: An Illustrated Companion* (1998; Aurum Press, 2003), p. 49.

Queen's Road

1 Cromer UDC *Register of New Dwellings.*

Quoits

1 *Cromer: A Descriptive Poem* (London: for J. Ridgway, 1806), p. 48.

Reading rooms

1 *Excursions in the County of Norfolk,* vol. 1, pp. 136-7.
2 Mr Stone's diary tells of frequent visits to Simons's newsroom in 1839, but when he wishes to get the latest part of *Nicholas Nickleby* he goes to Mrs Leak's library.
3 Rate card of 1836.
4 Letter to J. J. Gurney, postmarked 27 August 1842, now in Friends' House in London.
5 J. J. Gurney, letter to Elizabeth Fry 15 December 1842, in Friends' House library.
6 Cromer Museum: CCH 7/67/4 and slide 719.
7 Cromer Museum: CRRMU 1998.9.30.
8 Constance, Lady Battersea, *Reminscences* (London: Macmillan, 1922), p. 330.

Rectors of Overstrand

1 Walter Rye, *Some Rough Materials for a History of North Erpingham,* vol. 3, pp. 622-3.
2 Bishop Redman's visitation 1597 (Norfolk Record Society, vol. XVIII, p. 78); he is also included in a clergy list of 1592/3 printed in *Norfolk Archaeology* vol. xviii, p. 84.
3 NRO: DN/TER 24:31.
4 NRO: DN/TER 24:31.
5 Richard Mackenzie Bacon, *A Memoir of the*

Life of Edward, third Baron Suffield (Norwich: privately printed, 1838), p. 169.

Rectory

1 Glebe terriers in NRO: DN/TER 115/6.

Red Lion

1 Deed in NRO: MC 339/10.
2 Plans of 1885 in Boardman archive (NRO: BR 35/2/82/12).
3 Charles A. Munkman, *The Catholic Revival in North Norfolk: Centenary of Our Lady of Refuge Church in Cromer, 1895–1995* (privately printed), p. 16.

Ridge Way

1 Planning permission for the bungalows and roads was granted in 1986 (NNDC: PLA/19861236, 19861905).

Rocket House Gardens

1 Local Board minute book 3 (NLP: CR4), pp. 343-4.
2 NRO: DC 1/1/40 (Nissen buildings tender 1935). UDC Parks & Open Spaces Committee minute book (NLP: CR31), pp. 19, 22, 26, 32, 38, 48, 57, 89.

Roman Catholic church

1 Munkman says 1903; the Valuation Office fieldbook (TNA: PRO IR 58/62404, hereditament no. 1196) says 1904.

Romans

1 Norfolk Landscape Archaeology, site no. 6453 (grid ref. TG 2240 4090).

Rosebery Road

1 UDC minute book 9 (NLP: CR10), p. 187. Cf. Rochelle Mortimer Massingham *Up the Park! A History of Suffield Park, Cromer, Norfolk* (Cromer Museum, 1999), p. 15 of the original (A4) edition.

Royal Links Hotel

1 TNA: PRO BT 31/5411/37306.
2 *Norwich Mercury* 17 July 1895, p. 2, col. 5.
3 Charles Harbord, 5th Baron Suffield, *My Memories 1830–1913* (London: Herbert Jenkins, 1913), pp. 83-4.

4 Dent, *Reminiscences*, pp. 28, 63, 71, 73.
5 Ibid., pp. 26, 28.
6 J. E. Vincent, *Through East Anglia in a Motor Car* (1907).
7 Jean R. Grose, *Cromer: Those Were Their Days* (Ingatestone: R. S. Grose, 1999), p. 37.
8 Jamie Edghill and Keith Entwistle, *Cromer Fire Brigade 1881–2006* (Cromer: Poppyland Publishing, 2006), p. 63.

Royal Observer Corps
1 Derek Wood, *Attack Warning Red* (London: Macdoanld and Janes, 1976).

Royalty
1 C. Crawford Holden, *The Tragic Empress* (unpublished typescript in Norfolk Studies Library).
2 Reminiscence of Mr Self, notes by Crawford Holden (Cromer Museum: CCH 6/57/1, last page).
3 Programme in Cromer Museum.
4 Christopher Pipe, *The Story of Cromer Pier* (North Walsham: Poppyland Publishing, 1998), pp. 68–9; Crawford Holden's notes in Cromer Museum (CCH 7/67/8).

Runton Road
1 Norfolk Landscape Archaeology, Site & Monuments Record, site no. 25176; Norwich Castle Museum site no. 24SW/50.
2 UDC minute book 4 (NLP: CR5), pp. 415–17.
3 UDC Parks & Open Spaces Committee minute book (NLP: CR31), p. 125.
4 UDC Parks & Open Spaces Committee minute book (NLP: CR31), *passim*.
5 Cromer UDC *Contract Ledger*.
6 *Cromer Preservation Society Newsletter* 29 (2007), p. 2.

St Margaret's Road
1 UDC minute book 7 (NLP: CR8), pp. 2–3.

St Margaret's Terrace
1 A. D. Boyce, *Harmonious Houses in Exquisite Surroundings* (Cromer: Cromer Preservation Society, 2008), p. 3.

St Martin's church
1 Rochelle Mortimer Massingham, *Up the Park! A History of Suffield Park, Cromer, Norfolk* (Cromer Museum, 1999), pp. 13–14 of the original (A4) edition.
2 *Norfolk Archaeology* vol. xxxiii, p. 22.
3 Kelly's directory 1937 p. 432. The architect's design is in the RIBA library of drawings (PA514/13).

St Mary's Road
1 Local Board minute book 3 (NLP: CR4), pp. 11, 15; UDC minute book 4 (NLP: CR5), pp. 60–61.

Salisbury Road
1 Auction plan of building plots 1887, reproduced by Rochelle Mortimer Massingham in *Up the Park! A History of Suffield Park, Cromer, Norfolk* (Cromer Museum, 1999).
2 UDC minute book 5 (NLP: CR6), pp. 94, 104–5.

Sandcliff Hotel
1 Cromer Preservation Society publications.
2 Register of Lodging House Keepers, 20 September 1897 (NRO: PS 24/23/1).

Savings bank
1 Rules and Regulations in NRO: C/Scg/1/2. Pigot's directory 1830 and White's 1836 give the address and name George Pank as its actuary.

Schools
1 Wardens' report of 1838 (Goldsmiths Hall, R.III.170).
2 *Norfolk Archaeology* vol. xxxiii, p. 322.
3 T. Hugh Bryant, *Norfolk Churches: Hundred of North Erpingham* (Norwich: Norwich Mercury, 1900), p. 188.
4 Pigot's directory 1830.
5 John Griffin, *A Survey of Chapel Street* (Cromer Preservation Society, 2001), pp. 3–4.
6 Pigot's directory 1830, naming the mistress as Susan Warrington.
7 Bayne, *Royal Illustrated History of the Eastern Counties* vol. i, p. 212.
8 Kate D. L. Barrett, *A History of Cromer Girls' School, 1872–1949* (the author, 1977). The school log books are a primary source for Barrett and for Bronwen Phillips, *A History of Cromer*

Primary School in Relation to the Changes in English Elementary Education (unpublished college dissertation, ?1972; copy in the Norfolk Heritage Centre); the latter, though wider in scope, is not entirely reliable on the period before 1896.

Sea Marge

1 The Valuation Office fieldbook (TNA: PRO IR 58/62406, hereditament no. 1371) gives the date of the sale as 11 November 1902, and says the £8,000 spent subsequently was 'practically all for rebuilding house in 1903'. Cf. Pevsner/Wilson, which says 1908–12.

Sea walls

1 *Norfolk Chronicle* (21 September 1839), advertising sale of property on the West Cliff.
2 Christopher Pipe, *The Story of Cromer Pier* (North Walsham: Poppyland Publishing, 1998), pp. 22–30, 41–2, and sources there cited.

Sewage works

1 *North Norfolk News* (4 May 2000), p. 3.

Sheep's Pit

1 Savin, p. 132.

Shipden

1 *The Paper of Nathaniel Bacon of Stiffkey. Volume IV: 1596–1602* (Norwich: Norfolk Record Society, 2000), pp. 58–62, 69.

Shipden Abbots

1 Rye, *Cromer Past and Present*, pp. 36–7, citing Le Neve.

Shipden Avenue

1 Cromer UDC *Register of New Dwellings*.

Shipden Club

1 Valuation Office fieldbook (TNA: IR 58/62397, herreditament no. 446).

Shops

1 William Boyne and George Charles Williamson, *Trade Tokens Issued in the Seventeenth Century* (B. Franklin, 1970), vol. 2, p. 843. An earlier edition of the work read the name as Beaney.
2 NRO: MC 26/1, p. 115.

3 UDC minute book 5 (NLP: CR6), pp. 82–3.

Skates Hill

1 There were, of course, several men with the same name, but Domesday records include the following:
   • In Edgefield, Skeet, a free man, held 60 and 20 acres before 1066.
   • Skeet held Binham before 1066, 3 carucates of land.
   • Dersingham which Skeet, a free man, held before 1066 as a manor.
   • In Sloley . . . 20 acres which Skeet held in the lordship of Scottow.
For later examples see John Insley, *Scandinavian Personal Names in Norfolk: A Survey based on Medieval Records and Place-names* (Acta Academiae Regiae Gustavi Adolphi LXII, Uppsala, 1994), pp. 335–6.
2 Norfolk Record Society, vol. VI, p. 64.

Slavery

1 *Memoirs of Sir Thomas Fowell Buxton* (Everyman edition), pp. 53, 62.
2 Clare Midgley, 'Buxton, Priscilla (1808–1852)', *Oxford Dictionary of National Biography*, Oxford University Press, 2004 <http://www.oxforddnb.com/view/article/55183, accessed 27 Nov 2009>; *Daily News* (14 December 1871), p. 7, col. 2.

Smokehouses

1 Edmund Bartell, *Cromer Considered as a Watering Place* 2nd ed. (London: for J. Taylor, 1806), p. 11.
2 White's directory, 1836 and 1845.

Smuggling

1 Neville Williams, *Contraband Cargoes: Seven Centuries of Smuggling* (London: Longmans, Green, 1959), p. 21.
2 Rye, *Cromer Past and Present*, pp. 76–7.

Souvenirs

1 The first draft of this entry was compiled by the staff of Cromer Museum, where many examples of Cromer souvenirs are displayed.

Stained, coloured and decorated glass

1 Birkin Howard, *Nineteenth Century Norfolk*

Stained Glass (Norwich: Geo Books and the UEA Centre of East Anglian Studies, 1984).
2   *Eastern Daily Press* 4 August 1976.

Station Road
1   UDC minute book 5 (NLP: CR6), pp. 94, 104-5.

Stevens Road
1   TNA: PRO MAF 32/714/492 (National Farm Survey).

Stocks
1   *The Papers of Nathaniel Bacon of Stiffkey, Volume V: 1603-1607,* edited by Victor Morgan, Elizabeth Rutledge and Barry Taylor (Norwich: Norfolk Record Society, 2010), p. 295.

Stonehill Way
1   And on a map in the NRO (AYL 90) dating from the first half of the 18th century and on the 1838 Ordnance Survey map.
2   NNDC: PLA/19760484.

Street names and numbering
1   Local Board committee minute book (NLP: CR61), pp. 12-13.
2   *North Norfolk News* (21 March 1969), p. 1.

Suffield Park
1   Richard Mackenzie Bacon, *A Memoir of the Life of Edward, Third Baron Suffield* (Norwich: privately printed, 1838), p. 242; Jearrad's letter to Suffield, 24 June 1826 (NRO: GTN 22). For Jearrad and Cheltenham, see the summary in Dora Ware, *A Short Dictionary of British Architects* (London: George Allen & Unwin, 1967).
2   UDC minute book 5 (NLP: CR6), p. 44.

Suffield Park Hotel
1   Valuation Office fieldbook (TNA: PRO IR 58/62404, hereditament no. 1181), 1913, saying it had been 'built 20 years'. It had been sold on 11 December 1901 and 24 February 1902 for £500 (with land adjoining and opposite, hereditaments 1182 and 1617, which cost an extra £90) and £1,195 spent subsequently.

Suffield Park Preparatory School
1   Rochelle Mortimer Massingham, *Up the*

Park! A History of Suffield Park, Cromer, Norfolk (Cromer Museum, 1999), pp. 8-9 of the original (A4) edition. Cf. Valuation Office fieldbook (TNA: PRO IR 58/62405, hereditaments 1218, 1219).

Summer house
1   Gilbert Barclay, *Random Reminiscences* (1946 typescript in Cromer Museum, CCH 1/2/1), p. 8.

Summerhouse Close
1   NRO: AYL 90 (map not later than 1749).

Sussex House School
1   *Cromer, Sheringham & District Housefinder & Property Gazette* (broadsheet prepared by estate agents Elmes & Downing).

Taxis
1   Local Board minute book 2 (NLP: CR3), p. 379.
2   Ibid., p. 405.
3   Ibid., pp. 110, 119, 128, 143-4.
4   Ibid., p. 435.
5   Ibid., pp. 128-9, 429.
6   UDC minute book 9 (NLP: CR10), p. 298.

Tea rooms
1   *Mary Hardy's Diary,* with an introduction by B. Cozens-Hardy (Norwich: Norfolk Record Society, 1968), pp. 41 and 79.
2   *Norwich Mercury* 22 March 1817.
3   Valuation Office fieldbook at TNA: PRO IR 58/62396, hereditament no. 374.

Telegraph
1   J. F. Fone, 'Signalling from Norwich to the coast in the Napoleonic period', *Norfolk Archaeology* 42(3), pp. 356-61.
2   NHER no. 38942 (see <http://www.heritage.norfolk.gov.uk> - the site description, dated 1984, notes that the northern part of the site had already been lost to erosion by that date). Cf. J. S. Mannings, *Cromer: A Descriptive Poem* (1806), pp. 16-17. The telegraph station is not shown on the Overstrand tithe map of 1836, which shows a cottage in a rectangular plot at about the same position.
3   Steven Roberts, *Distant Writing: A History of the*

Telegraph Companies in Britain between 1838 and 1868 <http://distantwriting.co.uk> – accessed 9 December 2009.
4 Savin, p. 124. The 1861 census includes four young men with lodgings in Pump Street: telegraphists A. E. Bakker (born in Hanover) and J. G. Jorgensen (born in Holland) and a telegraph clerk and a messenger.
5 Steven Roberts, private communication.
6 *Manchester Guardian,* 21 December 1882, p. 8.
7 Eric Clayton, *The Early Days* (Norwich: Norwich Area Telephone Museum).
8 Local Board minute book 2 (NLP: CR3), p. 168.

Telephones
1 Eric Clayton, *The First Hundred Years of Telephones Viewed from Norwich* (British Telecom, 1980).
2 UDC minute book 4 (NLP: CR4), pp. 391–2.
3 Valuation Office fieldbook (TNA: PRO IR 58/62395), hereditament no. 236.
4 NTC telephone directory, 1899/1900. For UDC permission to erect telephone poles leading to the Links Hotel, in autumn 1898, see UDC minute book 6 (NLP: CR7), pp. 256–7, 275.
5 Clayton, *First Hundred Years.*
6 Ordnance Survey 1:10,000 map (1973; surveyed 1969).

Tennis
1 TNA: PRO IR 58/62399, hereditament 609.
2 TNA: PRO BT 31/32658/202418.
3 Crawford Holden's notes in Cromer Museum.
4 *Eastern Daily Press* 18 August 1979.

Thurst Road
1 Valuation Office fieldbook (TNA: PRO IR 58/62406), hereditaments 1303 and 1304.

Tithes
1 Rye, *Cromer Past and Present,* p. 127. Rye adds the figures for offerings at the festivals, and for 'secret tithes'.

Tourism
1 *Morning Chronicle* 17 June 1801.

Tourist Information Centres
1 Edmund Bartell, *Cromer Considered as a Watering Place* 2nd ed. (London: for J. Taylor, 1806), p. 9.
2 *North Norfolk News* 27 September 2007, p. 3.

Town criers
1 *Eastern Daily Press* 12 May 1952.

Town Hall
1 Skipper passed the final certificate on 27th August 1891 (noted in one of his sketchbooks in SKB 324 among the RIBA drawings housed in the Victoria & Albert Museum).
2 Skipper plans in Cromer Museum (CRRMU 1998.9.33).
3 TNA: PRO BT 31/40401/28516 and 31/40402/28516.

Trent House
1 Valuation Office fieldbook (TNA: PRO IR 58/62404, hereditament no. 1195).

Tucker Street
1 Local Board minute book 3 (NLP: CR4), p. 446.
2 UDC minute book 5 (NLP: CR6), pp. 105–6.
3 UDC minute book 4 (NLP: CR5), p. 253.

Tucker's Hotel
1 Map of lands belonging to Nathaniel Smith, in NRO (with photocopy FX 264/1).

Tucker's Hotel: George Cooke Tucker
1 Valerie Belton, *The Norwich to Cromer Turnpike* (the author, 1998), p. 1.
2 *Norwich Mercury* sale notice for the New Inn, 14 May 1830, p. 3, col. 2.
3 Diary of John Thornton, 1821 (Northamptonshire Record Office: Th 3183 & 3184). An extract from Th 3183 describing Cromer is printed in *The Observant Traveller: Diaries of Travel in England, Wales and Scotland in the County Record Offices of England and Wales* (HMSO, 1989).
4 NRO: MC 26/1, p. 116.

Tudor House
1 Dent, *Reminiscences of a Cromer Doctor* ed. Derek Barker, pp. 59–60. See also 'The Sad Case of Tudor House', *Cromer Preservation*

Society Newsletter 28 (Summer 2007), p. 3.

Tunnels

1 Personal communications from Bill (former barman at the Hotel de Paris), Nick (builder who had an office in Jetty Street), Brian and Pamela Clarke, Willie Cuff, Tony Gower, William Macadam and others.
2 Stan Jarvis, *Smuggling in East Anglia, 1700–1840* (Newbury: Countryside Books, 1987), pp. 144–5.
3 Walter Rye, *An Account of the Churches of St. Peter of Shipden and of St Peter and Paul of Cromer,* chapter IV.

Ufford's Hall

1 Domesday Book.
2 Rye, *Cromer Past and Present*, pp. 25–32.

Upton House

1 Abstract of title in NRO 27077.

Vicarages

1 Rye, *Cromer Past and Present*, pp. 81, 94, 122, 125. Glebe terriers of 1627 and 1709 (NRO: DN/ TER 52/3/1–2).
2 Visitation returns transcribed by Crawford Holden (Cromer Museum: CCH box 7/63).
3 CCH box 7/63/62, p. 2. Cf. original letters and map relating to the matter in the NRO: PD 523/72 and 85, plans and elevations by Thomas Jeckell 1853 (more elaborate ones by Edwin Nash had been prepared in the previous year) (PD 523/84).
4 Private communication from Nigel Weeks, grandson of Miss Herring who worked there as a kitchen maid in the late 1890s.

Vicars and Rectors of Cromer

1 TNA: PRO C 131/179/16.
2 Rye, *Cromer Past and Present*, p. xlviii.
3 Clergy list of 1592/3 printed in *Norfolk Archaeology*, vol. xviii, p. 84; Bishop Redman's visitation 1597 (NRS vol. xviii, p. 77); Venn, *Alumni Cantabrigienses*.
4 P. S. Barclay, *A History of Sir Bartholomew Rede, the Goldsmiths' Free Grammar School and the Cromer Exhibition Foundation* (1989), pp. 5–6.
5 Lambeth Palace Library: COMM/12B/4; NRO: ANF 228.

6 Will proved 1712 (NRO).
7 See NRO: MC 667/1, 792 x 2. Appointed sequestrator for the benefices of Cromer and Sheringham in 1768.
8 NRO: DN/REG 24:31, fol. 124v.
9 NRO: DN/REG 24:31.
10 Memorial inscription in Southrepps church, transcribed by Rye, *Some Rough Materials*, p. 339. For his politics, see William Cobbett's *Political Register* 45 (1823), 1 Feb. 1823.
11 Chadwick, *Victorian Miniature*, p. 22.
12 *Cromer, Sheringham & District Weekly Press* (5 August 1916), reporting that he was now considering an offer of the living of Brixton.
13 Philip Bligh, *A History of Cromer Beach Mission 1883–2007* (Lulu, 2008), pp. 111, 353. Bligh says he had a house in Cromer and wonders if he had retired here.
14 *Cromer, Sheringham & District Weekly Press* (3 June 1916), p. 1, col. 8.
15 *Crockford's Clerical Directory.*
16 *Crockford's Clerical Directory* (which calls him Gilbert Arthur Barclay).
17 *Crockford's Clerical Directory.*
18 *Crockford's Clerical Directory.*

Virginia Court Hotel

1 NRO: Hansells papers.

War memorial

1 Summary of newspaper cuttings, in Cromer Museum (CCH box 7/63/77).

Warren, The

1 *William Windham's Green Book 1673–1688* edited by Elizabeth Griffiths (NRS vol. LXVI) (Norfolk Record Society, 2002), pp. 208–9.
2 Karl Inge Sandred, *The Place-names of Norfolk* Part Three (Nottingham: English Place-Name Society, 2002), p. 27.
3 Gilbert Barclay, *Random Reminiscences* (1946 typescript in Cromer Museum), pp. 1–2.

Warren Court

1 The NNDC granted planning permission for flats for the elderly in 1978: PLA/19780651.

Watch House, The

1 John Varley's picture of Cromer beach in 1823 shows Webb's house, not the present Watch

House. For reports on the threat to the house by erosion in the late 1820s see TNA: PRO ADM 7/7, folios 34, 36, 44, 45.

Water supply
1 TNA: PRO E 326/3265. For the location of this rectory, see VICARAGE.
2 Walter Rye, *Norfolk Antiquarian Miscellany* vol. 2 (Norwich: Goose, 1883), p. 392.
3 Crawford Holden's notes of the recollections of a Mrs Balls, in Cromer Museum (CCH box 7/65/28).
4 Local Board minute book 2 (NLP: CR3), p. 174.
5 Local Board minute book 3 (NLP: CR4), p. 415.
6 NRO: MS 27077.
7 NRO: MC 97/38.
8 *Journal* 16 December 1977.
9 *Norfolk Weekly Standard* (25 August 1888), p. 6.
10 *Norfolk Weekly Standard* (1 September 1888), p. 8.
11 1892 plans for new works for Cromer Water Works Company Ltd in NRO (MS 4523), showing boiler house and engine house, the latter including borehole no. 1 (abandoned), borehole no. 2 and well no. 3, the latter with tunnels in the chalk extending to borehole no. 2 and to a spot outside the walls of the premises.
12 UDC minute book 4 (NLP: CR5), p. 188.
13 *North Norfolk News* (5 April 1974).
14 Cromer Water Act 1901; UDC minute book 8 (NLP: CR9), p. 141. P. E. Hansell was paid £250 compensation for loss of his job as secrerary to the water company: book 9 (CR10), pp. 120–23.
15 UDC minute book 8 (NLP: CR9), pp. 259-60 etc.; book 9 (CR10), pp. 120-23.
16 UDC minute book 9 (NLP: CR10), p. 440, and cuttings in Crawford Holden's box 5 in Cromer Museum.

Webb's House
1 Engraving after John Thirtle. Coast Guard papers in TNA: PRO ADM 7/7, folios 34, 36, 44, 45.

Wellington
1 *Norwich Mercury* 22 March 1817.

Wellington Street
1 Pigot's directory 1830.

Westcliff Avenue
1 Cromer UDC *Register of New Dwellings.*

Weylands
1 Rye, *Cromer Past and Present*, pp. 22-5.

Whaling
1 Rye, *Cromer Past and Present*, p. 51.
2 http://www.maritimeheritageeast.org.uk/themes/fishing/whaling-from-kings-lynn – accessed 27th July 2009.
3 *Universal British Directory*, p. 598.

Wheelwrights
1 UDC *Register of Factories & Workshops*, entry no. 52.

White Horse
1 UDC Fire Brigade Committee minute book no. 1 (NLP), p. 257.
2 Valuation Office fieldbook (TNA: PRO IR 58/62406, hereditament no. 1321); it was bought with other property on 11 October 1897.
3 Edward & Wilfred L. Burgess, *Men Who Have Made Norwich* (Norwich: E. Burgess, 1904), pp. 222-30.
4 Valuation Office fieldbook (TNA: PRO IR 58/62406, hereditament no. 1321).
5 *The Cromer Times* 260 (25 November 2006), p. 10.

White House
1 William Ashmore's will of 1712 in NRO (NCC Dawson, p. 213). In 1672 Ashmore had been taxed for five hearths, though it is not clear if these represented one large house or several smaller ones (Rye, *Cromer Past and Present*, p. xxxvi).
2 Deed of conveyance in Barclays archives: Benjamin Rust to bankers Henry Birkbeck junior of Bixley and Geoffrey Fowell Buxton of Thorpe (described in letter from company archivist 2 November 1978, of which there is a copy in Cromer Museum files); 1921 plans in

Boardman archive in NRO: BR 35/2/38/10.

3 *North Norfolk News* (2 November 2000), p. 3.

4 Valuation Office fieldbook (TNA: PRO IFR 58/62410), hereditament no. 1749.

White House Estate

1 Notice of public inquiry 31 July 1952, in NLP.

World War 1

1 Jean R. Grose, *Cromer: These Were Their Days* (Ingatestone: R. S. Grose, 1999), pp. 35, 38, 39.

2 *Norfolk Century* (Eastern Counties Newspaper Group, 1999), p. 107.

3 Robert Eaton, *A Hundred Years of Royal Cromer Golf Club*, p. 19.

4 Charles A. Munkman, *The Catholic Revival in North Norfolk: Centenary of Our Lady of Refuge Church in Cromer, 1895–1995* (privately printed), p. 33.

5 C. E. Knight, *The Auxiliary Hospitals of the British Red Cross Society & St. John Ambulance in Norfolk 1915–1919* (Norwich: Order of St. John of Jerusalem and the British Red Cross Society Norfolk County Joint Committee, 1989).

6 *Cromer, Sheringham & District Weekly Press* (30 September 1915), p. 6, col. 6.

7 *Cromer, Sheringham & District Weekly Press* (16 June 1916), p. 1, col. 4; and various earlier editions for similar reports of the difficulties.

8 *Norfolk Chronicle* (16 August 1918), p. 3, col. 6.

World War 2

1 Frank Meeres, *Norfolk in the Second World War* (Chichester: Phillimore, 2006), p. 93, citing Peter Brooks, *Coastal Towns at War* (1988), p. 12.

2 NHER nos. 38940, 38941. Smallhopes Hill, centred on Ordnance Survey map grid reference TG 2346 4085, is NHER 38921. See <http://www.heritage.norfolk.gov.uk>.

3 Robert Eaton, *A Hundred Years of Royal Cromer Golf Club*, pp. 24–5.

4 UDC Parks & Open Spaces Committee minute book (NLP: CR31), pp. 252, 260.

5 Maurice Doggett, *Eastern Counties: the First 50 Years* (Norwich: Eastern Counties Omnibus Company, 1981), p. 26.

Writers

1 Viator, in *La Belle Assemblee, or, Bell's Court and Fashionable Magazine* 1:1 (Feb.–July 1806), p.

323.

2 Julian Earwaker and Kathleen Becker, *Literary Norfolk: An Illustrated Companion* (1998; Aurum Press, 2003), pp. 142–3.

3 Karen Bethell, 'Henry's horror tale of life by the sea' in *North Norfolk News* 28 August 2008, p. 34.

4 Dent, *Reminiscences of a Cromer Doctor* edited by Derek Barker, p. 22.

5 *Penny Illustrated* 27 July 1889, p. 10. See also Elizabeth Jones, 'The Poppyland Poets' in *Norfolk Fair* 1984 (also on-line <http://jermy.org/poppy03.html> accessed 2 June 2008). The play *London Day by Day*, written here, was first performed at the Adelphi Theatre in London on 25 January 1890 but was never published (typescript copy offered for sale in 2008 by John Hart of Binham, who describes it as a romantic melodrama involving 'stolen jewels, money-lending and marriage entrapment').

X-rays: An interesting case

1 Based on Dr Dent's account (*Norfolk Chronicle* 22 July 1932; cf. *Eastern Daily Press* 15 April 2002 and www.softcode.com/X_Ray.html).

York Road

1 Rochelle Mortimer Massingham, *Up the Park! A History of Suffield Park, Cromer, Norfolk* (Cromer Museum, 1999).

2 UDC minute book 5 (NLP: CR6), pp. 94, 104–5.

Young Men's Christian Association

1 Charlotte Barringer and Peter Larter, *A History of the Young Men's Christian Association in Norfolk and Lowestoft* (Norwich: YMCA, 2007), pp. 87–90.

2 *Cromer, Sheringham & District Weekly Press* (23 December 1916), p. 1, col. 3.

3 Letter to F. H. Barclay from the National Council of YMCAs, 25 September 1933 (NRO: PD 523/154).

Zoo

1 *North Norfolk News* July 1981.

2 NNDC: PLA/19811316.

3 *North Norfolk News* 3 July 2008, p. 33.

FINDING OUT MORE

THE MAIN COLLECTIONS of material relating to Cromer history are held in Cromer and Norwich and are freely available to all those interested in finding out more:

Cromer Library. Reference and lending copies of many local books, including some scarce ones which must be asked for at the counter. Also original typescript copies of two unpublished works: *Some Notes Concerning Cromer Churches* by S. K. Clarke (a former verger), and C. Crawford Holden's *History of Cromer Lifeboats*.

Cromer Museum. Objects, pictures, books and ephemera, including Crawford Holden's collection of local books, photographs and cuttings and his card index of notes arranged under names of people, buildings etc. The catalogue of the collection (and of other Norfolk museums) is accessible on-line at <http://www.cult uralmodes.norfolk.gov.uk/projects/nmaspub5.asp>.

Norfolk Heritage Centre at the Millennium Library in Norwich – the main collection of printed material on Norfolk. Also holds microfilm and fiche sets of local newspapers and census returns, and a duplicate set of all the microfilms in the Norfolk Record Office.

Norfolk Record Office next to County Hall, Norwich. The main repository of archival material for the county. Also holds microfilm and fiche of parish registers and other documents.

North Lodge Park. Offices of Cromer Town Council, holding archives of the Local Board (1884-94), the Urban District Council (1894-1974), the Town Council (1974-) and the Cromer Protection Commissioners (1845-1948). Other archives have been deposited in the Norfolk Record Office.

C ORE PRINTED SOURCES for Cromer history (available in libraries and through the secondhand book trade) are:

Cromer Past and Present by Walter Rye (Norwich: Jarrold, 1889). This includes extensive summaries of what is known about Cromer in medieval times, and many transcripts of official documents and lists; it includes a useful index of names.

Cromer in the County of Norfolk by A. C. Savin (Holt: Rounce & Wortley, 1937; reprinted with additional material in 1950). Most useful for the 19th and early 20th centuries. Much of the book is derived from the published directories, but some statements are based on Savin's close personal knowledge of the town. His building-by-building description of the streets of Cromer is easily accessible (and partially corrected and updated) through paper file and card index in Cromer Museum, and is being put on-line at <http://www.museums.norfolk.gov.uk/defa ult.asp?document=400.600.10>.

Around Cromer by Martin Warren (Stroud: Alan Sutton, 1995). A collection of old photographs.

A Cromer Album by Brenda and Peter Stibbons (North Walsham: Poppyland Publishing, 1985). A collection of old photographs (excluding the beach area).

Poppyland in Pictures by Elizabeth Jones (Cromer: Poppyland Publishing, 1983). A collection of old photographs of Cromer, Overstrand etc.

Cromer Museum also sell a good range of inexpensive leaflets and booklets on specialised aspects of Cromer history, written for the general reader, whether local resident or holiday visitor. They include the Cromer Preservation Society's careful studies of individual streets and buildings. For Overstrand, Terence Richards' useful leaflet *A Visitors Guide to Overstrand Past and Present* (Overstrand Parish Council, 2001; amended reprint 2005) is available at the village shop.

References to other printed sources are in *A Bibliography of Norfolk History* by Elizabeth Darroch and Barry Taylor (2 vols., Norwich: University of East Anglia, 1975, 1984); a 1990s project to supplement this by the *Norfolk Bibliographical Database*, based at the University of East Anglia, was shortlived for lack of continuing funding, but in any case the Bibliography has been largely superseded for most purposes by the on-line catalogue of the Norfolk Heritage Centre.

The parish registers are deposited in the Norfolk Record Office, and are available there on microfiche. Copies of Crawford Holden's typed and indexed transcript are held at the parish church, in Cromer Museum and in the Norfolk Heritage Centre in Norwich.

O N-LINE RESOURCES are constantly expanding. They include transcriptions, indexes and digital scans of original documents, often available free or at very modest cost, as well as discussion forums for those interested in family history. Examples available at the time of writing are:

Norfolk Heritage Explorer <http://heritage.norfolk.gov.uk>, the on-line version of the Norfolk Historic Environment Record (formerly known as the Sites and Monuments Record), giving descriptions of buildings, archaeological sites, finds etc., searchable by place, date and description.

Rootsweb have an active Norfolk mailing list; the list archives are searchable at <http://archiver.rootsweb.ancestry.com/th/index/norfolk>.

FreeCEN volunteers have transcribed some 19th-century census and registration records for Cromer and Overstrand; see <http://www.freecen.org.uk> for details.

It is also possible to determine what documents are held in the main libraries and archives by searching their catalogues on-line; remote users can use these either to order on-line copies of certain documents, or to find out what published books might be relevant to their research (and then to order copies, perhaps, through inter-library loan or the secondhand book trade).

The catalogue of **public libraries in Norfolk** <http://norlink.norfolk.gov.uk> includes the main local history collection in Norwich and their collection of old photographs.

The catalogue of the **University of East Anglia library** can be accessed from <http://broadsearch.uea.ac.uk:1701/primo_library/libweb>.

The National Archives <http://www.nationalarchives.gov.uk> offers the facility to search not only for catalogue records of documents that can be seen at Kew, but also a rapidly increasing number of images of documents that can be downloaded over the web either free of charge or for quite a small charge. Catalogues are also accessible through the NA's website for archive repositories all over the country under the 'Access to Archives' scheme.

Norfolk Sources <http://www.norfolksources.norfolk.gov.uk> usefully makes available on-line a range of trade directories of Norfolk, the text of which can be searched.

Overstrand history is presented on its own website, which includes information from the 1838 tithe map overlaid on modern mapping for comparison: explore it at <http://www.thisisoverstrand.co.uk>.

Finally, the publisher of the present book maintains a website which includes not only details of **Poppyland Publishing** titles (which can set Cromer in the context of Norfolk history generally) but also a range of activities and extra resources based on them: <http://www.poppyland.co.uk>.

INDEX OF NAMES

The Story of Cromer Pier
by Christopher Pipe

Compiled from original documents.
Here are the first mention of a pier at Cromer
(in the first known document to use the very word 'pier' in its modern sense),
contemporary accounts of the storms which have damaged and destroyed one pier after another,
private diaries describing how the pier was used,
people's reactions to the entertainment offered – good, bad and indifferent;
and memories of famous people who have appeared on the pier.

1998   98 pages   A5 landscape   ISBN 0 946148 52 X

Overstrand: Our Village Past and Present

DVD including sections on prehistory, erosion,
a 3D reconstrruction of the village in 1836,
the Belfry School, fishing, late 19th-century mansions
and personal recollections.

Overstrand Parish Council   2009   60 mins   EAN 506156880081

Poppyland

The story in words, pictures and music of Clement Scott's journey
to north Norfolk and the creation of Poppyland.

Poppyland Productions   2006   60 mins   EAN: 5060156880012

The Cromer Lifeboats

Historic film, interviews maps and animations
illustrating the history of the Cromer lifeboats from 1804 to the present.

Poppyland Productions   2006   60 mins   EAN: 5060156880005